LABOR
AND CAPITAL
IN THE GILDED AGE

TESTIMONY OF THE TIMES:
SELECTIONS FROM CONGRESSIONAL HEARINGS

John A. Garraty, General Editor

LABOR
AND CAPITAL
IN THE GILDED AGE

Testimony taken by the Senate Committee upon the Relations between Labor and Capital — 1883

Edited by
JOHN A. GARRATY
Columbia University

LITTLE, BROWN AND COMPANY *Boston*

Contents

INTRODUCTION

During the second half of the nineteenth century the United States experienced one of the most remarkable periods of economic growth in all history: the national wealth increased from about $4.5 billion to nearly $64 billion in these years. Although every sector of the economy reflected this enormous advance, by far the most significant development of the period was the expansion of manufacturing. By 1850 the United States was still primarily an agricultural country, by 1900 it was clearly an industrial one. Statistics reveal the transformation. The output of pig iron rose from 631,000 tons in 1850 to 15.4 million tons in 1900. Steel production, almost nonexistent in 1850, exceeded 10 million tons in 1900. Whether one looks at textiles, petroleum products, or building materials — indeed, at anything from toys to tombstones — similar growth is seen.

This great industrial outpouring produced many benefits, both for capitalists and manufacturers, and for workingmen. Success of the kind achieved by multimillionaires like the steel baron Andrew Carnegie, the oil tycoon John D. Rockefeller, railroad magnates such as Cornelius Vanderbilt, Jay Gould, and E. H. Harriman, or bankers like J. Pierpont Morgan, was not of course typical. But thousands of figures emerged during these years who amassed less spectacular yet still substantial fortunes as a result of industrialization. Ordinary workingmen also profited. There were far more of them to begin with. For example, the number of persons engaged in the manufacturing and construction industries increased sevenfold in that half-century, while the total population merely tripled. More importantly, new technology increased labor's efficiency, with the result that real wages rose sharply, although the length of the average working day declined.

However, the speed and extent of industrialization also produced severe social and economic dislocations in the United States. As production expanded, the size of manufacturing establishments grew ever larger; soon a relative handful of corporate giants dominated many industries. The specter of monopoly loomed ominously, but at least the worst excesses of the monopolists could be curbed by government action. More knotty were the problems caused by bigness itself: the impersonality of great corporations; the separation of ownership (diffused among many stockholders) and actual management (more and more tightly controlled by small groups of bankers and industrialists); the inability of individual workers in huge industrial complexes to bargain on an equal basis with their employers over wages and working conditions; the monotony and danger of work in factories dominated by row upon row of mighty machines. Most ominous of all, according to many thoughtful observers, was the threat to democratic institutions posed by a society in which an ever-wider economic gap separated rich from poor, capitalist from worker.

Rapid industrial growth also made the United States steadily more urban; in 1850, 6.2 million Americans lived in towns and cities; in 1900, 30.1 million. While urban life offered marvelous new social and cultural advantages to city dwellers, it also produced grave problems. People poured into the cities faster than houses could be built to shelter them, faster than streets could be laid out and paved, water and sewage systems constructed. Overcrowding resulted, to be followed by revolting slum conditions. Disease, crime, and immorality flourished. Opportunity, in other words, went hand in hand with discouragement and decay.

Some contemporaries claimed that instead of representing the highest form of human civilization, cities were becoming monuments to social chaos. The insatiable demand for labor to man the new factories caused immigrants to flock to the United States by the millions, and most of the new arrivals settled in the cities. They huddled together in ethnic ghettoes, thus delaying their adjustment to American ways, and they were easily mustered into the political armies that cynical city bosses employed to control elections and to line their pockets with public funds. Essentially, immigrants were the victims, not the creators, of urban problems. Most criticisms of these newcomers — that, for example, they depressed American wage levels, that they were destroying the moral fiber of the country by importing strange new customs, that they were mostly political revolutionaries or nihilists — were patently unfair. But because of their ignorance of city ways, immigrants undoubtedly added to the burdens of social workers and others concerned with alleviating slum conditions.

Industrialization also exacerbated the effects of "normal" swings of the business cycle. Before the Civil War, depressions tended to be caused by agricultural real estate booms, which led to overproduction and glutted markets, and then to sharp declines in the value of land, which bankrupted speculators, caused bank failures, and eventually led to business stagnation in the towns and cities. In an agrarian society, however, bad times seldom spelled disaster. Men could usually get enough to eat, and seldom lost their homes. Even city workers often owned small plots of land, on which they could raise enough food to tide themselves over during periods of unemployment. But in an industrialized, urban society dominated by large business units, mass unemployment caused real hardship. Furthermore, the ups and downs of economic activity became more abrupt and violent. In good times the ever-more-efficient factories turned out mountains of goods; when demand collapsed, they closed down suddenly and remained shut until the surpluses were used up. The American economy, so vital, so complex, took on certain of the qualities of Frankenstein's monster. It became almost literally awe-inspiring, both in its power and in its incomprehensibility. Workers, businessmen, professional economists, and political leaders could neither control nor even understand the mighty forces they pretended to supervise and employ.

This last fact goes far toward explaining the political conservatism of the times and the tendency of government leaders and the major parties to avoid confronting pressing economic and social problems. Not knowing how best to deal with these problems, they hesitated even to try, lest in their ignorance they blunder and make things worse. At the same time, honest pride in the tremendous achievements of modern industry, achievements clearly related to the energy and imagination and daring of the great business organizers of the period, tended to make people hesitate to tinker with the machinery they had created or to employ the power of government to check or inhibit business leaders. The public's mood was a mixture of complacency and alarm, and statesmen, pulled in opposite directions by these feelings, preferred to adopt a wait-and-see attitude.

*   *   *

One area where government intervention in economic affairs was acceptable to most persons during the Gilded Age was the regulation of foreign imports by protective tariffs. In colonial times the British mercantilistic system had employed this device of taxing foreign products heavily in order to encourage the use of goods produced within the Empire. As early as 1816 the United States Congress had imposed high duties on foreign textiles and other manufactures to protect "infant" American industries that had flourished during the War of 1812, when European goods had been almost unobtainable. Tariff levels had fluctuated over the years, but in general, after the Civil War, most of the important American manufactured products enjoyed the protection of high duties on competing foreign goods.

Exactly how tariffs affected the total economy, however, was not easily determined. Manufacturers benefited directly, of course, but what of their employees? On the one hand, it could be argued that tariffs created jobs for American workers and helped maintain wage levels by raising the cost in the United States of goods produced by low-paid foreign workers. On the other hand, the tariff increased the cost of living for all citizens. Whether on balance, workers would be better off under free trade, perhaps earning less but spending less for the necessities of life, remained a debatable question. Less debatable was the effect of tariffs on American farmers. Since the United States raised surpluses of most agricultural products, these were not imported at all. Tariffs did not protect farm products. Yet farmers were consumers of manufactured goods that were protected. If duties were lowered or removed, the price of these goods would fall and farmers would benefit.*

---

*Protectionists, however, argued that farmers profited indirectly from high duties on manufactured goods. They claimed that if the wages of industrial workers declined, demand for farm products would slacken and prices would fall.

The tariff therefore triggered many spirited political debates during the post-Civil War decades. Both the Republican and Democratic parties tried to avoid declaring themselves too clearly on the issue because their supporters were divided. A preponderance of the Democrats, especially in the South, favored reducing the duties, but a well-organized minority, led by Congressmen from northern manufacturing districts, favored protection. Eastern Republicans tended also to be protectionists, but many western supporters of the G.O.P. desired to see the rates lowered. Since all concerned saw the connection between tariffs and other, more complicated industrial problems, and since the labor vote was becoming increasingly important, much of the discussion of the issue revolved around the effect of tariffs on workingmen. Opponents of protection assigned all the ills that beset labor to high duties, while the other side insisted that tariff cuts would cause mass unemployment and a sharp reduction in the living standards of all American workers.

This was the background for a resolution introduced in the United States Senate in the spring of 1882 by John T. Morgan of Alabama, which called for the creation of a committee to investigate the causes of recent industrial strikes. Morgan and other southern leaders had been alarmed by the establishment a few weeks earlier of a Tariff Commission to study the present schedule of duties. Most of the persons appointed to this commission were protectionists, which convinced these Southerners that it would recommend still further increases. To counteract this, they sought to demonstrate that high tariffs were not actually benefiting workers. A study of recent strikes, they reasoned, would reveal that workers were dissatisfied because they were not earning enough to pay for the necessities of life. Since duties were already high, the evidence uncovered in such an investigation could be used to persuade workers that protection was not helping them. Instead of striking for higher wages, which involved bitter struggles with their employers, they should support the effort to lower their expenses. Senators like Morgan had also an ulterior motive. The investigation, they hoped, would bring out evidence of political coercion of workers by their employers. If it could be shown that the bosses were controlling the voting behavior of their workers by threats and pressures, Republican charges that Southerners were subverting the political rights of Negroes would be counterbalanced.

The Republicans in the Senate considered it politically unwise to oppose Morgan's resolution. Since representatives of organized labor were already lobbying for a federal Bureau of Labor Statistics to study all aspects of the labor problem, they decided instead to try to steal Morgan's thunder. They urged that the Senate Committee on Education and Labor undertake a much broader study that would look into the whole subject of the relations between labor and capital. The protectionists, in other words, accepted Morgan's challenge, believing that a broad-gauged investigation would produce evidence which would convince workingmen that the system of high duties was necessary for their prosperity. On August 7, 1882, the following resolution was unanimously adopted:

Resolved, That the Committee on Education and Labor is hereby authorized and directed to take into consideration the subject of the relations between labor and capital, the wages and hours of labor, the condition of the laboring classes in the United States, and their relative condition and wages as compared with similar classes abroad, and to inquire into the division of labor and capital of their joint productions in the United States; also, the subject of labor strikes, and to inquire into the causes thereof and the agencies producing the same; and to report what legislation should be adopted to modify or remove such causes and provide against their continuance or recurrence, as well as any other legislation calculated to promote harmonious relations between capitalists and laborers, and the interests of both, by the improvement of the condition of the industrial classes of the United States.

Second. Said committee shall have leave to sit in vacation, and by sub-committees to visit such places in the United States as they may deem proper, to obtain necessary information under these resolutions; and said committee or sub-committees shall have power to send for persons and papers, to administer oaths, and to examine persons under oath or otherwise, and to cause depositions to be taken and certified under such regulations as they may adopt.

Third. Said committee shall have power to appoint a clerk, at a salary of $6 a day, and to employ such stenographic aid as may be necessary, and to appoint a sergeant-at-arms from the officers or employés of the Senate; and the actual and necessary expenses of said committees, properly incurred in the execution of these resolutions, shall be paid out of the contingent fund of the Senate.

As a result of this action, a parade of employers, union officials, workingmen, reformers, cranks, and ordinary citizens came forward to present their views. For the first time in American history a broad sample of opinion on industrial problems was collected and recorded. That part of this testimony presented on the following pages is only a fragment of the total, but a representative one. By the nature of the investigation, much of what was said was repetitious, rambling, and disconnected. Witnesses spoke on a variety of subjects and in no particular order. Wise men followed upon the heels of fools, conservatives followed radicals, dispassionate scientists followed fanatics. The connection between what one witness said in Washington, another in New York, a third in Boston, or between what a labor union official said one day and a corporation executive the next, can easily be lost when the thousands of pages of testimony are read seriatim. I have therefore selected what seemed to me the most interesting and important passages and arranged the material under major headings, bringing together various points of view on each subject so that the reader can weigh and compare the opinions offered and see the different aspects of the larger questions of late-nineteenth-century industrial relations relatively at a glance.

The first three chapters deal with the actual conditions of industrial workers in the 1880's: what it was like to work in a factory; what the

standard of living of laborers was; what their chances were to improve
their lot; what their homes and environment were like. Chapters 4
and 5 contain discussions of unions, the problems involved in organizing workers, and also strikes and other forms of industrial warfare.
Then, in Chapters 6 and 7, the conservatives and the reformers have
their day, discussing broad issues of social and economic policy, and
specific problems as well.

The testimony provides an incomparable picture of the American industrial world during the Gilded Age. This is the raw material of history,
the report of experienced eyewitnesses on the dynamic processes of industrialization and urbanization in which all were deeply entangled. Some
are smug, some angry, some merely frightened and confused; some are intelligent and possessed of great insight, others blind to the true nature of
the conditions they describe. But all were *involved:* all came forward
freely, hopeful of persuading the committee that their own views, myopic
or farsighted in the light of history, represented truth. All do represent
truth in the sense that they reflect the opinions of contemporaries and
thus enable us to understand the true character of the relations between
labor and capital in those times.

*　　*　　*

One of the most interesting aspects of this investigation, one which
forcefully illustrates the enigmatic and paradoxical element in human affairs, was the curious relationship between the motives of the Senate, and
especially of the southern Democratic members of that body, and the ultimate importance of the hearings. In the first place, the Tariff Commission, although dominated by protectionists, actually recommended broad
reductions in the taxes on foreign manufactures. It made its report even
before the investigators heard their first witness. Thus the pressure that
had led Senator Morgan to call for an investigation had largely disap-
peared before the hearings began. Many witnesses discussed the tariff and
the southern Senators made their own views clear, but the subject was by
no means emphasized. Secondly, despite their basic conservatism and
their mixed and generally selfish motives, the Senators who conducted
the hearings acted throughout with remarkable fairness. They listened pa-
tiently, heard all sides, asked searching questions, expressed deep concern
that the subject be discussed fully and from every angle. Particularly note-
worthy was the sympathetic hearing they gave to a procession of rank-and-
file craftsmen and laborers, men of a type who even in modern times
rarely appear before Congressional committees and whose testimony
is for that reason of inestimable value to historians.

Much of the credit for the manner in which the investigation was conducted belongs to Senator Henry W. Blair of New Hampshire (1834–
1920), the chairman of the committee. Blair was born in Campton, New

Hampshire. Orphaned early in life, he knew the grinding toil of farm work at first hand. Largely self-educated, he managed to become a lawyer. He enlisted in the Union army during the Civil War and rose to the rank of lieutenant colonel. After service in both houses of the New Hampshire Legislature, he was elected to House of Representatives in 1874 as a Republican. In 1879 he became a Senator. Blair's views on most public questions were conservative; like most northeastern Republicans, he favored sound money, liberal pensions for war veterans, and the protective tariff. But he was also an early and persistent advocate of federal aid to education, and, as his attitude during the investigation made abundantly clear, he was genuinely concerned with the welfare of industrial workers. Without being insensitive to the partisan aspects of the investigation, he sought to get the full story on the record, regardless of the political implications of any man's testimony, and he treated every witness, whatever his views, with kindness and respect.

Blair's exemplary behavior was adopted also by the southern Democrats on the committee. Whatever their ultimate intentions, their treatment of witnesses was scrupulously fair at all times. Never did they attempt to use the plight of northern workingmen to justify the southern attitude toward Negroes, nor did any of them try to turn the hearings to partisan advantage. One of the witnesses before the committee whose testimony is not reproduced on the following pages was an Arkansas cotton planter named John C. Calhoun, grandson of the famous Senator from South Carolina. Calhoun spoke chiefly about Negro farm labor; his views, moderate but definitely southern (when Senator Blair asked him: "Do you anticipate . . . any further difficulty from the race question?" he replied: "Not at all, and if we are left to ourselves things will very soon equalize themselves"), offered ample opportunity for these Southerners to drive home points embarrassing to northern Republicans. They did not take advantage of this opportunity. Indeed, they left the questioning of Calhoun almost entirely to Blair, interjecting only an occasional query related to some minor fact or opinion. One of the southern Senators even questioned Calhoun's use of statistics when he was arguing that Southerners, in general, lived longer than Northerners.

The most important of the southern members of the committee was James Z. George of Mississippi (1826–97). George was a veteran of both the Mexican War and the Civil War, having served as a colonel in the Confederate army. Although he was a typical states-rights Southerner and a leader of the fight to restore white supremacy in Mississippi, his concern for the welfare of workingmen was genuine and lifelong. In later years, for example, he fought unsuccessfully to have labor unions exempted from the provisions of the Sherman Anti-Trust Act. James L. Pugh of Alabama (1820–1907), who had been a prominent secessionist and a member of the Confederate Congress before entering the Senate in

1880, and Willkinson Call of Florida (1834–1910), another Confederate veteran and a Senator since 1879, also avoided partisanship and participated actively in the questioning of witnesses.

But the significance of the testimony and the behavior of both the witnesses and the investigators is amply revealed in the following selections. It is time to examine the evidence.

1 WORKING CONDITIONS

Testimony of Robert D. Layton

Robert D. Layton, an axe-maker by trade, was in 1883 Grand Secretary of the Knights of Labor, at that time the largest and fastest growing labor organization in the nation. The Knights advocated industry-wide, rather than trade-oriented labor unions, and were noted for their willingness to admit women, Negroes, and unskilled agricultural workers into their ranks. Many leaders of the Knights opposed strikes, but at least by 1883, Layton did not belong to this faction. He also favored permitting trade-union groups to join the Knights of Labor without surrendering their identity.

Sen. George: Can you tell us anything in regard to the physical conditions and surroundings of the working people, their food, their clothing, and whatever occurs to you pertaining to their mode of living? — A. There are differences, of course, in those respects, depending upon the amount of wages paid. The daily laborer perhaps lives more poorly than any of the others, has the least house room and the most illy-ventilated rooms, the least means of educating his children, and the least opportunity for society and other advantages. Then comes the coal miner, who receives more wages, but who generally lives in a little two-room house. These houses are built in long rows, not painted, with no grounds and no fences about the houses, and the men deal in the companies' stores, who tax them about all they can earn for their goods. . . .

Sen. Blair: Have you visited the homes of those people? — A. I have.

Q. In what places? — A. In Pennsylvania principally. I have left the subject of the laborer now, however, and gone to the miner.

Q. Don't you consider him a laborer? — A. Well, more skill enters into his occupation. A "laborer" is not supposed to be a miner or to be able to dig coal. A man must have been taught the business before he can be regarded as a miner, and the business is more intricate and difficult to learn in some places than in others.

Sen. Blair: As I am using the term laborer, it applies to all classes who perform manual work.

The Witness: It is all labor; but we usually divide it into skilled and unskilled labor. The work of the miner is skilled labor to a certain extent.

I have seen the laborers along the Monongahela and the Allegheny Rivers, and down the Pan-Handle Railroad toward Wheeling, and in fact at all points on the roads leading out of Pittsburgh. The houses of those men as a rule consist, as I have said, of two rooms — one upstairs and the other downstairs. The houses are built in long rows without paint on the outside. The kitchen furniture consists generally of a stove and some dishes, a few chairs and a table. They have no carpets on the floors so far as I have seen. I am speaking now about the lower parts of the houses; I don't know about upstairs.

Sen. George: Is the kitchen in the lower room of the house or is it separate? — A. In the lower room. In many instances there are no cellars under the houses. If there were cellars the miners would be enabled to lay in a stock of supplies.

Sen. Blair: Of what material are the houses usually built? — A. They are always frame houses. I cannot recall an instance of one being built of any other material than wood.

Sen. George: Are they plastered inside? — A. In some instances they are and in others they are not.

Sen. Blair: How are they as to warmth? — A. Living as these people do in the coal regions, the children can run out and gather enough fuel to keep the houses warm, and I never knew any of them to suffer from cold.

Sen. George: Can you describe the furniture a little more fully? — A. I think I have given you pretty nearly all the articles of furniture that they have in their house — a stove and the utensils that go with it.

Q. The sleeping apartment is upstairs I suppose? — A. Yes, sir; but in some instances where the family is large it is downstairs in the kitchen.

Sen. Blair: What kind of beds do the miners have? — A. I never slept among them and do not know.

Sen. George: Is the kitchen also the sitting room of the family? — A. Yes, sir; it is the sitting room, kitchen, and parlor.

Q. And library? — A. And library. Sometimes they have some little pictures on the walls.

Sen. Blair: What kind of pictures? — A. Oh, some little chromos or prints.

Q. Does the miner usually have a newspaper? — A. Yes, sir; wherever he can afford it.

Q. He is usually an intelligent man? — A. Yes; he generally can read.

Q. How are they supplied as to clothing? — A. Well, it is absolutely necessary for a miner to have two suits. The one that he wears when working in the mine is of the poorest quality, and usually very black and dirty, and then he has an ordinary suit of clothes besides.

Q. How are his wife and children clothed? — A. They are clad in the plainest possible garments, as a rule.

Q. What wages does the miner get generally? — A. The wages may average $2.00 or $2.50 a day; but, dealing in these truck-stores, when the end of the month comes around he generally has very little left. I have known some of them to receive in actual money at the end of the month $.35 after the rent was taken out.

Sen. George: Are they charged rent for those houses? — A. Oh, yes.

Sen. Blair: What amount of rent? — A. All the way from $4 up to $8 or $9 a month. Some of the houses have more rooms than two, but in the majority of cases they have only two rooms. If the upper floors are partitioned I don't know the fact.

Sen. George: What is the usual size of the lower room? — A. About 15 by 18 feet, or 18 by 20 feet, or something of that kind. I have no distinct recollection of ever seeing one of those houses with a cellar under it.

Q. How are they usually warmed, with a stove or with a fireplace? — A. Usually by a cook-stove.

Q. Is that the only heating apparatus they have? — A. Generally, I think. I don't know whether they have any upstairs or not, for I have never been upstairs in any of the houses, but that is the whole of the heating apparatus downstairs.

Sen. Blair: How are those people situated as to school privileges? — A. Usually the miner in the soft-coal regions, and I think in our hard-coal regions, too, puts his boys to work in the mine very young. I have observed boys of from eight to fourteen years of age working in the hard-coal region, and in the soft-coal mines boys of ten or twelve years of age are able to assist their parents materially in the mine, and unless the miner has a large number of them his boys are usually employed in that way helping their father. If there are only one or two boys in the family the father generally takes them into the mine with him. They go to school some, but their means of education is very limited.

Q. Is that because the father prefers that the boys should assist him in his work or because of a lack of school privileges? — A. The school privileges are generally good enough, but absolute necessity compels the father in many instances to take the child into the mine with him to assist in winning bread for the family.

Q. There is no compulsory school law in Pennsylvania, is there? — A. No, sir. . . .

Q. Do any of those miners ever accumulate any money? — A. There are some instances of that, exceptional cases — as there are in almost every occupation — cases where miners have accumulated a little funds.

Q. What are the personal habits of the miner generally as to economy or a disposition to save his wages? — A. He gets so very little to save from that he rarely saves anything. His desire may be to economize, but his opportunities for it are so poor that he seldom is able to accumulate any savings, let his desire for economy be ever so great.

Q. You call the miner a skilled laborer to some extent. Is there any other class of laborers in or about the mine whose wages are still lower than those of the miner? — A. Yes; but such work is usually done by young boys. Such work as driving the mules in the pit is done generally by the children of the miners. I am speaking of places where they use mules. Some places they do not use them, but dip the coal and permit the miner to push the car along. . . .

When you leave the miner and go to the iron-worker, the man who works in the iron-mills, you find the social condition and surroundings somewhat improved — more home comforts, more of the little things that go to make a home comfortable and pleasant. The iron-worker has usually more room and better furniture, carpets, and so on, and his children are better clothed, in garments neater and of better quality. The iron-workers have the advantages of the markets in the large centers of industry, the cities, so that they can get a greater variety of food and are not confined, like the miners in isolated situations, to perhaps a visit from the butcher once or twice a week. They eat more fresh beef as a general thing, and as I have said, have usually more living room and that more comfortably furnished. But if you go among the laborers employed in the iron-mills you will find them huddled together in tenement houses and no more comfortable than the miners.

Sen. George: Please state the distinction between the iron-worker and the laborer in the iron mills. — A. The laborer there performs the heavy work, the unskilled work, and waits upon the skilled worker, the iron-worker. The laborers receive from $1.00 to $1.25, or perhaps sometimes $1.75, a day. When we speak of a "laborer" in the iron-works, it is understood that we do not mean a man who performs any skilled labor. When you get above the laborer the men are designated by the character of the particular work in which they are engaged; they are called "rollers," "finishers," etc., and are skilled laborers. . . .

Q. To go back to the houses, you have described them as being in very close juxtaposition and very near the works. What grounds have they around them, what shade, what grass, what opportunities for the children of the family to have outdoor recreation? — A. If there is any grass on the south side of Pittsburgh attached to a tenement house it is in a little box sitting on the windowsill. I do not know of any existing on the earth. They would have to take up a brick to sow the grass, if they had any. I know numbers of houses where the backyard of each is not more than 8 feet by 10, and that is allowing more territory than many of the landlords do.

Q. What opportunities have the children under ten or twelve years of age, who are too small to work in the factories, for outdoor recreation? What playgrounds have they? — A. They have to play right on the street.

Q. They are street children? — A. They are compelled to play on the streets. They have no other place. For outdoor exercise they take the pavement in the middle of the street. What little ball-playing they indulge in is done on the streets at the risk of breaking windows and being stopped summarily by the police.

Q. They are exposed to danger, too, from carriages, wagons, and drays, I suppose? — *A.* Yes, sir; and there are occasional accidents. Usually, though, the little shavers are on the look-out for anything of that kind and contrive to avoid it.

Q. Playing in the street is common? — *A.* Yes, sir; there is no place else to play. When they go to school they have a large yard to play in during the recess.

Q. What opportunities have men who live in these tenement houses and their families for recreation on Sundays and holidays? What resorts have they? Where do they go to? Do they stay in their houses, or do they go out into the country, or into the parks? . . . I want to know what they usually do? — *A.* Well, usually they are tired and they stay at home. They may walk around sometimes on Sunday to see a friend, or they may go to church, but if they don't do that they stay at home and rest. . . .

Q. I have an idea that the life of a coal miner is very disagreeable. Now, why do men go into that business? Is it because of the high wages paid, or what is the reason? — *A.* Well, some person has to dig our coal, and the only way to get it out is to go down into the bowels of the earth after it.

Q. Then it is the exceptionally high wages that induce men to engage in the business? — *A.* No; men are born to it; their fathers worked in the mines, and they began life in that way and never did anything else; they inherited it, as you may say.

Sen. Blair: Really, then, they are an utterly helpless class so far as they are themselves concerned; they must remain in their present position unless others lift them out? — *A.* I do not know how you can lift them out of the dirt of the businesss. I do not know how coal can be got out cleanly.

Sen. George: I had the idea that men were seduced into that sort of employment by extraordinarily remunerative wages? — *A.* The average miner's earnings, as I think will be shown to you, do not amount to more than $350 a year. That is the seductive compensation given to the miner for spending the greater portion of his life in utter darkness. In Pennsylvania the miners and other citizens had a law enacted at the last session of our general assembly prohibiting these truck stores of which I have been speaking — "pluck-me" stores, as the operatives call them; they are known universally by that name in the mining regions — we had a law passed, I say, to prohibit such stores, but our able constitutional lawyers, I believe, found holes in it, and the institutions continue. . . .

Sen. Blair: The effect of these "pluck-me" stores is, I suppose, to largely decrease the actual rate of wages received by the men, by reason of the higher prices that they are compelled to pay for everything they buy? — A. Yes, sir. I know a miner who told me that when flour was selling for $2.00 a sack in the city he was paying at one of these stores, eight miles from the city, $2.50 a sack.

Q. How many pounds are in a sack? — A. Fifty.

Q. That was a difference of 25 percent? — A. Yes, sir.

Q. The transportation that distance could scarcely amount to anything? — A. No, sir; the cost of it must have been very slight.

Q. I suppose that the meats and provisions of all kinds, the clothing and the material for clothing, and all the necessaries of life are subject to the same rule? — A. Yes.

Q. Do the operators furnish everything? — A. Yes, sir; everything that the miners may need, their groceries, boots and shoes, calicoes, and everything of that kind. The "pluck-me" store is a general store. . . .

Q. Can you give us some instances of the obnoxious rules of which you speak? — A. Yes; one instance was on the part of a large firm of carriage manufacturers at Rochester, N.Y. — James Cunningham, Sons & Co. Just a year ago this month their men rebelled against certain rules that they had established in their works — rules degrading to human nature. For instance, the faucets in the water sinks were locked up, and when an employee wanted a drink of water he had to go to the foreman of his department and ask for a drink; the foreman went and unlocked the faucet and gave him a cupful of water, and whether that was enough to satisfy his thirst or not, it was all he got. When the men entered in the morning they were numbered by checks. A man lost his identity as a man and took a number like a prisoner in a penitentiary. The checks ran up to five hundred and something. If a man worked in the third or fourth story of the building (it was a large, high building), and if he was an old man — for they had a good many old men doing light work — when the bell rang for dinner he was obliged to walk down several pairs of stairs, take off his check and then walk up stairs again to eat his dinner, and when he got done he had to walk down again and put on the check before the bell rang for afternoon work. In that way they knew just when a man came in or went out. Then, if a man was a pieceworker there, and got through his work at half past two or three o'clock, he was not permitted to leave the building until the regular time — six o'clock. No matter when he got through with his work, he had to stay there in dirt and discomfort, and could not go home or go out until six o'clock in the evening. Another obnoxious rule was that if a man was half or even quarter of a minute late he was shut out. They had a gate and it would be shut down upon a man even when he was going in, sometimes so quickly that he would hardly have time to draw his foot back to keep it from being crushed by the gate, and that man would be kept out until nine o'clock, so that he would make only three-quarters of a day's work. The rule was that the men had to be *in* the works before the whistle blew. . . .

Our miners almost universally complain of being cheated in the amount of coal that they take out. That is another cause of great aggravation and disturbance. In some mines, they dig and get pay for the "run of the bank" — that is, slack and lump and nut coal all go in together at so much a ton. In other mines the miners are paid for simply the lump coal; and all the rest is deducted. The men have to dig the other kinds for nothing, getting so much a bushel for the lump coal only — coal that is not large enough to go through the screen. The size of the screen is regulated by law in Pennsylvania, but as you proceed in this investigation we will produce witnesses who will prove that the screens are often half an inch larger than the size the law prescribes. The screen is made of long bars of iron, and the coal runs down, over, and between them. . . .

Q. Go on and give us the "true inwardness" of the thing, so far as you can, in your own way. — A. As to wages, I presume there always has been, and to a certain extent always will be, a difference as long as self-interest controls. . . . But so far as we can understand our wants, and describe them, as I learn from gentlemen with whom I am in communication, there is a large lack of confidence existing between the employers and the employed. It is a truth so self-evident that there is no hiding it at all, that as a rule the employed can never get an advance in wages without either entering upon a strike, of longer or shorter duration, or at least threatening a strike. That I believe would be the universal testimony of all who have ever been connected with labor organizations. We have known the employers to go on prospering, to grow richer and richer, to live in larger residences and travel more extensively, with their family expenditures constantly increasing, yet all the time, when approached for an increase of wages, they would declare that they were making nothing. That one fact alone destroys the confidence that should exist between employer and employed and causes many of the strikes in this country.

Sen. George: The employee thinks, as I understand you, that his prosperity ought to increase with that of his employer? — A. He not only thinks so, but he absolutely knows that it should. That thought, however, is never realized except by either striking or threatening to strike. The great majority of cases are controlled in that way. . . .

Testimony of Samuel Gompers

Samuel Gompers, who was soon (1886) to become one of the founders and the first president of the American Federation of Labor, was a cigar-maker. English by birth, he migrated to the

United States in 1863, settling in New York City. He was much influenced by the writings of Karl Marx and other socialists, but after taking part in a bitter but unsuccessful strike in 1877, which had been called in an attempt to force the abolition of sweat-shops, he decided that workers could best improve their lot not by seeking broad social reforms but by organizing into strong trade unions. By creating such organizations, he believed, workers could force their employers to raise wages, reduce hours, and otherwise improve working conditions. Although for a time a member of the Knights of Labor, Gompers insisted that effective unionization could only be achieved on the basis of individual skilled trades.

The Witness: . . . I will not start with the organizations. I would rather speak first of the general condition of labor as I find it, as I know it and believe it to be.

Sen. Blair: Well, take up the subject in your own way, but before you get through I would like you to answer the question I have put with regard to the extent and the actual objects and results of these organizations. — A. Oh, certainly; I shall endeavor to give you that to the best of my ability. The condition of the working people appears to be coming to what may rightly be termed a focus. On the one hand it would be well to note the underlying motives that frequently break out in what are generally termed strikes. Strikes are the result of a condition, and are not, as is generally or frequently understood, the cause. For instance, in the State of Massachusetts they have a ten-hour law, intended to benefit the female and child operatives there, yet the employers (and the same is true in Cohoes, in this State, and other places where the hours of labor are recognized as settled) or their agents start up the mills several minutes, sometimes seven, eight, nine, or ten minutes, before the time for commencing to work according to rule and law. In other instances they close them at "noon" several minutes after twelve o'clock and open them again several minutes before the hour, or half hour rather, has elapsed, closing again for the day several minutes after the rule requires. These employers are pretty well described by some of the English economists and labor advocates — not labor advocates, but men who have made economic questions a study; they call them "minute thieves." . . .

In the branch of industry in which I work we have a bane to contend with, a curse, known as the manufacturing of cigars in tenement houses, in which the employer hires a row of tenements four or fives stories high, with two, three, or four families living on each floor, occupying a room and bedroom, or a room, bedroom, and an apology for a kitchen. The tobacco for the work is given out by the manufacturer or his superintendent to the operatives who work there, the husband and wife, and they seldom work without one or more of their children, if they have any.

Even their parents, if they have any, work also in the room, and any indigent relative that may live with them also helps along. I myself made an investigation of these houses about two years ago; went through them and made measurements of them, and found that however clean the people might desire to be they could not be so. The bedroom is generally dark, and contains all the wet tobacco that is not intended for immediate use, but perhaps for use on the following day; while in the front room (or back room, as the case may be) the husband and wife and child, or any friend or relative that works with them, three or four or five persons, are to be found. Each has a table at which to work. The tobacco which they work and the clippings or cuttings, as they are termed, are lying around the floor, while the scrap or clip that is intended to be used immediately for the making of cigars is lying about to dry. Children are playing about, as well as their puny health will permit them, in the tobacco. I have found, I believe, the most miserable conditions prevailing in those houses that I have seen at any time in my life.

Q. How many families are thus engaged in the manufacture of cigars in this city? — A. Between 1,900 and 2,000. The lowest ascertained number was 1,920 families. That was about five or six months ago.

Q. About 10,000 people, taking the average to a family of five? — A. Probably. These rooms I found to be, the main room, in which they work, about 12 feet by 8 or 9; the height of ceiling generally about 7 feet 6 inches to 8 feet 2 inches. It may probably be in order for me to state how I ascertained the height of these places. If I had gone in my true character as an investigator of the conditions pervading these houses I would not have been admitted into them. I, however, assumed the character of a book agent, and endeavored to sell Charles Dickens's works; and, by a practice of calculating the dimensions of small rooms, that I had undertaken and continued for several weeks, I found that the rooms in those tenements varied so very little that the differences between the different rooms could easily be estimated.

Sen. George: What was the size of the bedrooms? — A. The bedrooms were generally 6 feet by 8, or, in some instances, less. The kitchen was generally what is known in New York tenements as "dark" — an intermediate room. There is, first, the front or back room, as the case may be, then the kitchen, which has no light, and then another room in the back, which has no ventilation whatever except an aperture about 2 feet square in the side, and leading into a hall which leads into the street or the yard.

Q. The kitchen is not so large as the front room? — A. Not so long; it is as wide, generally.

Q. There is a narrow hall, making four families on each floor? — A. Four families on each floor.

Q. In what condition were the yards? — A. I made an investigation into that also, and found that the yards were all dirty. The halls were kept very dirty with tobacco stems and refuse that accumulates from the tobacco. In one instance it bordered on the ludicrous. There was a sign, "Keep off the grass!" The only "grass" that I could see was the green paint on the walls and the tobacco stems lying around by the hundred weight. The water closets are all vaults, in very few places connected with sewers, vaults in the backyard, around which a few boards have been nailed and the places termed "water closets." The water supply is very meager indeed.

Q. How many stories high are the buildings? — A. Four, generally; sometimes higher.

Q. Is there a water closet for each family? — A. No; there are generally two or three private closets, which are locked and keys given to, probably, one closet for two, three, or four families, there being not more than three or four water closets for all the families in the building. On the lower floor or basement generally in those houses there are stores, sometimes grocery stores or lager-beer saloons, or second-hand furniture stores, or Chinese laundries.

Q. Do you mean to say that about 1,900 families, engaged in the manufacture of cigars, live in the manner which you have just described? — A. Four-fifths of them, I think. Within this last year one of the manufacturers has endeavored to build a row of houses that are an improvement upon the old ones; but notwithstanding all attempts to keep these places clean, that is impossible, in consequence of the long hours of toil and the fact that all of the family are employed right at the work of cigar-making. . . .

The Cigar-makers' International Union adopted a system of agitation against the tenement-house cigar manufacture some years ago, believing that it was a public nuisance, and the press of the city of New York, together with that of the entire country, took this matter in hand, discussed it ably, exposed the iniquity of the system and the greed and avarice to which many men will resort in unfair competition, even with their fairer rivals in the trade. The opinions of the press, several of them, were extracted and printed by us and spread broadcast. I do not know that they may be of any importance, but this one from the *New York Sun* says, speaking of certain of these tenements:

From cellar to attic the business carried on is the stripping of tobacco or the manufacture of cigars; women as well as men, girls as well as boys, toiling for life in an atmosphere thick with tobacco dust and reeking with odors too foul to be described. All this illustrates how one may start an extensive cigar and tobacco factory without investing in buildings and appliances.

The New York *Staats Zeitung* said:

The manufacture of cigars is one of the most important industries in our city, and tens of thousands of our working population make, directly or indirectly, their

living in the tobacco industry. Circumstances impeding this industry must therefore affect also the prosperity of the city in general.

That the manufacturer in tenement houses can underbid other tobacco manufacturers is in the first place possible by compelling their workmen to pay the rent
for factory rooms. Every other manufacturer has to pay high rents, taxes, etc., for
his factory rooms; while the manufacturer in tenement houses not only pays nothing therefor, but the subletting of the rooms yields him perhaps a surplus income.
In addition to saving his expense he makes additional extra profits by means of low
wages. He is not, like other manufacturers, confined to certain working hours;
the law against the employment of children under fourteen years of age is a dead
letter for his tenement-house factories; the workingman, whose landlord he is at
the same time, is much more dependent upon him. The workingman cannot quit
work without being thrown into the street; when he is refractory, the manufacturer
raises the rent, or assigns him to poorer rooms; in short, he has a great many more
means to oppress the workingman. The wages are so regulated that the whole
family must assist in working; that women, young girls, and children, without regard to age, bodily development, mental education, must year after year, on Sunday and weekday, work hard in an atmosphere pestered by poisonous tobacco
dust to earn the money necessary for the high rent and the direct necessities of life.

The manufacturer is getting rich, though he sells cheaper than his competitors.
But he obtains his favorable position at the expense of the health, morals, and
manliness of his workingmen, and the system thereby becomes an aggravated nuisance. The system is not only a pecuniary injury to a great many; to enrich a few
it is a social as well as an economical evil. Hundreds of medical testimonials prove
the injurious effects which the work has in ill-ventilated factories upon workingmen, and all these consequences are much stronger in tenement houses where the
working room is at the same time used for dwelling purposes. This kind of work is
especially injurious to the health of women. Out of 100 girls of the age of twelve
to sixteen years, 72 in the average become sick after six months' work. In tenement
houses where cigars are manufactured there are only 1.09 to 1.63 children to every
married couple, and the mortality is about twenty per cent. greater than in other
tenement houses. Surely this evil ought to be remedied. It endangers the whole
society, inasmuch as infectious diseases, as scarlet fever, etc., when occurring in
such houses, may be spread all over the city by means of cigars manufactured in
the room of sick cigar-makers. One physician states from his own experience that
in the same room where persons were suffering from small-pox the manufacture of
cigars was continued until the board of health interfered. Other physicians have
seen that persons suffering from diphtheria continue to make cigars. This is a
direct danger to all citizens.

Furthermore, the children in such houses grow up without sufficient education;
the dense population, the working in dwelling rooms, the unreasonable extension
of the working hours, the working on Sundays, endangers the morals and the education of adult persons. Low wages and insufficient control induces to smaller or
greater embezzlements and evasions of the revenue laws.

Continually dirty surroundings prove also in this case to be detrimental to good
morals. These evils are so apparent that, as the House-owners' Association has dem-
onstrated, a tenement house in which cigars are manufactured decreases the value
of the adjoining real estate. . . .

Q. What is your personal observation as compared with that statement? — A. I think there are a larger number of children to a family, and that this is rather an underestimate. . . .

I visited Cohoes, N.Y., during the strike there, about a year ago. That strike was organized against a proposed reduction of 10 percent in the operatives' wages. There were certain conditions surrounding the people in Cohoes that struck me very forcibly. On meeting the committee who received me (as I had been invited to attend), I made inquiries as to an immense building which I saw in the town, that being the first time I had visited Cohoes, and upon all hands was I informed, "That belongs to the Harmony Mills." Inquiring further as to another building, I was told, "That belongs to the Harmony Company." Everything belonged to the Harmony Company. The hotel was the Harmony Hotel. The boardinghouses were Harmony boardinghouses; the tenements in which the people lived belonged to the Harmony Company. The water is controlled by the Harmony Company. The waterpower by which the mills are run, the water which the people drink, the water which the other manufacturers are compelled to use, all is under the control of the Harmony Company.

Sen. Pugh: How many persons are there in the employ of that company? — A. Over 5,000.

Q. Where is Cohoes? — A. It is within an hour's travel from Albany, on the Mohawk River. As to the church there, I am informed that the minister in that church is a brother-in-law of the superintendent of the Harmony Mills. When the Harmony Company are in want of water to run their mills, and the people want water to drink, they have to go thirsty and the mills are run.

Sen. Blair: Is the water supply of the town taken from the river? — A. From the river; supplied through works first constructed by the Harmony Company.

Q. Are the city and the Harmony Company substantially identical? Does the company own the city pretty much? — A. Pretty much.

Q. Has not the city, the municipality, any reasonable opportunity of freeing itself of this dependence for water upon the Harmony Company? Can they not get a supply of water elsewhere? — A. Not very easily. I think it would require a great outlay, more than the people of Cohoes would be able to bear, outside of the interest of the Harmony Company. I was informed while there that several attempts had been made to start competitive mills in Cohoes, but that in consequence of the ownership by the Harmony Company, and their control of the water supply of Cohoes, competition was strangled at once; and while I have not traveled very extensively, I have seen some mills, and I am of opinion that no greater water facilities exist in this country than in Cohoes for the running of mills.

Q. I interrupted your statement to draw closer attention to your assertion that when water was scarce the people went thirsty in order that the mills might run. You, perhaps, were never thirsty in that city your-self, but you may know of the complaints of people who reside there. I would like to know what your information is on that point. — A. The complaints were general. Of course scarcity of water in a place of so few inhabitants is not apt to occur very frequently, but when it does occur, and it has occurred several times, then complaint is general.

Q. Then the dearth is of water for purposes of cleanliness and ablu-tion, rather than for drinking? — A. Sometimes it is.

Q. But still you do understand that the corporation restricts the people in the necessary amount of water for sanitary purposes? — A. No, sir, I do not; but I say that when there is a natural drought or scarcity of water they do. I do not wish to be understood as saying that the Harmony Company are willfully depriving the people of water, but that when there is a natural scarcity of water they first run the mills, even though the peo-ple have to go dirty and thirsty.

Q. That you understand from common conversation and from com-plaints that you have heard yourself? — A. Yes, sir.

Q. Complaints that you have heard on the ground? — A. Yes, sir; during my visit there.

Q. Was that a time of scarcity of water or not? — A. I could not an-swer that question.

Q. Do you believe that statement? — A. If I did not believe it, if I did not place some credit in it, I would not mention it.

Q. You think it is a fact? — A. Yes, sir.

Q. It satisfies your own judgment as a true statement? — A. Yes, sir; I believe it to be a truth; I have no reason to doubt it; I made inquiries after the persons told me that, and the statements were verified. I will say, by the way, that so much was I impressed with the information con-tinually given that this and that and the other thing belonged to Harmony Mills, that although I am not on a poetical turn of mind I paraphrased Tennyson's "Charge of the Light Brigade," so that instead of "cannon to right of them, cannon to left of them," it was "Harmony to right of them, Harmony to left of them." The operatives there were striking against a reduction of 10 percent in wages which was proposed, notwith-standing the fact that during that period we had had the greatest era of prosperity that this country had known. . . .

I will proceed now to another branch of inquiry, in reference to one of the most hardworked class of people under the sun, the freight-handlers of the city of New York. They are a body of men, very sinewy, working for $.17 an hour for the railroad corporations. Last year they had the hardihood to ask for three cents more an hour, making $.20 an hour, when the railroads informed them that they would not pay it. The freight-handlers were, after a struggle, starved into submission, and are working now for $.17 an hour.

Q. Now, you are here and see these people: what sort of life does a freight-handler have on $.17 an hour? — A. He generally lives in very poor quarters; his home is but scantily furnished; he can eat only of the coarsest food; his children, like too many others, are frequently brought into the factories at a very tender age; in some instances his wife takes in sewing and does chores for other people, while in other instances that I know of they work in a few of the remaining laundries where women are still engaged, the work not having been absorbed by the Chinese. By this means the home, of course, is broken up; indeed there is hardly the semblance of a home, and in these instances where the wife goes out to work no meal is cooked. Many of the stores have for sale dried meats or herrings, cheese, or some other article which does not require any cooking. Of course, when the wife is at home although the living is very poor, it is cooked; she cooks what can be purchased with the portion of the $.17 per hour remaining after the payment of rent, and the cost of light, fuel, etc. . . .

The car-drivers of the city of New York are working from fourteen to sixteen hours a day in all weathers, and receive $1.75 a day.

Q. Now, why is not that enough? — A. Because it will not purchase the commonest necessaries of life.

Q. You understand, of course, that my question is designed to draw you out fully in regard to that class of workmen, their condition, etc. I understand your assertion to be that it is not enough; it does not seem to me, either, that it is enough; but I want to know from you what chance a man has to live on $1.75 a day? — A. He has this chance: his meals are served to him by his wife or friend or child, as the case may be, in a kettle, while he is driving his team, and at the end of the route he may possibly have two or three minutes to swallow his food. It is nothing more than swallowing it, and when he comes home he is probably too tired or perhaps too hungry to eat.

Q. There is no cessation in his work during the day of any consequence, then? — A. If there is, that which is termed relays or switches, he has still the same number of hours to work.

Q. Do you mean that that is deducted from his fourteen or sixteen hours? — A. Yes, sir.

Q. Then, if the relays amounted to an hour, he would be absent from his home seventeen hours? — A. Yes, sir.

Q. And if two hours, eighteen? — A. Yes, sir. And in the matter of these relays, in some instances men who do not and cannot live, on account of the meagerness of their wages, on the route of the railroad, are compelled to live at some distance, and when they have these relays or switches it takes them sometimes twenty or thirty minutes to reach their homes, and to return again takes another half or three-quarters of an hour.

Q. Then, do I understand you that these relays and the time occupied morning and evening going to and returning from their work are to be added to the fourteen or sixteen hours of actual service required? — A. The actual service is from fourteen to fifteen hours. Then there is the looking after their horses and cleaning the car besides.

Q. From the time that a car-driver leaves home in the morning until he returns for the night how much of the twenty-four hours will ordinarily be consumed? — A. I cannot tell you exactly as to how long a time they have at home, for the reason that it depends to some extent upon how far they live from the route of travel.

Q. State it approximately as near as you can. — A. Well, I do not believe that they have more than seven and a half hours out of the twenty-four.

Sen. Call: At what hour in the morning do they commence ordinarily, and what time do they quit? — A. Several of the street railroads of this city run all day and night; and on those, of course, the men commence at various hours. During the day the traffic on some routes is not so much as on others, and then they will be relayed; and, although they may go on to work at five o'clock in the morning, they probably would not get off before eleven or twelve o'clock at night, or probably later still. I would not say later still positively, but I think in some instances later.

Sen. Pugh: Have they ever been paid higher wages? — A. Yes, sir. About two years ago they were on a strike to obtain, I think, $2.00 a day, but were starved into submission.

Q. What do they get now? — A. One dollar and seventy-five cents.

Sen. George: Does the conductor get the same wages, or more? — A. I think he gets $.25 more, by reason of his position of trust.

Sen. Blair: Have you any knowledge with regard to those who operate the elevated railways? — A. The men who work at ticket collecting or at the boxes where the tickets are deposited receive $1.25 a day, I think. I would rather wait until I can give you information definitely. I think I can do so now, but I prefer to wait.

Sen. George: Are the car-drivers allowed to have seats? — A. They are not. They have to stand all the time.

Sen. Call: How many hours do they stand? — A. Fourteen or fifteen.

Q. Do you mean fourteen hours' standing without intermission? — A. Very little intermission. They sometimes rest back against the door of the car for a while. They also, in some instances, have to act as conductors; that is, give change, count the passengers, and register the number of passengers on an indicator. And then they are sometimes held responsible when somebody is run over on account, perhaps, of their having to perform two men's work. The greed of the horse-railroad companies has been such that they have introduced on several lines what is known as the bobtailed car, and have dispensed with the services of a conductor.

Sen. Blair: Don't you think that is because they cannot afford to pay any more? — A. I hardly believe that. Judging from the traffic, they are capable of paying it, and judging from what is currently reported as their dividends, they are more than capable of paying it. I must acknowledge, though, that so far as their dividends are concerned, I am personally uninformed. I take merely current rumor and the appearance of the traffic, the number of passengers I see on the cars.

Among some of the tailoresses in the city I have made a personal investigation. They make a regular heavy pantaloon, working pants, for $.07 a pair. They are capable of making ten pairs per day of twelve hours. Boys' pantaloons they make for $.05 to $.06 per pair, making fourteen to sixteen pairs per day of twelve hours. They work mostly seven full days in the week; sometimes they will stop on Sunday afternoon, but all work on Sunday, and their average weekly wages is about $3.81, providing no time is lost.

They are compelled to provide their own cotton out of this, and their own needles and thimbles, and other small things that are necessary in the work. Overalls and jumpers (a kind of calico jacket used by laborers in warm weather sometimes, to prevent the dirt getting to the shirt or underclothing) they make for $.30 to $.35 per dozen. They generally work in "teams" of two, and they make about three dozen per day, or in a working day of thirteen to fifteen hours they earn from $.45 to $.52½ each. They work generally in the shop, but usually finish some work at home on Sunday.

In the manufacture of cigars in shops there is a branch termed "stripping." I am not sure as to these statistics that I am going to give you, but I believe them to be correct. Nine-tenths of these strippers, or about that proportion, are females. Their average hours of labor are ten per day. Their wages range between $3 and $7 a week when at work. About one-half of these girls are employed at the former wage, but two-thirds at $5 a week, and the remaining third at a higher wage.

They lose days and weeks' work frequently, or have lost them in the past more than at present, and in very rare instances are they paid for loss of time, even when it is caused by national or other holidays. In the shops, more especially the larger ones, they are prohibited from holding any conversation under pain of fine or dismissal. Even if they were disposed to converse they could not. The very positions in which they work, or are placed to work (which are not necessary to the work), in long rows, in which each faces the back of the girl in front of her, precludes them from holding conversation. They suffer in every way the disciplinary measures of imprisonment at hard labor. They cannot hold conversation. One sits with her face to the back of the other, and that is the rule in almost all the factories. Where there are only a few of them of course it makes very little difference. It is believed that this plan of placing them gets more work out of them. . . .

Q. Now, about the newsboys and the other little fellows that we see around the streets, the bootblacks. Those little waifs seem to be pretty busy doing something all the time. What pay do they get out of their labors — how do they live? — A. Well, the newsboys earn very small sums. I do not believe more than one-half of them live at home with their parents. The others, out of the papers they sell or earn, try to purchase a ticket for some variety show, and buy cigarettes, of course, and keep just sufficient to get a meal in a five-cent restaurant and to pay their lodging in a newsboys' lodging-house, which costs about half a dollar a week.

Q. What chance is there of their attending school? — A. Without answering that question I would like to make a statement that I read in one of the papers (and the paper said that the superintendent of the Newsboys' Home acknowledged it to be true) that the newsboys were required to pay for one week's lodging in advance; that one boy was taken sick while in the lodging-house, and sent to the hospital after the second night of the week for which he had paid, and when he came out of the hospital he thought that he had five nights good yet to sleep in the lodging-house, but when he came there he was informed that he had forfeited that money by not sleeping in the lodging-house during the week. . . .

Q. Are the newsboys employed by the newspapers, or do they just get so much for every paper they sell? — A. They get so much for every paper they sell, and sometimes a man can buy two-cent papers for a penny. Some will offer you two papers for a cent.

Q. When they have a supply left which they do not sell what becomes of it? — A. It is their own loss.

Sen. George: They buy the papers themselves and make what they can? — A. Yes, sir; and it is quite a sight to see some of the boys running after the wagons that contain the papers, the evening papers more especially; to see one hundred or two hundred of them, and as one drops off that has been served with his papers another one takes his place, the others coming up continually and keeping up the crowd. If the poor boys were on the point of starvation and their only hope of life was in that wagon I do not believe they could run much faster or risk their lives much more than they do sometimes.

Q. How about the bootblacks? — A. How the bootblacks do I cannot say, any more than their position in life is very hard.

Q. Does the newsboy get a chance for school at all? — A. I do not see where that comes in, except that possibly one here and there may have an opportunity of going to a night school, and that, I think, is not generally taken advantage of by them. The boy fails to see the importance of an education himself, and there are very few who are willing to lend a hand to guide him. . . .

Sen. Pugh: What is your opinion as to whether that idea of regarding the laborer as a machine exists more now than it has existed in the past?

— A. I think it exists now in a greater degree than it did formerly. Not only do I think that, but I am forced to the opinion that it is increasing and intensifying even as we go along.

Q. Anyhow, that, you say, is the view that the employees take of the sentiments entertained towards them by their employers? — A. Yes, sir. They find that employers are no longer — when I speak of employers I speak of them generally — that they are no longer upon the same footing with them that they were on formerly. They find that where a man who may have worked at the bench with them employs one or two hands they and he may have full social intercourse together, but as that man increases his business and employs a larger number of hands they find that his position has been removed so far above that of his old friends that they meet no more socially. Probably they may meet occasionally in the factory, when there will be a passing remark of "Good morning" or "Good day"; and then, after a while, the employer fails to see the employees at all; the superintendent does all the business and the employer does not bother himself any more about the men. That is how the position of the two has been changed since both were workingmen at the bench. The difference is considerably greater when the employer and the employee did not know each other before, and when the employer's resources are already large. In such cases he and the men do not know each other at all, and in most such instances the employees are not known as men at all, but are known by numbers — "1," "2," "3," or "4," and so on. . . .

Testimony of John S. McClelland

In 1883 John S. McClelland, a telegrapher, had been practicing his trade for about fourteen years. He was a member of the Brotherhood of Telegraphers.

Sen. Blair: I would like to have you give us whatever information you possess as to his opportunities for intellectual improvement, for suitable and proper amusement and recreation, and any other information which bears upon the actual condition of the city telegraph operator and his mode of life? — A. Well, I will instance two cases, the case of the night operator and that of the day operator. The day operator works from eight o'clock in the morning until half past five o'clock in the afternoon. Living, as he generally does, at some distance from the place of his employment, either in the uptown districts of the city or in the outskirts of Brooklyn, or perhaps in some of the New Jersey towns, he is compelled, in order to reach his place of employment at eight o'clock, to rise at six o'clock in the morning. He is then continuously employed, I may say, from six o'clock in the morning until six o'clock in the evening, and his dinner-time is spent in the telegraph building as a general rule. The company have a restaurant in the top floor of the building, and he is allowed half an hour or perhaps forty or forty-five minutes for dinner, according to the length of time that he is willing to wait for his dinner. When his day's work is done and he is ready to leave the building it will be close to six o'clock. He will reach home probably in the neighborhood of eight o'clock in the evening, and then he will have an hour and a half or two hours for social enjoyment, mental improvement, recreation, rest, and the enjoyment of whatever other luxuries he can command, when he will be forced to retire in order to be ready to rise again at six o'clock in the morning; and he pursues this routine from one end of the week to the other. That is the life of the day operator. I have always considered that the night operator has in some respects the best of it. I may be wrong, however, for a great many of the men who work in the daytime would rather do so, while a great many of the night men also are anxious to get on the day force.

Q. Is the pay the same? — A. About the same. The hours of service of the night operator are less. He goes to work about half past five o'clock in the evening. In order to do so, if he lives at any distance from his place of employment he has to leave home at, say, four o'clock. He then works his regular hours, until one o'clock in the morning, or sometimes until two o'clock or half past two o'clock, and in many instances when business is heavy he will work on until eight o'clock in the morning. But, taking the average hour of quitting as three o'clock, he starts for his home and reaches it probably about half past four o'clock or 5 o'clock. He then retires to rest, and in order to satisfy the wants of nature will probably sleep if he can until two o'clock in the afternoon.

Q. Does he take his breakfast before retiring to rest? — A. Sometimes, I suppose. It is the rule, however, after coming out of the office, whatever the time may be, to get a light lunch and then go home and go to bed. Then, waking up at two o'clock in the afternoon, he will have time to get his dinner and catch the next train or car and reach the office so as to go to work again at half past five o'clock; so that his opportunities for enjoyment are perhaps about the same as those of the day operator, except that the night operator, by denying himself sleep, can have a greater portion of the afternoon to walk around and enjoy himself as he sees fit. But if he takes the proper amount of rest his opportunity for such enjoyments will be limited at the most to two or three hours.

Q. How is it as to vacations or an occasional day off? — A. No vacations are known in the telegraph business. If a man wishes to go off for a day, a week, or a month he may possibly get leave of absence, but he will lose his pay during the time he is absent. If he cannot secure leave of absence he can hire a colleague to work for him, paying that substitute usually at a much higher rate than he would receive for the work himself. . . .

Testimony of Conrad Carl

Conrad Carl, a resident of New York City, had been a tailor for nearly thirty years.

Sen. Pugh: Please give us any information that you may have as to the relation existing between the employers and the employees in the tailoring business in this city, as to wages, as to treatment of the one by the other class, as to the feeling that exists between the employers and the employed generally, and all that you know in regard to the subject that we are authorized to inquire into? — A. During the time I have been here the tailoring business is altered in three different ways. Before we had sewing machines we worked piecework with our wives, and very often our children. We had no trouble then with our neighbors, nor with the landlord, because it was a very still business, very quiet; but in 1854 or 1855, and later, the sewing machine was invented and introduced, and it stitched very nicely, nicer than the tailor could do; and the bosses said: "We want you to use the sewing machine; you have to buy one." Many of the tailors had a few dollars in the bank, and they took the money and bought machines. Many others had no money, but must help themselves; so they brought their stitching, the coat or vest, to the other tailors who had sewing machines, and paid them a few cents for the stitching. Later, when the money was given out for the work, we found out that we could earn no more than we could without the machine; but the money for the machine was gone now, and we found that the machine was only for the profit of the bosses; that they got their work quicker, and it was done nicer. . . . The machine makes too much noise in the place, and the neighbors want to sleep, and we have to stop sewing earlier; so we have to work faster. We work now in excitement — in a hurry. It is hunting; it is not work at all; it is a hunt.

Q. You turn out two or three times as much work per day now as you did in prior times before the war? — A. Yes, sir; two or three times as much; and we have to do it, because the wages are two-thirds lower than they were five or ten years back. . . .

Sen. Blair: What proportion of them are women and what proportion men, according to your best judgment? — A. I guess there are many more women than men.

Q. The pay of the women is the same as the pay of the men for the same quantity of work, I suppose? — A. Yes; in cases where a manufacturer — that is, a middleman — gets work from the shop and brings it into his store and employs hands to make it, women get paid by the piece also. If the manufacturer gets $.25 for a piece, he pays for the machine work on that piece so many cents to the machine-worker, he pays so many cents to the presser, so many cents to the finisher, and so many to the button-sewer — so much to each one — and what remains is to pay his rent and to pay for the machinery.

Q. What is your knowledge as to the amount that workers of that class are able to save from their wages? — A. I don't know any one that does save except those manufacturers.

Q. As a class, then, the workers save nothing? — A. No.

Q. What sort of house-room do they have? What is the character, in general, of the food and clothing which they are able to purchase with what they can make by their labor? — A. They live in tenement houses four or five stories high, and have two or three rooms.

Q. What is the character of their clothing? — A. They buy the clothing that they make — the cheapest of it.

Q. What about the character of food that they are able to provide for themselves? — A. Food? They have no time to eat dinner. They have a sandwich in the middle of the day, and in the evening when they go away from work it is the same, and they drink lager or anything they can get.

Q. They are kept busy all the time and have but little opportunity for rest? — A. Yes.

Q. What is the state of feeling between the employers and their employees in that business? How do you workingmen feel towards the people who employ you and pay you? — A. Well, I must say the workingmen are discouraged. If I speak with them they go back and don't like to speak much about the business and the pay. They fear that if they say how it is they will get sent out of the shop. They hate the bosses and the foremen more than the bosses, and that feeling is deep.

Q. Why do they feel so towards the foremen? — A. They know that they do a wrong onto them; they know that.

Q. Do not the foremen act under the instruction of the bosses? — A. Well, it seems so.

Q. Could not the boss correct the wrong that the foreman does, if it is a wrong? — A. Well, when we complain that the foreman is so and so, the boss says, "Oh, I have nothing to do with it; I don't know; go to the foreman; it is the foreman's business." Then when we go to the foreman he says, "Oh, I can't pay more; these are my rules; if you don't like it, go to the boss."

Q. And when you do go to the boss he sends you back to the foreman? — A. Yes; he says, "I have nothing to do with this; that is my foreman's business; go to him." Therefore the workmen hate them both.

Q. But can you explain why they hate the foremen, as you say they do, more than the bosses, when the bosses keep the foremen there and could discharge them and get better ones in their places if they desired? — A. Gentlemen, if I say all this here — if it is made public I come out of work.

Sen. Pugh: Then you are testifying here under the apprehension of punishment for what you have stated? — A. Well, I have no fear for anyone, you know, and if you think it is better that I say it, I do so.

Q. What is your feeling of restraint in testifying? What injury would you be subjected to for telling the truth? Would the workingmen in your business testify under a fear of being punished by their employers for telling the truth? — A. Yes. It is nothing but fear. . . .

Sen. Blair: Have you any objection to giving us the names of some of the bosses and foremen that you know, who control a large number of laborers of the class to which you belong? This committee desires to obtain such information as you can give in regard to the condition of those engaged in your trade, and if there is any attempt to punish you for giving such information I think you can find protection from the country, or from some source. We cannot compel you to give the information, but we desire you to state, if you will, the names of some of these bosses and foremen, so that if they do not think proper to come here and speak for themselves the country will understand that you have told us the truth. — A. Now, sir, if I lose my work who can give me another work? I am an old man now, you know, and the young ones, they get the work and they say, "He is an old man; what can he do?" . . .

Testimony of Robert S. Howard

Robert S. Howard, a Fall River, Massachusetts, textile worker, was secretary of the local union and a former member of the Massachusetts legislature. Before migrating to the United States he had worked for seventeen years in English textile factories.

The Witness: Now there is one remarkable thing in Massachusetts, and that is that if ever a bill is brought before our legislature for the redress of some grievance which may exist, or if the workingmen come to the legislature asking for some law which may be beneficial to their interests as workingmen, such as a law providing that they shall be paid weekly, or a law providing for boards of arbitration, or a law to make the ten-hour rule more stringent — if ever there is a bill of any of these kinds brought before our legislature you will always see the corporation detectives there, particularly from Lowell and from Lawrence. Lowell wishes itself to be looked upon as the workingman's Paradise of Massachusetts, but it is the worst place in Massachusetts, and pays the lowest prices to its workingmen. The Lowell manufacturers always have a ring of men down at the State House, and they always wish to make it appear that their city is a Paradise and an Eden. It was that Merrimac corporation that got us reduced 10 percent in 1880. When the Board of Trade met the others said to us, "You make that Merrimac company pay the same as we are paying; they can undersell us as things are." There are men there running 1,500 spindles for about $9.50 a week, while in the other New England mills they can get $12.00 a week. They have a man named Moses Sargent who is there at the State House every week, and when I was on the legislative committee I used to see him watching every man that came in; so that a Lowell man that had to earn his bread in the mills dare not put his head into the committee room. The same is true in Lawrence. They had a detective named Filbrook always watching to see if any Lawrence men came before the committee to give testimony. Then, after the meetings were over, they would say, "There are those Fall River fellows; they are a turbulent set." It is not that we in Fall River are turbulent; it is because we had manhood enough and nerve enough to go and ask and demand what was our right that they say that about us. There are no Fall River detectives at the State House. I went to a meeting of the mule-spinners at Lawrence some six or seven weeks ago. I wanted to get all the mule-spinners out from the Pacific Mills where the wages was reduced about a year ago, and I called a meeting by circular and had the circular distributed through the Pacific and the Atlantic and the Pemberton Mills. When the time came that was appointed for the meeting, there across the road stood Filbrook, the corporation detective, and Russell, the overseer, watching every man that came in. There was one man at that meeting who was looking out of the window at them, and he said, "I never belonged to a union in my life, Howard, but nothing does so much as the presence of those men there to convince me that there must be some good for the workingmen in unions, for unless there was, those men would not stand there spying us as we come in." That is the condition of affairs. Those manufacturers have their detectives employed permanently. I will not vouch for the statement I am going to make, but I have been told that Filbrook gets a salary of $6,000 a year from the Pacific Mills alone. However, I do not vouch for that as true. . . .

Sen. Blair: In regard to the actual physical condition of the operatives in Fall River and elsewhere, can you give us any information? — A. The condition of the operative in our city is a very unenviable one. The work there is very hard and the wages are very low — low in proportion to what they used to be some ten years ago, before the financial depression set in. Our females in particular are overworked; their strength is entirely overtaxed by the labors they have to perform. I have often argued myself that if our manufacturers would give over preaching so much about temperance and other things and try to bring about a reform in the condition of their operatives, it would be better than all the many thousand temperance lectures and temperance tales. . . .

The work is too severe. Nobody would credit the amount of labor that a cotton operative has to perform. You may take a girl, boy, or man, from outside and put him in there to walk by the side of one who is employed in those mills, and I tell you that unless he has a very good constitution you will soon perceive a failure — that is, on account of the mere traveling, irrespective of the peculiar labor they have to perform. It is dreadful to see those girls, stripped almost to the skin, wearing only a kind of loose wrapper, and running like a racehorse from the beginning to the end of the day; and I can perceive that it is bringing about both a moral and physical decay in them. I do not want to say a word that would reflect disagreeably on my city or its people, because I think others are quite as bad, but I must say that I have noticed that the hard, slavish overwork is driving those girls into the saloons after they leave the mills in the evenings; and you might as well try to deprive them of their suppers; after they leave the mills you will see them going into saloons, looking scared and ashamed, and trying to go in without anyone seeing them — good respectable girls, too, but they come out so tired, and so thirsty, and so exhausted, especially in the summer months, from working along steadily from hour to hour and breathing the noxious effluvia from the grease and other ingredients that are used in the mills, and they are so exhausted when the time comes to quit, that you will find that all their thoughts are concentrated on something to drink to allay their thirst. I know of one girl in particular that lived close by me; her father died in the war and she lives with her widowed mother, who is receiving a pension from the state. The girl's health began to fail her some time ago and she had to go round the country trying to recruit her strength, and finally the doctor told her that the work was too hard and tried to keep her out of the mills, but the mother found it hard to get along, because it is so difficult to get occupation outside of the mills, and the doctor advised the mother to tell the girl to get a glass of beer or something to stimulate her appetite, as she could not eat anything; for beer, with all its bad faults — and I do not believe it is a good thing for anybody, still it has an effect sometimes in stimulating the stomach and creating the desire for something to eat, and without they do eat they won't work long in the mills. I would not put a child of mine in to be a mule-spinner for anything — I think I would sooner put it to a chimney sweep to learn his trade. It is a trade and it is no trade, mule-spinning, and if the manufacturers would only try it a little they would think so too, because it is a continual race from morning till night, and there is not one man in twenty not brought up in the business who could follow a mule-spinner from the beginning of his day's work to the end, even considering nothing but the walking. . . .

It is a constant race from morning to night after this machinery; and you may know as well as I can tell you, how a man must feel in this hot weather following such an occupation as that. He just feels no manhood about him. He can only take a glass of beer to stimulate him, to give him a little appetite so that he may eat, in order to be able to go through his daily drudgery. I have been there and I know it. From the time I was very young I was fond of reading, and I remember many occasions when I have gone to my supper and taken my daily paper and have fallen asleep with the paper in my hand, and have slept there until about eleven o'clock. Then I have been determined to read it, and have put my lamp beside me when I went to bed, and have gone to sleep again with the paper in my hand and lain there just as I put myself down, without stirring, until morning, the result of exhaustion.

Now we can never expect to advance civilization among such a class of people until we get a reform of this miserable condition of affairs. We must get our people to read and think, and to look for something higher and nobler in life than working along in that wretched way from day to day and from week to week and from year to year. . . .

But there is one thing that needs rectifying in Massachusetts, and that is the blacklisting system — the system of blacklisting men who have the courage to speak their opinions. In Lowell some two years ago I went to start the men to ask for more wages, because we in Fall River could not do anything until Lowell made some advance. I went down there and we had a petition drawn up. No name was signed to it, because all of the men were afraid, but the petition was sent in asking for an advance in wages. In about two weeks after that petition was presented to the Lowell manufacturers the three men that had had the drawing up of the petition were discharged from the mills. That is a fact. I made this same statement before the legislature of Massachusetts; I told it to Mr. Ludlam and the representatives of the three corporations and they could not deny it. Then their detective came walking across and said to me, "If you have any charges you should make them in writing"; and I turned to him and said, "It was you that tracked those men." One of those three men is now dead; another is tending bar, and the other we do not know where he is. The same practice exists in Lawrence. I know a man who left the Arlington Mills. They had an imported superintendent from England and he wanted to show our Americans that he could make people do anything he pleased, and he sent down to one of our mills to have the man blacklisted, and that man is now working in the city under an assumed name. I may say also in the same connection, that in my own city we had thirty-three men discharged about two years ago for asking for an advance of wages, and they are working now under assumed names. The bosses hired a detective in our city (for they have adopted the Lowell and Lawrence system), and I am told that he goes around with his list to see if he can find those men.

Q. What do you say those men were blacklisted for? — A. Merely for having courage enough to ask for an advance of wages when the state of the trade warranted it. . . .

Testimony of John Hill

In 1872 John Hill, an Illinois woolens manufacturer, migrated to Columbus, Georgia, to become manager of the woolens division of the Eagle and Phoenix Mills. In 1883 he was in charge of the company's cotton division, which processed nearly fifty 500-pound bales of cotton daily.

The Witness: The hours of labor in cotton manufacture in the Eagle and Phoenix Mills average eleven per day, but in many mills they average twelve per day. In New England, in some of the states, the law prescribes ten hours as a day's work. That is so in Massachusetts, but not in New Hampshire. . . .

Sen. Blair: At some point in your statement I should like to ask you to state your experience as to the wages paid now and at other times since you have been in this southern country for all classes of labor in the South. — A. There is no uniform scale of wages in the South. While there is none in the North either, the relation between capital and labor there, and the antagonism of the two at times, exert influences of which the result is a very considerable uniformity of wages for equal labor in the North. Here, on the other hand, each manufacturer establishes his hours of labor and regulates the amount that he shall pay. I am talking now about common labor. If he can afford to be liberal on account of profits, wages will advance. The profit on manufacturing has been heretofore so great that the prosperous manufacturer has been willing that a portion of the profits should be divided among the operatives. If there was a disposition on the part of manufacturers at the South, as there is on the part of some of them, to employ labor at less prices than are now paid, they could do it — more especially in the isolated mills; but in Columbus and Augusta and at other points where there is considerable competition and considerable opportunity for employment, the prices paid for labor in the mills regulate themselves, the law of supply and demand coming in and governing in that as in other things. The average wages paid in Columbus and Augusta for really proficient help may be stated to be equal to the average wages paid at the North. The unskilled labor being less profitable, is probably employed in the South at less wages than at the North, but it is usually paid for about in proportion to its proficiency.

Q. I would like to have you state the wages actually paid in the construction of the mill which you superintended, and then the pay which the operatives receive? — A. The labor question in this portion of the South, in fact in the whole South, has radically changed within the last ten years. Ten years ago, and previous to that, back to the close of the war, there was an enormous percent of unemployed labor. That was the case, first, because there was little demand for labor; and, secondly, because, from the results of the war and the changed conditions and necessities of labor, it was not appreciated, because there was a lack of capital and of enterprise which would call for the employment of large amounts of labor. Owing to the changes that have taken place, this condition of things does not now exist. There is no able-bodied man, woman, or child, who desires employment, permanently unemployed in the city of Columbus. Everybody that desires employment may obtain it at fair, reasonable, and profitable rates; the demand being about equal to the supply. The construction of our new mill in 1876 was the first step in the movement which has resulted in a radical change in this respect; and that, together with improved conditions all round, has changed the question of the price of labor, and the question of supply and demand here. In 1876, at the commencement of the construction of this mill, the supply of labor was so great that the price paid for it could have been made anything within reason that we chose. For some time after the commencement we employed several hundred laborers at $.50 a day. The river banks were lined black with men every morning seeking employment at that price, and we had probably one hundred applications every morning.

Q. From laborers of both races? — A. Yes, sir; from both races. We employed them both together at that time. We didn't know any better then. We found, however, that low wages did not pay, and that while an abundance of labor could be procured at that price, the remuneration was too small an inducement to call out the best men so we found our labor very irregular. Sometimes we would have twenty, thirty or forty hands who had worked yesterday who would not be at work today, and while we were able to fill their places without any trouble, yet we found that these continued changes were undesirable. Therefore, for the purpose of securing the most desirable labor and rendering it more permanent, we advanced the wages to $.60 a day, which was then considered a high figure.

Q. Did that remedy the evil of irregularity and instability? — A. Yes, sir; we were then able to secure the best labor, and it became comparatively permanent, with very few changes. Labor here today is very much more proficient than it used to be. We have no vagabonds or loafers now, comparatively speaking, and at present, unlike that time, when a man hires a man to do a day's labor, he expects to perform the labor. At that time he expected to get his pay without working if he could. The men are the same now that they were then. The average price today is probably on the same basis as before, $.75 a day; but, owing to experience and to other causes, the labor has become much more intelligent and in many instances $.90 and $1.00 and $1.25 a day are paid. It is not really, however, an advance in wages, but an advance in capability and in general proficiency which renders the labor more valuable. The laborers are smarter now, and they are worth more money than they were then. . . .

Q. Now, what have you to say to us in regard to child labor in factories? — A. Well, the child labor question is different here from what it is in the North, for sundry reasons. In the first place, it is a lamentable fact that parents here do not recognize the necessity of education to the extent that they do in the North. In the North all the people, including all the laboring classes, think it a duty to have their children educated, and the facilities which the free-school system gives them for that purpose are very largely used. Perhaps the laws of the northern states regulate the matter somewhat; but laws are second to facts, and if the sentiment of the people did not justify such laws they would not be made. Then, too, a law that would be good in that regard in Massachusetts would not be good for anything in Alabama. You must adapt your laws to the state and conditions of society. Suppose you should pass a law in Alabama that, up to a certain age, children should not work because they must go to school; it wouldn't be good for anything; for the reason that, in the first place, even if they did not work, they would not go to school, because the parents would not want to send them, and also because if they did there are no schools to which they could send them generally. . . .

In regard to the small children, more especially those in our spinning room, they are worth all they are paid, and the fact is that the wages they earn are a necessity for the support of the families from which the children come; so that if they were turned out there would be suffering upon the part of those families for want of that income. We do not really employ those children as a matter of preference, but as a matter of necessity. When a family comes here and a portion of them go to work in the mill they are sure to make application for employment for all their children who are of sufficient age to go to work in the mill, and they persist in those applications until those children are employed.

Q. At what ages are the children employed? — A. About ten years, I believe, is the youngest age at which we employ them.

Q. What do children of ten years and upward do? — A. They do this very light work, attending the spinning and winding machinery — very light work. There is no work that those children do that is sufficiently arduous to overtax them or to interfere with their health or development. Their work is all light, and the only thing that can tax them is perhaps the hours of labor.

Q. Are they generally as healthy as other children of the same age? — A. I think they are. Of course, the dust and all that kind of thing in a cotton mill is not quite so healthy as the air that comes unpolluted from the Gulf, but still, I think, their health generally is very good.

Q. Does their health average well compared with that of other children who are not employed in the mills? — A. Yes, sir; I think their health is, if anything, a little better, for the reason that they are not exposed in cold weather so much as other children, but work in the mill where it is warm and pleasant. They are better housed and better regulated than those outside as a general rule. . . .

Testimony of Addie Priscilla Jones

Addie Priscilla Jones was one of several relatively skilled female operatives from the Eagle and Phoenix Mills who testified before the committee.

Sen. Blair: You began working in the mill twelve years ago? — A. Yes, sir; at $.30 a day.

Q. How long did it take you to learn to weave? — A. Four weeks.

Q. Did you commence weaving at the end of four weeks? — A. No, sir; I was spinning until I was large enough to weave. I was spinning for three or four years.

Q. How old were you when you began to weave? — A. I think I was fifteen.

Q. When you began to work in the mill you were about eleven years of age? — A. Yes, sir.

Q. Have you worked in the mill all the time since? — A. I have.

Q. Has your health been pretty good? — A. I have had very good health.

Q. Are there many others who have worked as long as you have, or about as long, in the mills? — A. Yes, sir; a great many others.

Q. How are the factory girls, generally, as to health? — A. They have good health, I believe.

Q. Do you think they enjoy as good health as other young women? — A. Yes, sir.

Q. How about the work itself? Do you like it, and do the girls generally like it? — A. Yes, sir; I like it very much.

Q. I suppose you feel rather attached to the mill? — A. I do.

Q. You do not object to the number of hours you have to work? — A. No, sir. That is to our advantage, you know; we are piece weavers, and we make more the longer we work.

Q. What can you earn now? — A. I earn $1.50 every day.

Q. What do you do with the money? — A. I support myself and my mother, and save some, too. . . .

Q. What chance have you had to attend school? — A. I have never had much chance to attend school since I went to work. Before I went to work I went to school. . . .

Testimony of Timothy D. Stow

The background and experience of Dr. Timothy D. Stow are explained in the evidence he presented before the committee.

Sen. Blair: You are a physician? — A. Yes.

Q. You live at Fall River? — A. Yes.

Q. Won't you state how you happen to appear before the committee, what your object is in coming here, and at whose request you come; and then give us the benefit of any observations you choose to lay before us? — A. Mr. Robert Howard, of our city, called on me yesterday, and desired me to appear here today before your committee to give whatever testimony I could relating particularly to the physical and mental and perhaps the moral condition of the operatives and laboring classes of Fall River. I have made no notes, and I hardly know what your plan is; but I would as soon answer questions as to make any detailed statement.

Sen. Blair: We want to find out how the working people of Fall River are living and doing. You can tell us that in the way in which one gentleman would talk to another, the one understanding the subject and the other not understanding it. Just tell us the condition of the operatives there, in your own way, bearing in mind that we would rather have it without premeditation than as a prepared statement.

The Witness: I have been in Fall River about eleven years, though I have been one year absent during that time. As a physician and surgeon, of course, I have been brought into contact with all classes of people there, particularly the laboring classes, the operatives of the city.

With regard to the effect of the present industrial system upon their physical and moral welfare, I should say it was of such a character as to need mending, to say the least. It needs some radical remedy. Our laboring population is made up very largely of foreigners, men, women, and children, who have either voluntarily come to Fall River, or who have been induced to come there by the manufacturers.

As a class they are dwarfed physically. Of course there are exceptions to that; some notable ones. On looking over their condition and weighing it as carefully as I have been able to, I have come to the conclusion that the character and quality of the labor which they have been doing in times past, and most of them from childhood up, has been and is such as to bring this condition upon them slowly and steadily.

They are dwarfed, in my estimation, sir, as the majority of men and women who are brought up in factories must be dwarfed under the present industrial system; because by their long hours of indoor labor and their hard work they are cut off from the benefit of breathing fresh air, and from the sights that surround a workman outside a mill. Being shut up all day long in the noise and in the high temperature of these mills, they become physically weak.

Then, most of them are obliged to live from hand to mouth, or, at least, they do not have sufficient food to nourish them as they need to be nourished. Those things, together with the fact that they have to limit their clothing supply — this constant strain upon the operative — all tend to make him on the one hand uneasy and restless, or on the other hand to produce discouragement and recklessness. They make him careless in regard to his own condition. All those things combined tend to produce what we have in Fall River.

Now, first, as to the moral condition of the operatives of Fall River. I think so far as crime is concerned we have quite as little crime there as in any city of its size. We have a population rising on 50,000. There is a disposition at times, and under certain pressure, for some operatives to violate the law, to pilfer, or something of that kind, and I think it grows out of not what is called "pure cussedness," but a desire to relieve some physical want. For instance, a man wants a coat and has not the means of earning it, and he is out of employment, and being pinched with the cold, and with no prospect of getting employment, or of getting a coat by honest means, he steals one. Or perhaps he steals food on the same principle.

But so far as crime is concerned, we have comparatively little. But what I do say, and what has been on my mind ever since I came to Fall River, with reference to operatives there, is the peculiar impress they seem to bear, a sort of dejected, tired, worn-out, discouraged appearance, growing out of the bad influences of long hours of labor, the close confinement of the mills, the din of the machinery, their exclusion from social intercourse, except at night.

And I think we can look for a solution of the problem which the country at large is endeavoring to solve — that with reference to the intemperate habits of the laboring classes and the operatives — in those facts that I have mentioned.

I have questioned many thoughtful men and women in regard to that. I have said, "Why is it that at night particularly you frequent the dramshops? Why is it that by day you drink; that you store enough even for the day in your houses?" The answer is, "Well, doctor, I tell you the fact is this, there is a sense of fatigue over us which we do not know how to overcome, and which we must overcome for the time being if we are to have any social qualities of an evening, and we can't do it without taking something which will bridge over the time and make us equal to the emergency of the evening or the occasion." . . . But I have said, "How does this make you feel? You say you have been feeling fatigued in the evening and discouraged; that your future does not look bright; how do you feel when you get the liquor?" "Why," he will say, "it covers that all up; we lose all thought of that, and for the time being we feel well." And so they go on from day to day, and from night to night.

Now, after all, I do not know of many drunkards in Fall River, but this is true: the operative spends his five, ten, or fifteen, or twenty-five cents a night for liquor, and it is so much lost money to him, and yet he feels impelled to it, because he does not know how otherwise to adapt himself to the circumstances of the evening. . . .

Now, it is invariably the testimony of the more intelligent men and women in answer to the question, "Why do you persist in drinking?" "It makes us feel better; we are relieved of the ennui of life; we are relieved of mental depression for the time being, and after the evening's social engagements are over we get home and go to bed, and think nothing of it, and next day resume our day's work." And so it goes on from day to day.

Now, there are other things which hinge upon low wages and long hours of labor to demoralize the operative. For instance, his food. I think it is safe to say that the great mass of operatives there are forced to buy the cheapest food. They go to the meat stores and purchase joints, which, of course, made up into a soup, generally makes good food, but it does not do to have soup all the time. Then they purchase the cheapest vegetables and endeavor to make the money go as far as it possibly will to supply their wants. But all that produces this condition: they lack that sort of nutrition which is essential to an increase of fiber and flesh, and to maintain that elasticity which they ought to have for the performance of a fair amount of labor. I think if the food of the operatives could be increased it would be better.

Q. You mean increased in quantity, in quality, or both? — A. I mean both.

Q. You mean that they do not have enough to eat? — A. Many of them do not, they are limited in amount. I have occasion almost every day to see the manner in which the average operative has his table spread, and certainly it seems to me eminently proper that if it be within the scope of human legislation, or within the scope of the religion which men and women profess, to alleviate the condition of the laboring classes who are our producers, it should be done. . . .

Testimony of Thomas O'Donnell

When he appeared before the committee, Thomas O'Donnell, a native of Ramsbotham, England, had been for eleven years a mule-spinner in the textile factories of Fall River, Massachusetts.

Sen. Blair: Are you a married man? — A. Yes, sir; I am a married man; have a wife and two children. I am not very well educated. I went to work when I was young, and have been working ever since in the cotton business; went to work when I was about eight or nine years old. I was going to state how I live. My children get along very well in summer time, on account of not having to buy fuel or shoes or one thing and another. I earn $1.50 a day and can't afford to pay a very big house rent. I pay $1.50 a week for rent, which comes to about $6.00 a month.

Q. That is, you pay this where you are at Fall River? — A. Yes, Sir.

Q. Do you have work right along? — A. No, sir; since that strike we had down in Fall River about three years ago I have not worked much more than half the time, and that has brought my circumstances down very much.

Q. Why have you not worked more than half the time since then? — A. Well, at Fall River if a man has not got a boy to act as "back-boy" it is very hard for him to get along. In a great many cases they discharge men in that work and put in men who have boys.

Q. Men who have boys of their own? — A. Men who have boys of their own capable enough to work in a mill, to earn $.30 or $.40 a day.

Q. Is the object of that to enable the boy to earn something for himself? — A. Well, no; the object is this: They are doing away with a great deal of mule-spinning there and putting in ring-spinning, and for that reason it takes a good deal of small help to run this ring work, and it throws the men out of work because they are doing away with the mules and putting these ring-frames in to take their places. For that reason they get all the small help they can to run these ring-frames. There are so many men in the city to work, and whoever has a boy can have work, and whoever has no boy stands no chance. Probably he may have a few months of work in the summer time, but will be discharged in the fall. That is what leaves me in poor circumstances. Our children, of course, are very often sickly from one cause or another, on account of not having sufficient clothes, or shoes, or food, or something. And also my woman;

she never did work in a mill; she was a housekeeper, and for that reason she can't help me to anything at present, as many women do help their husbands down there, by working, like themselves. My wife never did work in a mill, and that leaves me to provide for the whole family. I have two children. . . .

Q. How much have you had within a year? — A. Since Thanksgiving I happened to get work in the Crescent Mill, and worked there exactly thirteen weeks. I got just $1.50 a day, with the exception of a few days that I lost — because in following up mule-spinning you are obliged to lose a day once in a while; you can't follow it up regularly.

Q. Thirteen weeks would be seventy-eight days, and, at $1.50 a day, that would make $117, less whatever time you lost? — A. Yes. I worked thirteen weeks there and ten days in another place, and then there was a dollar I got this week, Wednesday.

Q. Taking a full year back can you tell how much you have had? — A. That would be about fifteen weeks' work. . . .

Q. That would be somewhere about $133, if you had not lost any time? — A. Yes, sir.

Q. That is all you have had? — A. Yes, sir.

Q. To support yourself and wife and two children? — A. Yes, sir.

Q. Have you had any help from outside? — A. No, sir.

Q. Do you mean that yourself and wife and two children have had nothing but that for all this time? — A. That is all. I got a couple dollars' worth of coal last winter, and the wood I picked up myself. I goes around with a shovel and picks up clams and wood.

Q. What do you do with the clams? — A. We eat them. I don't get them to sell, but just to eat, for the family. That is the way my brother lives, too, mostly. He lives close by us.

Q. How many live in that way down there? — A. I could not count them, they are so numerous. I suppose there are one thousand down there.

Q. A thousand that live on $150 a year? — A. They live on less.

Q. Less than that? — A. Yes; they live on less than I do.

Q. How long has that been so? — A. Mostly so since I have been married.

Q. How long is that? — A. Six years this month.

Q. Why do you not go West on a farm? — A. How could I go, walk it?

Q. Well, I want to know why you do not go out West on a $2,000 farm, or take up a homestead and break it and work it up, and then have it for yourself and family? — A. I can't see how I could get out West. I have got nothing to go with.

Q. It would not cost you over $1,500. — A. Well, I never saw over a $20 bill, and that is when I have been getting a month's pay at once. If someone would give me $1,500 I will go. . . .

Q. Are you a good workman? — A. Yes, sir.

Q. Were you ever turned off because of misconduct or incapacity or unfitness for work? — A. No, sir.

Q. Or because you did bad work? — A. No, sir.

Q. Or because you made trouble among the help? — A. No, sir.

Q. Did you ever have any personal trouble with an employer? — A. No, sir.

Q. You have not anything now you say? — A. No, sir.

Q. How old are you? — A. About thirty.

Q. Is your health good? — A. Yes, sir.

Q. What would you work for if you could get work right along; if you could be sure to have it for five years, staying right where you are? — A. Well, if I was where my family could be with me, and I could have work every day I would take $1.50, and be glad to. . . .

Q. You spoke of fuel — what do you have for fuel? — A. Wood and coal.

Q. Where does the wood come from? — A. I pick it up around the shore — any old pieces I see around that are not good for anything. There are many more that do the same thing.

Q. Do you get meat to live on much? — A. Very seldom.

Q. What kinds of meat do you get for your family? — A. Well, once in a while we get a piece of pork and some clams and make a clam chowder. That makes a very good meal. We sometimes get a piece of corn beef or something like that. . . .

Q. What have you eaten? — A. Well, bread mostly, when we could get it; we sometimes couldn't make out to get that, and have had to go without a meal.

Q. Has there been any day in the year that you have had to go without anything to eat? — A. Yes, sir, several days.

Q. More than one day at a time? — A. No. . . .

Q. What have the children got on in the way of clothing? — A. They have got along very nicely all summer, but now they are beginning to feel quite sickly. One has one shoe on, a very poor one, and a slipper, that was picked up somewhere. The other has two odd shoes on, with the heel out. He has got cold and is sickly now.

Q. Have they any stockings? — A. He had got stockings, but his feet comes through them, for there is a hole in the bottom of the shoe.

Q. What have they got on the rest of their person? — A. Well, they have a little calico shirt — what should be a shirt; it is sewed up in some shape — and one little petticoat, and a kind of little dress.

Q. How many dresses has your wife got? — A. She has got one since she was married, and she hasn't worn that more than half a dozen times; she has worn it just going to church and coming back. She is very good in going to church, but when she comes back she takes it off, and it is pretty near as good now as when she bought it.

Q. She keeps that dress to go to church in? — A. Yes, sir.

Q. How many dresses aside from that has she? — A. Well, she got one here three months ago.

Q. What did it cost? — A. It cost $1.00 to make it and I guess about a dollar for the stuff, as near as I can tell.

Q. The dress cost $2.00? — A. Yes.

Q. What else has she? — A. Well, she has an undershirt that she got given to her, and she has an old wrapper, which is about a mile too big for her; somebody gave it to her.

Q. She did not buy it? — A. No. That is all that I know that she has. . . .

Q. Do you see any way out of your troubles — what are you going to do for a living — or do you expect to have to stay right there? — A. Yes. I can't run around with my family.

Q. You have nowhere to go to, and no way of getting there if there was any place to go to? — A. No, sir; I have no means nor anything, so I am obliged to remain there and try to pick up something as I can.

Q. Do the children go to school? — A. No, sir; they are not old enough; the oldest child is only three and a half; the youngest one is one and a half years old.

Q. Is there anything else you wanted to say? — A. Nothing further, except that I would like some remedy to be got to help us poor people down there in some way. Excepting the government decides to do something with us we have a poor show. We are all, or mostly all, in good health; that is, as far as the men who are at work go.

Q. You do not know anything but mule-spinning, I suppose? — A. That is what I have been doing, but I sometimes do something with pick and shovel. I have worked for a man at that, because I am so put on. I am looking for work in a mill. The way they do there is this: There are about twelve or thirteen men that go into a mill every morning, and they have to stand their chance, looking for work. The man who has a boy with him he stands the best chance, and then, if it is my turn or a neighbor's turn who has no boy, if another man comes in who has a boy he is taken right in, and we are left out. I said to the boss once it was my turn to go in, and now you have taken on that man; what am I to do; I have got two little boys at home, one of them three years and a half and the other one year and a half old, and how am I to find something for them to eat; I can't get my turn when I come here.

He said he could not do anything for me. I says, "Have I got to starve; ain't I to have any work?" They are forcing these young boys into the mills that should not be in mills at all; forcing them in because they are throwing the mules out and putting on ring-frames. They are doing everything of that kind that they possibly can to crush down the poor people — the poor operatives there.

Testimony of R. Heber Newton

R. Heber Newton was an Episcopal clergyman, one of the founders of the Social Gospel movement.. Much concerned by the failure of the churches to respond to the new needs of urban industrial society, men like Newton tried to apply Christian principles to social problems and persuade religious leaders to work toward improving the living conditions of the unfortunate, not merely preparing souls for a future life. Newton advocated a long series of practical reforms, including strict regulation of railroads, an income tax, tenement-house legislation, and other labor laws.

The Witness: Concerning the uninterestedness of labor and its too common lack of any identification with capital we must also look beyond labor itself to find the full responsibility of this evil.

The whole condition of industrial labor has changed in our century. Contrast the state of such labor a century ago with what it is now. Then the handicraftsman worked in his own home, surrounded by his family, upon a task, all the processes of which he had mastered, giving him thus a sense of interest and pride in the work being well and thoroughly done. Now he leaves his home early and returns to it late, working during the day in a huge factory with several hundred other men. The subdivision of labor gives him now only a bit of the whole process to do, where the work is still done by hand, whether it be the making of a shoe or of a piano. He cannot be master of a craft, but only master of a fragment of the craft. He cannot have the pleasure or pride of the old-time workmen, for he *makes* nothing. He sees no complete product of his skill growing into finished shape in his hands. What zest can there be in this bit of manhood? Steam machinery is slowly taking out of his hands even this fragment of intelligent work, and he is set at feeding and watching the great machine which has been endowed with the brains that once was in the human toiler. Man is reduced to being the tender upon a steel automaton, which thinks and plans and combines with marvellous power, leaving him only the task of supplying it with the raw material, and of oiling and cleansing it.

Some few machines require a skill and judgment to guide them proportioned to their own astonishing capacities, and for the select workmen who manage and guide them there is a new sense of the pleasure of power.

But, for the most part, mechanism takes the life out of labor as the handicraft becomes the manufacture, or more properly, the *machino*-facture; and the problem of today is, how to keep up the interest of labor in its daily task, from which the zest has been stolen.

37

2 LIVING STANDARDS AND THE POSSIBILITY OF IMPROVING THEM

Testimony of Frank K. Foster

Frank K. Foster, a printer by trade, was a member of both the Knights of Labor and the International Typographical Union. Although only twenty-seven in 1883, he was a prominent figure in the labor movement, one of those trying to reconcile the narrow craft-oriented concepts of the trade unions with the broader perspectives of the Knights.

The Witness: I do not think that at the present time there is, to any considerable extent, opportunity given for the members of the printing trade to raise themselves from the condition of wage-workers, if they have any family ties or expenses, owing to those periods of sickness and necessarily extraordinary expense that are incident upon the care of a family. That has been my experience, and I have no doubt it is the experience of most of my fellow-workmen. . . .

Sen. George: You have not answered as fully as I should like to have you answer in regard to the social condition of your craft. Are the social relations of the printers mostly among themselves or do they extend to other classes? — A. To some extent, both; but I suppose the majority of the social acquaintances and intimacies of printers and their families is among themselves or among those who work in trades corresponding to theirs. The skilled trades and the various miscellaneous occupations, and the people employed in mercantile business in the smaller departments of it very often mingle together by means of their fraternal societies, and in that manner become acquainted; but it is not possible for any extended sociability to exist among those people in the centers of industry, owing to their inability to bear the necessary expense of dress and amusements that would be incident to it. Their circles of acquaintance, therefore, are generally small.

Q. What is the *nature* of their social intercourse, so far as it exists, as regards visiting and dining with one another, for example? How is it conducted? — A. Among the married and the unmarried, I suppose you mean?

Q. Yes; all. — *A.* The unmarried printer finds a large share of his so-cial enjoyment among members of his own trade, so far as he meets or mingles at all with his fellowmen in the capacity of a social being. It is customary for a little group of friends to form something of coterie or an informal club and attend places of amusement together. The printers patronize the theater, I think, to a considerable extent, many of them at least once a week; and if a man belongs to a fraternal society of any de-scription he of course attends the festivities, the "sociables," or dances that are organized by the society. But he has a very small visiting list outside of the two sources I have named. He is generally a reader — al-most universally, I think — and where possible he patronizes the li-brary and reading room to a considerable degree. The reading rooms and the various places provided for intellectual gratification are taken ad-vantage of, I think, by a larger percentage of printers than of those be-longing to any other trade. The nature of his pursuit gives the printer a taste for knowledge, and unless prevented by intemperate habits or un-usual social conditions he pursues information through all available chan-nels as far as he can conveniently and consistently with his physical comfort and his command of time. I may say, however, in this connec-tion, that the occupation as a general thing leaves the body and mind in a condition of lassitude, so that after a day's work or a night's work it is difficult, unless the individual possesses extraordinary stamina, to do a great deal in the way of acquiring knowledge. There is a peculiar mo-notony incident upon setting type that I do not know has its exact equivalent in any other trade. That feeling, from my own observation and from the reports that I have read, particularly that of the British commission which was appointed some years ago to investigate into the causes of the social discomfort and the degree to which the nature of the occupation influenced the members of a trade, exists largely among printers, and the desire after a day's work is rather for some amusement, something that will not put any strain upon the acquiring faculties. On the other hand, a man with a family of course finds that solace in his family which the unmarried man is deprived of and, from the nature of his surroundings, cannot have. This in many instances goes further than anything else to alleviate the trials and tribulations of the world; but of course those trials are aggravated when misfortune overtakes the man and sickness and death come into the family circle, not only injuring him in his affections, but causing great discomfort from the inadequate means at his command to meet the necessary expenses of the coming in and the going out of life. The married man, the man of family, has of course the advantages of social enjoyments which the unmarried man does not generally have, because he has a home where he can return any social privileges that may be offered him by others, and therefore is not con-tinually a debtor in the social balance account.

Sen. Blair: I would like to call your attention to a remark that we often hear made, that, as a rule, people who live by ordinary employments, assuming the responsibilities of married life, are able to support themselves by the joint efforts of the two as well as or better than if they remained single; that most unmarried young men earn enough to support families, and that, failing to marry, the surplus, which would otherwise go to the support of the family, is expended or frittered away in amusements, frivolities, or indulgences; so that after all the married life is as economical as any other, if not the most economical mode of living. You have undoubtedly heard that suggestion many times, and I should like to have your views in regard to it, based upon your own observation.

The Witness: I think that depends so much upon the individuality of the person in each case that it would be very hard to strike an average or to make any statement which would apply generally. We can draw the picture of the individual whose interests might be advanced by marriage, a man with strong domestic tastes, strong home proclivities, with fondness for children — a man who has in general the faculties for the enjoyment of home life, and I think that as a rule such a man would be better off if he did marry and make a home of his own, because the same social faculty that finds its gratification in the home, if it has no means of exercising itself there, is apt to seek social enjoyment that is not conducive to the man's welfare. But I can safely say that, so far as we look at the matter from a financial standpoint, no man working at printing, or working in any mechanical occupation, who desires to become wealthy, or who even sets before himself as the aim and object of his existence the gaining of a competence — no man who entertains those predilections should marry; because in the present condition of society I think it is in the realms of improbability, not to say impossibility, for the married mechanic to do more at best than to support his wife and his little family in the most ordinarily comfortable manner, and even that he can do only upon condition that no misfortune befall him. That is a social question which lies probably a little out of the range of the observation of most of us, but of course we form our opinions regarding it, and I find the view I have stated to be common among young men in the trade — the view that they cannot in justice to their probable posterity take upon themselves the responsibilities of a family.

Sen. Blair: A condition of society which makes it economically wrong for men to marry is of course one requiring attention.

Sen. George: Upon this subject of the social privileges and advantages of the printers you have not answered as fully as I desire to have you answer. I want to call your attention to certain points and you may answer generally with reference to all the working people of whom you have knowledge. I want you to tell us what are the opportunities of association between the laborers and the non-laborers. Is there any barrier between them? Is social intercourse free between the laborer and the capitalist or other non-laborers? — A. Where there is any such intercourse it is the exception, not the rule. Speaking further upon the social question, I find it to be a peculiar feature of the time, especially in New England, that we are rapidly developing classes in society as well as in the industrial world, and that these classes are becoming more and more fixed in the particular positions that they claim in the social life of the country. The walls are being erected higher and higher. The old New England idea of the nobility of labor is fast passing away. We have among our manufacturers, in the majority of cases, an aristocracy no less rigid in its demands for what it deems to be its due than, so far as I am able to learn, is the aristocracy of any other country. . . .

Testimony of Henry George

Henry George was probably the best-known writer on social and economic problems of his day. During his career as a newspaper editor in California, he became increasingly disturbed by the growing disparity between the rich and the poor in America. Study of economics convinced him that most authorities possessed little insight into the true causes of social problems, which, he decided, were rooted in the control of land. His great book, Progress and Poverty (1879), *quickly won him an international reputation as an economist and reformer.*

Sen. Pugh: I would like to get your views (if you have thought upon the subject, and I have no doubt you have) as to this question: We understand that production results from the joint efforts of labor and capital. Now I wish to get your idea as to the proper distribution of the product between capital and labor, as a general rule, under our system of industry. Does labor get its fair share now? If so, how? And if not, why?

The Witness: No, I think that labor does not get its fair share. Neither do I think that capital, unless it has some monopolistic advantage, gets as much as it ought to get. The average earnings of capital are indicated by the current rate of interest, and you will find that the large profits made have in them always some element of monopoly. For instance, one of the largest manufacturers in the United States and one of the largest employers of labor said to me not long ago, "On our regular business we make really nothing; it is on some peculiar things in which we have special advantages that we make our money." Labor does not get its fair share. There are workingmen in this country who are as much peons as the peons of Spanish America. Get the reports of the Massachusetts Bureau of Labor Statistics (and they are corroborated by the investigations of independent inquirers) and you will see that a very large proportion of the operatives in New England cannot make enough to support their families, even, in the poorest fashion. They are absolutely compelled to rely upon the labor of their little children, children whom the law strives to prevent going to work. In an article published in the *Atlantic Monthly* two months ago by Miss Emma E. Brown on the subject of child-labor in factories in Massachusetts a good many of these facts were stated. She instanced cases in which mothers came crying and begging of the factory overseers that their children might be permitted to go to work, even though it was against the law, on the ground that it was absolutely necessary for the support of the family. I think that in all the manufacturing states where these laws have been passed like instances can be found. Even in the last report of the Illinois Bureau of Labor Statistics the same fact is stated, that in a large number of industries it is impossible for a man to earn a living for himself and his family; and, speaking generally, wages are higher in Illinois than in Massachusetts or in any of the eastern states. . . .

Testimony of Robert D. Layton *

The Witness: Our iron-masters live, in many instances — there may be a few exceptions where their aspirations do not find vent in that direction, but, as a general thing, they live in very elegant palatial residences, they have carriages and horses, and fine grounds, and servants, and everything that a person would suppose would go to make life enjoyable. I know a man who lives in that condition now who was a warehouse clerk at Pittsburgh at the outbreak of the rebellion. He now owns three iron mills; I think he owns three wire-works for making barbed wire; and he controls or owns most of the stock in one of our railroads in the city. I know that to be a positive fact.

Sen. George: That is an exceptional case, is it not? — A. Yes, sir; he is the only man now within my recollection who has sprung up to this condition by reason of being an employer; and of course the times were propitious for that sort of advancement. I know another man who in 1862 was working for $3.00 a day as a saw-maker — a man who is not recognized among his fellowmen generally as possessing any superior ability, who is now a part-owner in three large establishments, who lives in a very fine residence and has everything about him to make life comfortable and enjoyable. On the other hand, I may state that I have known

* See above, page 1.

some of his employees to have earned nice comfortable modest homes of five or six rooms, and to have paid for them and also educated their children well.

Sen. Blair: Which do you believe is the happier man, the employee or the master — which gets the most out of this life? — A. I cannot give any positive information on that point, but I can state my belief. If I were to judge by the actions of these men, I would consider that the man that had the most money was the happier, from the way they grab at it and the sordid means they use to get it. . . .

Testimony of Frederick Smyth

Frederick Smyth, a former governor of New Hampshire, describes his career before 1883 in the following selection from his testimony, which was taken at Manchester in that state.

Sen. Blair: Where were you born? — A. In Candia, 10 miles from here.

Q. Where have you spent your life? — A. In Manchester, since I was twenty years of age.

Q. That is how many years ago? — A. That is about forty-four years ago.

Q. In what business have you been engaged during your lifetime? Give us a little of the story of your life. — A. Well, I was brought up on a farm until I was seventeen years of age. Candia is a very rough, stony place. I had only the privileges of the winter time at school. At eighteen, I got a school to keep, at $12 a month; and with that money the next season, I went to Andover to school. In the summer of 1838, I got out of money, and thought I would come to Manchester and work a while, to get money to finish my education. I let myself for $125 a year to a man named George Porter, who kept a store here. . . .

Manchester was then a perfect sandbank. I think one Stark Mill was running, and another was building at that time, though I cannot be exact about that. Elm Street was laid out. There were but four or five buildings on this side of the street. There were no buildings in Manchester excepting the Stark Mill and a few boarding-houses, but they were building the second mill, I think. . . .

I used to get up early in the morning and work until eleven o'clock at night, on an average, and sometimes till twelve. For the whole year, it would average that. I had only $4.50 when I came here, and had no relatives, nor anybody on earth to help me. I had a certificate from my minister, saying that I was a "pretty clever boy," as he put it. I worked that year intending to go back to school, but at the end of the year my pay was raised to $250; and the third year it was doubled. Then I went into business for myself, and was in that business ten years. Then I was elected city clerk of Manchester, and served in that office three or four years. I was then elected mayor, and reelected three years. That was my official record up to about 1855. I then went into the banking business. In 1864 I was elected mayor of the city again. Up to that time I had always been a party man, and was still; but in 1864, I was elected without any opposition from either party. In that same year — in war times — I was nominated for governor, and elected in 1865 and reelected in 1866. . . .

Q. You say that Manchester was a sandbank almost when you came here? — A. Yes; it really was.

Q. What has made the difference between Manchester as it was then and as it is now? — A. Labor. Of course capital was in the mills, but all the work that has been done here has been generally by men who came here poor, as I was. The first year I came here I did not know a single resident of Manchester who was worth $2,000. There might have been one, but I think they were all like me, worth nothing. We came here with only our hands and heads. The place owes its prosperity, first, to capital from Massachusetts; that established the mills here, and from that the people who came here have built the city on this side of the street (of course, the corporations built the other side), as you see it today, with their own hands and heads, not with capital; and those who have been industrious, who were not imprudent, have accumulated a comfortable competency. I do not know that I can show better what Manchester was when I came here than to relate an instance in my experience to show you how sandy and dry it was. You could not see a tree anywhere except on Elm Street; not a single tree. In the parks there was not a tree to be found except on this park right here by the Manchester House. It was such poor soil that it immediately dried up after a rain. Elm Street was so deep with sand that the girls who worked in the Stark Mills, as they crossed Elm Street and got to the store steps, would sit down and take their shoes off and turn the sand out of their shoes. . . .

Q. Won't you go on and describe the gradual growth and development of the place, the construction of new mills, and the order in which their construction took place, as nearly as you can remember, so as to give us an account of the history of the place? — A. Since our first rise we have had sometimes rise, sometimes progress, and sometimes standing still. For several years after I came here they continued building mills, but it was ten or fifteen years, I think, before any buildings were on the other side. I was one of those hopeful fellows who thought we were going to have a town here, but the majority of the people were probably of a different opinion. I remember hearing a question asked by somebody, "Do you suppose there will ever be any buildings on the left side of Elm Street?" And I immediately said, "Yes; and you will live to see it." The answer to such remarks generally was that they would not live to see it. But finally we got one building over on this side, and that started them. The people who came here at that time were a different class to those now. The Stark Mills, of which Mr. Bourne is agent, were running, and I do not think there was a foreigner in them; possibly there might have been, but all the foreigners that we had then, I think, were Irishmen, who were digging the canal. The operatives were Vermont and New Hampshire blooming girls. Perhaps, being a young man of about twenty at the time, I may have appreciated them a little more; but I remember, as we kept a drygoods store, after the mills let out in the evening, they came to our store, and it was crowded with them. And all of our men, so far as I know, were Yankee men. There being so few places about, the store was the only gathering place. . . .

Everybody worked in the mill then except a few carpenters and the Irishmen who were digging the canal. The three stores formed really the exchange, and in the evening the people would come up to the stores and sit around the steps, and the general impression was that we would be some day five or six thousand. But we got along by labor entirely. No capitalists ever came to Manchester, so far as I know, except the capitalists of the mills. The merchants who came here came poor; the mechanics came poor. I think it has been the most industrious place in the world. It is seldom that, during my life of forty-four years here, I have, during labor hours, seen a man standing on the sidewalks, except on holidays and evenings; I have very seldom seen anybody "holding up posts," or loafing around the streets. We have all been at work, and have all been busy. There may be now a few more idle men than there used to be, but for many years there were none, and wages were low, too. I got $125 a year when I first came, and I saved $120 of it. I will not trouble you by a recital of the circumstances under which I came to save that much. Hundreds came here and got about $100 a year and saved it all except $5 or $10.

Q. How was that — it might be interesting to know? — *A.* Well, I will tell you. I got $125. Now, how did I get my clothes? I clothed myself. I mended my own stockings; my employer used to give me a pair of socks sometimes. We had no new clothes as boys have nowadays. During the whole year that I was first in this place I never paid one dollar for a carriage, nor did anybody else: spent no money for cigars; no money for rum; we had no amusements, no holidays. I never heard of such a thing as a vacation for ten years. That is the way we grew up here — by con-

stant labor, day after day. I think the prosperity of the place is more
due to that than to anything else — with the starting of the capital in
the mills, of course. Labor is the foundation of our prosperity. . . .

There is another thing here that I have not observed anywhere else:
We do not know what you call an aristocracy, unless there is a little of
it now. I think that within the last few years a little of it has cropped
out once in a while, but it cannot live. I remember a man who was an
educated man, and a fine gentleman, who came here thinking that he
was a little smarter than the rest of us, and I suppose he was. He
wanted to get an office, the position of city clerk, but his aristocratic
tendencies were the death of him. The moment a man shows his hand
in the way of aristocracy here it is the death of him. The girls in the mill
were just as good as the ladies of Washington — as a Senator's wife —
to us. The idea that a girl in the mill was not as good as anybody would
astonish us. I remember Mr. Gillis, of the Amoskeag Mills, and such
people, would invite me, a poor boy, working for $.50 a day, while they
were agents of the mills and had control of all these people — would
invite me to their houses, and would invite the factory girls to their houses
at a reception or entertainment. I do not say but what there is a little
more aristocracy now, but I think we owe our prosperity in great measure
to the fact that all the men in Manchester have worked together. These
men that we call rich men here today — look over the city and see our
best residences — call the roll — and I don't think you will find a man
among them that is not a worker. There is not a harder working man in
the city than Nathan Parker. We are all working hard today, perhaps
not as hard as we used to do, but there is not a day that we are not attending to our business. I suppose I could find now and then a loafer
among the wealthy, but very few. . . .

Q. You have, of course, observed the industrial character of the operatives all the way along. You spoke of their being Americans in the
early days. Won't you give us some idea of the transition from the
American help to the present? I should also like to get an idea of the
way in which labor and capital have harmonized throughout the history
of the city. — A. All the operatives, at first, were Yankees. Then the
Irish came directly from Ireland with their families, and after they had
dug the canals — of course we employed them for all that sort of work —
we commenced gradually working them into the mills; machinery was
improved, and as the young children grew to be old enough to do any
kind of work, we gradually got them to tend some of the machines. So
then we had first the Irish, and we had no other; then came the Germans. There were not yet any French. As the foreigners worked in,
the Yankees worked out; they were crowded out; some of the old overseers after a while had left for other parts, while some remained, and
what we call the "second hands" worked up to firsts, and then by and
by the third hands worked up. As the Irish came in they took the

under work, and gradually rose up till they had places of importance. That has been going on gradually till the Germans commenced coming, and then the French. It is going on all the time, until this day, for, as you know, a very large part of the help now is foreign.

As to the American help you may ask me what is become of them. Many of them, after they had got a competency, went out, and went onto farms. Many of them went West, and foreigners naturally came in and took their places. The Yankee girls got married and made splendid wives, as a rule, and there was a demand then for the Yankee girls in other departments. As female labor has been advanced, and as the sentiment has been growing to employ foreign labor, the Yankee girls have worked out of the mills to a large extent.

Testimony of Jay Gould

Jay Gould, a self-made tycoon, began life on an up-state New York farm. Hard work and shrewdness that approached knavery made him rich before he was thirty. He was one of the most notorious stock-market speculators of his generation and a prominent railroad organizer. In 1867 he won control of the Erie Railroad and soon managed to milk the corporation of millions of dollars. After being forced out of Erie in 1872, he turned his attention to western lines, obtaining control of the Union Pacific, the Kansas Pacific, and other roads. In addition, he controlled the Western Union Telegraph Company and an influential newspaper, the New York World.

Sen. Blair: We have had a man six feet high, who has driven a truck team, and who has more intellectual capacity than half, or perhaps any, of the members of Congress, offering here before this committee to agree under contract to work diligently and faithfully for the next twenty years for anybody who would give him employment and agree to maintain himself and his family. That man said he had been unable to get anything ahead, and could not find a chance to work; that he was hungry, and his family were hungry, and that he didn't know what to do; and it was represented to us here that he was one of a large class. He said that folks told him to go West; but such a man cannot go West, if he tells the truth about his situation, and even if he were to adopt the plan you suggest, his family certainly could not accompany him, driving a mule on the canal tow-path. . . . — A. Well, I know there are a great many cases of actual suffering in a large city like this, and in all large cities. It is a very difficult thing to say exactly how you are to ameliorate everybody's condition. I have noticed, though, that generally if men are temperate and industrious they are pretty sure of success. In cases such as the one you describe I could almost always go back behind the scenes and find a cause for such a person's "misfortunes."

Q. There has been testimony before us that the feeling generally between employers and employees throughout the country is one of hostility, especially on the part of the employees toward those whom they designate as monopolists. From your observation, what do you think is really the feeling as a general rule between those two classes? — A. I think that if left alone they would mutually regulate their relations. I think there is no disagreement between the great mass of the employees and their employers. These societies that are gotten up magnify these things and create evils which do not exist — create trouble which ought not to exist.

Q. Of the men who conduct business enterprises and wield the power of capital in this country today, what proportion do you think are what are called "self-made men"? — A. I think they are all "self-made men"; I do not say *self*-made exactly, for the country has grown and they have grown up with it. In this country we have no system of heirlooms or of handing down estates. Every man has to stand here on his own individual merit.

Q. What is the proportion of those men who have made their own fortunes pecuniarily, such as they are? — A. I think they are nearly all of that class. I think, that according to my observation in the field that I have been in, nearly every one that occupies a prominent position has come up from the ranks, worked his own way along up.

Testimony of William Steinway

The piano manufacturer William Steinway describes his rise in the following selection.

The Witness: I was born in Brunswick, Germany, in 1836, and came to the city of New York in the spring of 1850, when fourteen years of age, with my father, mother, and the rest of our family. We worked for three years in the factories here, learning the language and the customs of the people, and in March, 1853, started the business of Steinway & Sons — my father, my two brothers, and myself — which has now become the most extensive establishment of its kind in existence. We have three distinct establishments, manufactories rather, our New York factory, at Fourth Avenue and Fifty-second and Fifty-third Streets; a large establishment at Astoria, N.Y., opposite One hundred and twentieth Street, where we employ over 400 men, and where we have carried out our ideas of improving the condition of the workingmen by giving them light and air and good houses to live in, building them public baths, and laying out a public park, keeping up at our own expense in the public school a teacher who teaches German and music free of charge, and various other advantages. We employ about 1,000 workmen, a great majority of whom are skilled workmen. I will remark that in the first three years when I worked as an apprentice and journeyman, and in the first few years when our business was small, I had ample opportunities of studying the lot of the workingman by actual experience, also the way that workingmen worked, and I can say that skilled artisans today are far better off than they were a third of a century ago. At that time but very few people, even skilled laborers, were able to save money and put it in bank. Today the skilled laborers, more especially in the pianoforte trade, and the woodworking establishments, have wages double what they were in those times; and from my experience also as director in savings banks, etc., I find that a great many skilled artisans, those blessed with health, have constituted a great portion of the depositors in banks. . . .

The introduction of machinery in our business, and in the woodworking establishments, has been of great benefit by doing the hard work which formerly imperiled the health and lives of the skilled artisans. I will further state that of the about one hundred pianoforte manufacturers of the United States, which are chiefly concentrated in the four cities I have named [New York, Boston, Baltimore, and Philadelphia], nearly all have been workingmen themselves. . . .

Sen. Blair: The resolution calls attention to the relative conditions of all working people abroad, and working people in America, specific and general classes. What is your observation in that respect? — A. I have paid a great deal of attention to the condition of the workingmen, and, as I before stated, in our own business and kindred trades I find that first-class skilled artisans in this country earn from double to three times as much as skilled artisans of the same rank do in Europe. In unskilled labor I find the proportion is not so favorable to the American laborer. It is true that they earn more money here, but the cost of living, especially rents, is so much enhanced that they are not much better off in a pecuniary way than the workingman in Europe. But their social position here is much higher than that in Europe, and they have a much better chance here to get along than they have in Europe where everything is more limited. But the skilled artisans are far better off in this country; they wear better clothing, have better food, and have a chance to live better, move in better society, and in fact their condition is in every way far superior. Still there remains a great deal to be done, and a great deal could be done to improve their condition in this country in the way I have indicated. . . .

Testimony of John W. Britton

John W. Britton boasted to the committee that he had been a worker for forty-eight years. "Having been a worker myself, I have mixed with working people, and I know them pretty thoroughly." Actually, in 1883 Britton was the president of a New York bank and an executive in a carriage-making firm that employed over 500 men.

Sen. Pugh: Are not our most successful merchants and traders and financial and manufacturing men, and even men in the professions, largely men who made themselves? — A. Yes, sir; I think there is hardly a question of the truth of that.

Q. The self-made men are the leading men in all these pursuits and industries? — A. In a country like this I think that follows generally; but you must understand that we are not now trying to elevate the leading men, it is the rank and file we are talking of. As I said to you, the boy that is taught to make a beautiful curved line is elevated by even that simple thing.

Sen. Blair: We are not trying to make the leading men, but common men? — A. Yes.

Sen. Pugh: I mean by "leading" men the men that move the world; that give direction to the thought and energy of the country. I do not mean "bosses." — A. I understand that. This is certainly a glorious country for opportunity. A man has no stone upon his head here unless he carries it voluntarily. He has a clear road if he wants to go up.

I should like to say a few words more on the subject of trades unions. A man once asked me this question: "Do you think that trades unions have been a necessity in England?" I said, "Yes." "Well, why do you think they are not a necessity here?" "Well," I said, "the great choice of occupations in this country will prevent any class from becoming oppressed for any length of time. A man here may be a common day laborer, but if he has the right material in him there is no reason why he should not occupy the best place in the nation. My father was originally a shoemaker, and afterwards a public cartman in the city of New York. That was no reason why I should be a cartman or a shoemaker. But, if I had lived in England and my father had been a cartman or a shoemaker, the chances are that I would be one. When great bodies of men are born and brought up in cities and have not had any opportunities for outside observation, and employers combine to regulate the hours and prices of labor, I tell you that these men are justified in organizing against the employer. But in this country I do not see the necessity. The right is unquestionable, but the necessity does not exist. If a man is oppressed in one occupation, this whole wide country is open to him and he can change his occupation." . . .

Q. There are very few men that have not the ambition to become employers; that is a great incentive to the general worker, is it not, the ambition to become an employer? — A. Yes; when he ceases to have his ambition he is not so good a workman, as a rule. Now, the opening up of new communities — the enlargement, for instance, of our trade — drains us of a lot of our best people. They see opportunities to go into new communities where they will get more rapid advancement. The journeyman that leaves us and goes to a growing western city is apt to come back four or five years hence as the head of a great establishment. Out there, I think, they rate a man a little differently from here. In a Western city it is not the quality of his clothes, or even the amount of money that he has, that they measure him by. If he is an industrious, pushing man, there is somebody there who will take hold of him. I remember presiding at the convention held in Chicago in 1880, and one of the liveliest debaters on the floor, who gave more real entertainment to the debate than anyone else, was a young fellow whose countenance was familiar to me, but I didn't know his name. He was from Oshkosh. After the meeting was over he introduced himself to me and said, "You don't remember me; I used to work for you four years ago." He had gone out there, and having more than average ability was taken right hold of. That is the advantage that new settlements have for ambitious young men. A man goes out there who is a little better equipped than his fellows and he soon goes to the top. There are so many at the top here that there is no opportunity. . . .

Testimony of Thomas M. Miller

Thomas M. Miller was general manager of the Atlas Company of Pittsburgh, which manufactured rolling-mill machinery for steel mills and other heavy equipment.

Sen. Blair: As a rule, do you think that the working people devote more time to labor or less time than the employers? — A. Less, I think.

Q. On the other hand, I suppose, the working people have less to hope for from the results of their labor? — A. That is true, unless they are skilled and ambitious. I find, at least in our city, that nearly all the men who are now capitalists have been workingmen.

Q. How have they come to be capitalists? — A. By evolution, development, according to capacity and opportunity.

Q. It is the result of thrift and hard work? — A. Thrift, hard work, and economy. As an illustration of that, the present manager of the Edgar Thomson Steel Works, Mr. Jones, was an ordinary workman, and he has now control of those works as general manager, and is receiving a very large salary — $20,000 a year. He grew up from being an ordinary roller. Being more skilled and ambitious than others, he commanded better wages when he was a workingman, and finally he reached the highest position in the trade.

Q. I suppose, however, you would not present such a case as illustrations of what the mass of the workmen can do, because the condition of the mass of the men must be regulated by different considerations. They cannot all expect to be superintendents. — A. No. That is the reason that I think the regulation of the hours of labor will operate against the men themselves instead of being a benefit to them, except where they may have been required to work excessive hours. . . .

3 THE TENEMENT
AND THE SLUM

A Visit to New York City Tenements

New York, August 7, 1883

The committee, having determined to visit and inspect personally some of the tenements inhabited by the working classes in certain sections of the city, obtained the services as a guide of a gentleman connected with the detective branch of the police department. In the course of a preliminary consultation with this gentleman he made a general statement, of which the following is a brief summary:

The settlements of this city began at the southern end of the island, around the Battery, and in the territory now included in the first and the fourth wards. The majority of the houses in that region are three stories high and built of brick. Most of them have been altered into business houses, but there are still people who continue to live down town on account of old associations, and you will sometimes hear a man say, with a certain amount of pride, "I am a first-warder yet." Of course houses down there, built sixty or seventy years ago, are not such houses as are being built now. If you gentlemen want to see the real tenement-house life of this city, about as good a place as you can go for that purpose is along either the east or the west side. I will show you through the fourth ward and through the portion of the city where the Italians are to be found, so that you may get an idea of how they live. I will also give you a chance to see life in Baxter Street. That will probably interest you, but it will hardly give you a fair idea of tenement-house life in New York, or of the way the working people live, because that is a street that is occupied almost entirely by Jews and others in the second-hand business, mostly dealers in second-hand clothing. Baxter Street is almost wholly devoted to that class of people, and they live there huddled up together like sheep. When you see that street you see the best sample of that kind of life in this city. In the tenement region, where I propose to take you, you will find blocks of houses which are all tenements, supposed to contain all the modern improvements, and having from two to four families on a floor.

Sen. George: How many rooms are there on a floor, or how many rooms does each of the families occupy?

The Detective: The number varies in different cases; from three to five rooms generally.

Sen. George: Is there a family in each room?

The Detective: Oh, no. But I will take you into the houses, so that you can see for yourself.

Sen. George: Can you get us into the houses?

The Detective: I will engineer that. I will find means to let you see as much of that kind of life as you wish. As to the portion of the city that the Italians inhabit, they have it almost wholly to themselves. Other people do not want to live there, because it is extremely dirty. The Italians have selected a section of the city which is quite old, and you will probably want to visit that neighborhood, but if you wish to see the dwellings of the working classes, the people who really live by labor, then you must go into the regular tenement-house district. The working people live in those tenement houses in rooms for which they have to pay from $10 to $25, to $35, or even $40 a month.

The committee determined to set out at once on this tour of inspection, and, by the advice of the detective, in order to attract less attention, decided not to take carriages, but to go on foot.

Messrs. Ormsby and Gibson, representing respectively the *New York Sun* and the *New York Tribune*, accompanied them.

The first house visited was a cheap lodging-house on Chatham Square, with a sign offering lodgings for $.15 a night. The house was quite large, containing 156 rooms, so called. The "rooms" were very small, about 6 feet long by 4 or 5 feet wide. The small cot-beds appeared to be clean and comfortable, and in each room there was a little closet. The house was provided with a fire escape and with water in the halls, and was under the charge of a superintendent. In the office or reading room below there was a placard prohibiting smoking. In conversation with Senator Blair, the chairman, the proprietor of the house stated that although most of his patrons were casual lodgers, yet he had a class of lodgers, mechanics and others, who stayed in the house all the year round.

Sen. Blair: What do the people who lodge with you here do for a living?

The Landlord: Oh, I can't tell you that. Some of them are peddlers and some of them are bricklayers, carpenters, and other mechanics, but there are plenty of them that I could not tell you what they do.

Sen. George: Do any common laborers lodge here?

The Landlord: No; I think not.

The Detective: No; they generally live up town.

Sen. Blair: This, I understand, is a lodging-house merely; you give no meals here?

The Landlord: No meals; only lodging.

Sen. Blair: How many men do you employ to look after this house?

The Landlord: Three men and a woman.

Sen. Blair: How many rooms have you?

The Landlord: One hundred and fifty-six.

Sen. Blair: When a man is taken sick here what do you do with him?

The Landlord: Summon an ambulance and send him to the hospital.

Sen. Blair: Do any people who are employed in stores as clerks lodge with you here?

The Landlord: No clerks. We have mechanics and watchmen, and also a number of ragpickers, who work at night and sleep in the daytime.

Sen. Blair: I suppose there are a good many such houses as this in New York City?

The Landlord: Oh, yes.

Sen. Blair: Do any married people live here?

The Landlord: No.

Sen.Blair: Have you bathrooms in the house?

The Landlord: No.

The Detective: These lodging-houses are all under the supervision of the board of health, and the officers go around once a week and inspect the houses and see that they are kept clean and that there is plenty of water for washing, and so on.

The Landlord: The people can get a bath outside, if they want it, for fifteen cents.

The next place visited was a Chinese grocery on Mott Street. The chairman began a conversation with the proprietor, who was at first disposed to talk, but suddenly became reticent when he noticed that the stenographer of the committee was about to take note of his remarks. However, in reply to the chairman's questions he stated that he liked New York very well. The chairman asked him whether many of his countrymen were now coming to New York, to which he replied, "Some come, some go; just same as steam-car." The chairman asked him whether he intended to stay in New York. He answered, "Can't tell — don't know — can't tell."

Next the committee walked through a portion of Mulberry Street, where the Italians were very numerous. Members of the committee expressed surprise at seeing so many men idle in the middle of the day, but the detective accounted for it by stating that they were mostly ragpickers, who worked at night and rested during the day.

Passing along Bayard Street the committee stopped at a butcher's shop and inspected the meat offered for sale, which appeared to be of good quality, and was sold at the following prices: round steak, $.18 a pound; porterhouse steak, from $.23 to $.25 a pound; lamb, $.14 a pound; sausages, $.14 a pound. The woman who attended the shop stated that they sold their meat sometimes in very small quantities, one or two cents' worth for instance, and their green groceries in the same way, some of her customers buying, say, two cents' worth of meat and one onion.

In the course of the walk through this and adjacent streets the detective called attention to the fact that this quarter was inhabited, as he said, by "Jews, Gentiles, Irish, Americans, and Germans, all living in peace with each other."

In this ward, the sixth, the committee visited a public school building. It being vacation time, the school was not in operation, but the janitor conducted the committee through the building and answered intelligently the questions that were put to him. . . .

Sen. Blair: Of what nationalities are the parents of the children who attend school here?

The Janitor: They are of nearly all nationalities.

Sen. Blair: From your observations of the children of parents of different nationalities, Irish, French, Italians, Germans, Jews, and other classes of foreigners, which do you think are the brightest children as a class?

The Janitor: We have got mostly Jewish children here. They are about the brightest I know of. There are very few Germans and no Italians in this school. The rest are Irish or American born. We have had one or two Chinese here, and I believe they got along very well.

Sen. Blair: Do you find any prejudices manifested among the children of different classes or nationalities against each other; do they divide into classes in the schools?

The Janitor: No. We have two or three colored children. At first it seemed a little odd, but now all the children play together without any trouble.

Sen. Blair: How do those colored children get along?

The Janitor: They get along in their books very well, I think. But they have not been here very long. The children generally agree very well indeed. The Jews advance very rapidly; they take a great liking to drawing, and they are very good readers and very good in arithmetic.

Sen. Blair: Have you many French children here?

The Janitor: Very few.

Sen. Blair: Have you many American children — I mean of the old American stock?

The Janitor: I don't believe there are any of them. . . .

The committee visited next a six-story tenement house in Mott Street, which presented a very gloomy and uncomfortable appearance, but was well provided with fire escapes, as required by law. One of the tenants, in reply to questions by the chairman, stated that the building was occupied mainly by Irish and Jewish families. She was herself a native of

Ireland, had been in this country seventeen years, and was the mother of nine children, born in New York. Her husband, she said, was a laborer, getting from $2.25 to $2.50 a day. His business was tearing down houses and sometimes helping masons in erecting others. The detective explained that this business of tearing down houses was one which required a certain amount of skill, and that a man who was expert at it would not rank exactly as a common "laborer."

Next the committee visited a ten-cent lodging-house on Hester Street, $.10 being the regular charge for a night's lodging, though some of the beds brought as high as $.15 a night. The lodging-room in this house was simply a large dormitory, with cots ranged along at certain distances apart. There were no partitions between the beds. The washing facilities were out in the hall. The house seemed clean, and the accommodations furnished appeared to be very good for the prices charged.

From here the committee went uptown to visit a tenement house on Second Avenue near Eightieth Street. This was a modern four-story building, the rooms on the ground floor being used as stores. The detective stated that this and most of the houses of the same kind were occupied by the laboring classes, men whose work might be anywhere in the city; from the Battery to the extreme upper end, and explained that men whose employment was regular and at one place generally contrived to get apartments as near their work as possible, so that they could go home to dinner, while those whose work was irregular and in different localities usually selected their apartments with reference to cheapness, as they traveled to and from their work by the cars and generally carried their dinners with them.

Another large tenement house was visited in the same neighborhood. Each set of apartments was four rooms deep, and on each floor there were two sets, with a hall separating them. In one set of these apartments which the committee inspected, in the second story, the front room was used as a parlor, the rear room as a kitchen and dining room, and those intervening as bedrooms. The "parlor" was about 16 by 12 feet, quite comfortably furnished, and adorned with some thirty cheap pictures, including several of a religious character. The committee inspected the sanitary arrangements as far as was practicable under the circumstances, and the detective explained that the board of health exercised a vigilant supervision over all such matters in tenement houses and lodging-houses. A conversation took place between the chairman and the wife of the tenant, in part as follows:

Sen. Blair: You do your own cooking, I suppose? — A. Oh, yes.

Q. How much rent do you pay for these apartments? — A. We pay $14 a month for these four rooms.

Q. What is your husband's business, and what wages does he get? — A. He is a stonecutter, and he gets $4 a day when he is employed, but he is not employed all the time. He cuts brownstone altogether.

Q. How old is he? — *A.* Forty-three.

Q. Is he an American? — *A.* He is American born, of Irish parents, and so am I.

Q. How many children have you? — *A.* We have had seven. We lost the first; the others are alive.

Q. Are they healthy? — *A.* They are.

Q. Have you lived in these same apartments all the time you have lived in New York? — *A.* Oh, no; our first child died when we lived on Ninth Avenue.

Q. Do you find this location healthy? — *A.* Very healthy, indeed.

Q. You are Catholics, I judge, from some of your pictures? — *A.* Yes, sir.

Sen. George: Are the rents for the apartments in this building the same on the different floors? — *A.* No; they are cheaper as you go up.

Q. Do your older children go to school? — *A.* Yes, sir.

Q. How many months of school are there here? — *A.* This year there is a vacation of twelve weeks. All the rest of the time there is school.

Q. What does it cost you to live? — *A.* It takes pretty much all my husband makes for us to live; we can't save much.

Q. If your husband had work all the time you would be able to save something, would you not? — *A.* Yes, I think we would; but in winter the work is pretty dull. If he had regular work we might be able to save something.

Sen. Blair: You manage to live and be tolerably happy in this world, though? — *A.* Yes, sir; we are quite happy. . . .

Next the committee visited some new tenements lately erected on Seventy-first Street by the "Improved Dwellings Association." This is an association composed of wealthy ladies and gentlemen who take an interest in the improvement of the dwellings of the working classes in New York, and who have had these houses planned and built with a view of safety, comfort, and economy. The apartments are rented at certain fixed rates, said to be about 10 percent below the rents charged for inferior accommodations in the ordinary tenement houses, and the stockholders of the association have agreed among themselves to devote the surplus income above 5 percent on the capital invested, to further improving the tenements in respect to comfort and convenience. The houses occupy a whole square, and are built around a spacious courtyard, which is used for drying clothes by a certain portion of the tenants, and also as a general playground for the children. Under the guidance of the agent of the association (whose office is in the building) the committee visited and inspected several of the sets of apartments. The first visited consisted of three rooms, two bedrooms and a living room, the whole renting for $12.75 per month. The living room (which has to serve as kitchen, diningroom, and parlor) is in the middle, so that in winter the

heat from the cooking stove will heat the whole three rooms. Attached
to these apartments were three large closets. Another set, consisting
of four rooms, with large closets, and having stationary tubs for washing, rented for $13.25 per month. The agent stated that the entire
block of tenements cost about $300,000, and the rents of the apart-
ments ran, he said, from $7.25, the lowest, to $15.50 per month, the
highest. The storerooms for wood and coal are in the cellar, and there
is an elevator to carry the supplies to the upper stories. There is a de-
pository in the cellar to which the ashes are carried from all parts of
the building by tubes. There is also a clubroom and a reading room
provided by the association for the use of the tenants. In the reading
room were found *Harper's Weekly*, the *Scientific American, Puck*, and
other illustrated papers. The laundries for the tenants on the first,
second, and third stories are in the cellar, the clothes being dried in
the courtyard. For the fourth, fifth, and sixth stories the laundries are
on the sixth floor. Two hundred and eight families occupy the apartments contained in this block. The list of tenants showed that among
them were stonecutters, telegraphpole men, bakers, cabinetmakers,
barbers, painters, stablemen, windowcleaners, carpenters, seamstresses,
engineers, coopers, plumbers, laborers, butchers, piano-makers, cigar-
makers, rubber-workers, clerks, shirt-makers, etc. In letting their apartments the association insists that the number of rooms hired by each
tenant shall equal the number of children in his family. Thus, a
family having four children will be required to take four rooms, and so
on. A calculation made by a member of the committee showed that
the families averaged about four and one-half persons.

New York, August 8, 1883

The committee resumed its tour of inspection this morning, and visited
first a tenement house of an inferior class on the east side of the city,
along the line of the Second Avenue Elevated Railroad. On the second
story of the tenement the committee found a family consisting of a husband, a wife, and three children living in three small rooms. The only
light admitted to these apartments came through the window of the
front room, facing the street. The partition between this room and the
one immediately behind it (which was used as a kitchen, dining room,
etc.) extended only about halfway to the ceiling, so as to admit the
light, but the woman said it was necessary to keep a lamp burning in
daytime in order to have sufficient light to do her work. The third room,
the bedroom, in rear of the kitchen, was really a dark pantry, with no
light or ventilation except what could be obtained through the doorway
connecting it with the kitchen. The woman stated that they paid $12.50
per month for the three rooms. She had a baby fourteen months old,
a delicate-looking child, and in reply to a member of the committee

she said that it was "all the time sick." Senator George suggested that what the baby needed was fresh air, and that the mother ought to take it to Coney Island, but she seemed amazed at the suggestion and exclaimed, "Oh, we could not do that." In reply to further questions this woman stated that her husband received $2.00 a day when he was at work, but that he was often idle, and that sometimes even when employed he had work during only four days in a week. A member of the committee asked her whether she liked her apartments; she replied that she did not, and that the elevated railroad made her sick. . . .

A cursory glance at the quarter inhabited by the colored people in South Fifth Avenue and thereabout closed the committee's tour of inspection.

Testimony of Emmons Clark

Colonel Emmons Clark was secretary of the New York City Board of Health, a post he had held since 1866. He was also commander of New York's famous Seventh Regiment.

The Witness: A department of health has two objects in view, one entirely of a public character, and another of a humanitarian character. The lives of laboring men are supposed to have a public or a business value. It is estimated, I think, that every person that comes to this country as an immigrant, and every laboring man, has a productive value of $1,000 or more. That, I believe, is the minimum which has been fixed by the gentlemen who devote themselves to that line of thought. That being so, it is to the public interest that the lives of laboring men should be preserved, and also that their health should be preserved, in order that they may settle their families and keep them from being subjects of charity. A board of health, therefore, in a city like this, and, indeed, anywhere, has for its primary object to preserve the health of the people, to prevent contagious diseases from spreading, to prevent malarial diseases, and also to preserve the lives of the people from the various other diseases which belong to a community like this. On its organization the New York board of health found that no particular attention had been paid to sanitary matters in this city.

Sen. Blair: When was the board of health organized? — A. In 1866.

Q. Until then there had been none in this city? — A. No, sir. At that time the streets had been very indifferently cleaned; the slaughterhouses, and other houses connected with the consumption of slaughterhouse material, were located in all parts of the city — in fact, in some of the tenement districts there were large butchering establishments where animals were butchered in view of men, women, and children, as they passed through the streets, and the blood ran into the gutter in the sight of everybody. The city was suffering from many establishments whose business produced offensive odors. They found that in most of the houses, excepting very modern houses, the only accommodation for the necessary purpose of life were large privies, which were very foul in the summer season, and were not connected with sewers. They found at that time, also, that no provision existed to prevent the spread of contagious diseases. When contagion occurred, measures were inaugurated to put a stop to it, but no preventative measures had been exercised. I mention these things to show what progress the board has been able to make in this city in the way of securing improvements. The public mind (and by the public mind I mean the property owners) was not much disposed to make improvements in the interest of health. There was a prejudice, also, among the laboring people against what seemed to be an interference — a prejudice against people coming about their habitations for information, or anything in the nature of inquisitorial intrusion. For several years that was a difficulty. That, however, has been removed, and the inspectors of the board of health are now welcomed to all parts of the city, not only by the rich who suffer in any way from defective drainage equally with everybody else, but also by the very poor. That is a very gratifying progress in public opinion.

Soon after the establishment of the board of health there was a tenement-house law passed, giving the board of health special powers to look after the habitations of the very poor. The tenement-house population of this city is very large — larger than that of any other city in the world. By a tenement house, under the law of the state, we mean a house that contains more than three families. Under the law of New York any house is a tenement house that has four or more families.

Q. Can you give anything like the approximate number of persons who live in these tenement houses? — A. Yes; I had that in mind when I came here. . . . When this board came into existence there were two kinds of tenement houses; one built on purpose for the occupation of many families — four, eight, or twenty families, as the case may be. Another class of tenement houses were those which had been originally private dwellings built for one family, and as the city changed in the business locations and in the location of people able to have a house in a large town like this, the private house became the boarding-house, and finally became the tenement house. Now, houses built for tenement houses at that time were mostly built on lots 25 feet by 100. The object of the builders was, apparently to cover space so as to crowd as many families into it as possible, and the question of light and air had received very little attention.

Q. Had these houses been built without any legal supervision? — A. Without any legal supervision whatever.

Q. According to the will of the owner? — A. Yes; the way lots are laid out in this city; they are in the form of 25 feet front by 100 feet deep. The result was, in regard to the tenement houses, that all the sleeping rooms — all excepting the rooms fronting on the street and the rooms in the rear of the house — would have no light and no ventilation.

The new tenement houses built at that time, and, in fact, for some time after that, were all of a character in which light came only from the front and rear, and sometimes the rear was obstructed and gave little or no light. But in any case the sleeping apartments were altogether destitute of light and air.

At that time, also, there were tenement houses built two on a lot 25 by 100, leaving a space of 10 or 15 feet between the two houses; and in this space would be a privy, the smell from which in the hot weather would be very offensive to people living in the neighborhood. In many cases these privies were not connected with the sewers, and of course the system of scavengering at that time was of the crudest nature; open carts or buckets were used once a month, or, perhaps, only once in a season, and the whole neighborhood would be made uncomfortable on the emptying of cleaning of these privies. Previous to the existence of this board of health there was no provision by which the owner of the house could be compelled to take care of his property, if it were out of repair or in a filthy condition. . . .

The number of tenement houses in this city at that time — four years ago — (in 1879) was 21,163. In those 21,163 tenement houses there were 160,362 families, making an average, as you see, of about 7½ families to each of the tenement houses of this city. Statistics collected at that time show that the average number in each family is about 4½ — 160,000 families in tenement houses, with 4½ to each family, make 720,000 people living in the tenement houses of this city in 1879. . . .

In 1879, a very stringent tenement-house act was passed by the legislature, instigated by the board of health and a great many gentlemen of this city interested in sanitary reform, who believe that the interests of the city require that inasmuch as we are obliged to have these tenement houses here to a greater extent than in any other city, they should be made as comfortable and healthful as possible. This law requires that before the foundation of a house is laid the party proposing to build it must submit to the board of health an exact diagram showing the elevations and ground plan, and showing exactly how each room is to be ventilated.

This law requires that there shall be no room in a house erected after the passage of that act without an opening directly into the open air. That is a very important point, as you must observe. This law requires that a house shall cover only a certain percentage of a lot. Formerly a house might cover a whole lot. Now they can only cover 65 percent of it, but if the plan secures ventilation and light in a proper manner the board of health can increase the extent which the house may cover to 78 percent of the lot, and no tenement house can be built within 10 feet of the rear line of the lot. . . .

Q. What spaces are there on the exterior of the lot? — *A.* The general tendency is to build on each side, midway, a large shaft, into which all the interior rooms, such as bedrooms, can open, and that shaft either opens directly into the open air or has at the top of the shaft a covering with louvres, giving an air space equal to the entire space of the shaft.

Q. There would be no party-walls, as they are called, but a space between the tenements? — *A.* Well, no. There would be a party-wall for a part of the distance; for instance, a party-wall running back 20 or 30 feet, then a large shaft, then again the party-wall would continue.

Sen. Call: You mean by a "shaft" an open space? — *A.* An open space running from top to bottom.

Sen. Blair: Like a chimney? — *A.* Yes.

Sen. Call: When you have not that you have it open at the top? — *A.* The shaft may be open at the top and with a drainage at the bottom, so that the air and rain may come in, or they generally have it covered and with louvres or openings at the side like a window shutter. The law requires that that amount of opening in the louvres shall be the same size as the shaft itself. That is the way with the cheap houses, but in the large apartment houses instead of having a shaft they have a slot running in; what I mean by a slot is something from the rear running right in. In the large houses they run large slots, as I would call them, into a house to give light, but in these smaller houses shafts are built.

Sen. Pugh: That law does not affect tenement houses built before its passage? — *A.* No, sir. . . .

Sen. Call: Does your board regard the covering of 78 percent of a lot, and leaving only the remainder open as sufficient for pure air, ventilation, and health? — *A.* Well, it is regarded as reasonable in this city, where the land is so valuable and the people are so crowded.

Q. Suppose the land was not valuable, would it be sufficient then? — *A.* Well, we should like every man to have about ten acres about his house if we could.

Q. But ten acres are not necessary for air, are they? — *A.* No, of course not. Perhaps I ought not to have answered your question in that way. But in this city, situated as we are, if everything else is properly done, covering 78 out of a 100 feet gives proper ventilation. . . .

Sen. Blair: You had stated the condition in which the board of health had found the city, and were going on to state the changes that had been accomplished by the board, when a diversion in another direction took place. I should like you now to please go on and state first what improvements you made, and afterwards I will ask you to state what further may be done.

The Witness: I think I stated that about three years ago there was

an act passed by the legislature which placed the plumbing of new buildings in the hands of the board of health; that is, so far as the preliminary
approval of the plans was necessary. In a general way the board of health
has looked after the plumbing in tenement houses, and also, when complaints have been made, in private houses, during the whole period of its
existence. . . .

A great improvement has also been accomplished in the matter of these
large open privies. When such a privy is now within 15 feet of any
window they require it to be removed, and what are called "school sinks"
to be substituted in place of them. In many of those large tenement
houses there are many objections to the kind of plumbing which you
would have in a private house; that is, the habits of the people are such
that the water closets would be obstructed and injured. The people are
not found careful enough for some of these improvements, therefore the
privies in the yards are continued, but they are made upon a different
principle.

I will explain to you, if you please, what is the approved principle
for an outdoor privy. It is called a school sink, because that class of
sinks were first introduced in the schools of this city. It is a large iron
trough with the seats above it. These troughs are kept filled with
water. The janitor of the building who has charge of it overnight re-
moves the plug from this trough and lets the water in to fill it, and then
the next morning adjusts it. Of course, the feces dropping into this
water, there is no smell from it, and, being removed every day, there is
no fermentation and no odor arising from fermentation. So that a school
sink between two tenement houses on the same lot, if properly cared
for, gives no smell any more than if it did not exist; whereas, with the
old privies they were a constant source of trouble, and gave forth odors
that are known to be detrimental to health. That has been a great improvement effected in tenement houses. . . .

As far as the water supply is concerned, that is an element at the
present time of great danger in the city of New York. As the city has
increased in population, and on account of the elevated railroads, a
deal of water is used, and large manufacturing establishments are constantly growing up so that the water supply which a few years ago was
abundant is now short. That is, in many of the houses where it used to
reach the third or fourth floor it will now rise only to the second and
perhaps only to the first floor, and in some parts of the city, at certain
times in the day, you will only be able to turn the water on in the basement.

We attribute much of the disease of the past two or three years to
the want of an efficient water supply. You are probably aware, however, that arrangements are being made to add largely to the water supply
of the city.

The device of water meters has been introduced with a view to prevent wastage of water, but it has not entirely accomplished the result; there is still a great waste of water. For people have had so large a supply for many years that it is very difficult to teach them not to waste the water; and in the winter season nearly every householder is guilty of an offense against the public interests in letting the water run all night from the faucet in order to prevent the freezing of the pipes, and sometimes the whole storage of water has been nearly exhausted by people allowing the stream to run all night. . . .

Q. Do you think that the tenements as they existed in 1866 have been so modified that they are as healthy as they ought to be for occupation by human beings? — *A.* Well, I could hardly say that they are as healthy as they ought to be.

Q. Is there anything further that the board of health could, under the law, accomplish in that direction without the tenements themselves being replaced by new and better structures? — *A.* Well, in some cases — indeed in many cases — the tenements might be improved by removing the tenants and making very great and expensive changes in the building, but the board of health has not ventured upon that.

Q. You have not the power to direct the tearing down of premises, I suppose? — *A.* Not except in an extraordinary emergency. In such an emergency they might do it. In many cases we have vacated buildings — had the tenants all removed — but that was only where the building was infected by contagious diseases, or where the building was in such repair as to make it dangerous for people to live in it.

The spirit and tendency of the law under which we act, however, is that we are not to do anything of that kind, but that simply, if a place is dirty or wants repair, to see that that is remedied — not subject the owner to great loss by closing up his building, by tearing it down, or anything of that kind. In fact the law limits us, as I have said, to these two contingencies — where the house is infected by contagious diseases, or where the repair is such that the house is dangerous. . . .

Sen. Blair: I remember that we went into one tenement house that seemed to have, I should think, 400 or 500 people in it, and they all, so far as I saw, seemed to be living in such rooms as you describe. The house must have been built before 1866. It had a front room and back room and a connecting room, a dark apartment, which was a sleeping room, and from this same sleeping room was a room with a stove in it on which stood a kerosene lamp, and a woman was doing the day's cooking on this stove in the center of the room.

The Witness: That is a difficulty in New York. No other city is like it because no other has such a large tenement population.

Sen. Blair: It requires considerable power to be able to take down such a building. On the exterior, this building that I speak of, looked rather like a comfortable building.

The Witness: To gentlemen like you of the committee, who have seen the rooms and the air that people have in the ordinary cities and villages of the country, and then go through our city tenement houses here, it looks, of course, as if they must be very crowded, and so they are. One would hardly think they could exist in such crowds, and yet there seems to be no remedy, no way of giving them more room. . . .

Testimony of Charles F. Wingate

Charles F. Wingate was a New York sanitary engineer whose work, he told the committee, provided "very unusual advantages for studying this problem of the condition of the working classes."

The Witness: I suppose a small library has been published on the subject of the tenement-house problem in New York City. I do not propose to talk mere sentiment on this matter, or to exaggerate its evils; I wish simply to state some facts, and rather to soften them down than to exaggerate them; and while I shall speak specifically of tenement houses in New York, I must repeat that these conditions are to be found in Boston, in Philadelphia to a less extent, in Savannah, Ga., which I lately visited, and even in the smaller places like, Newark, Paterson, and manufacturing towns generally where there is a large operative population. . . .

It is impossible to ventilate the ordinary tenement house, because they call a ventilator a shaft which is open simply at the top. They build a skylight or light shaft and put an opening at the top, which is not always open, and then allow the tenants to close all the windows connected with it. Then the halls are closed in on all sides, so that there is no possibility of any fresh air getting in. Then there is always a "living room" for such families, which is an interior room, and it is impossible to secure a draft of air through it. Yet, by securing air below and having an opening at the top of the shaft, you would secure a great deal of air, and sufficient ventilation, or by making the shaft larger you would get more air.

Damp cellars are also a great trouble, yet that is entirely curable. It is nearly fifty years since cellar occupation was forbidden in this city. Yet you see many people living in cellars today, and business carried on in them. It is perfectly feasible to have dry cellars, and if you had them you would win half the battle. From my experience I should say that damp cellars are the chief cause of sickness in cities. While a large number of the tenements of New York have plumbing in the house a large portion have not, and the people are compelled, if they are going to be cleanly or decent, to carry up all the water they use from a hydrant in the yard, which, in the winter time, is apt to be frozen. It is manifestly unjust to expect that with such labor anybody can be cleanly. The mere fact of carrying water up four or five stories for cooking purposes is as much as can be expected — if they have to carry all the waste water back, four or five stories. Furthermore, these four or five stories representing eighty or ninety persons, there is sometimes nothing in the way of sanitary conveniences except four or five or six water closets, or "privies," in the yard. . . .

Another evil is that the rooms of the poor are so contracted that they can do nothing. When a woman wants to do anything, or carry on any little occupation, there is no room in which to do it. If you can supply homes where the people can carry on labor, washing or sewing, or a little light manufacturing, you assist the tenants or workingmen very much. It is considered one of the great reasons of the prosperity of the workingmen of Philadelphia that they have small homes and can carry on such industries; and even in this city, as I notice in hot weather, when people leave their windows open, as you ride along the Third Avenue Elevated Road, you will see scores, if not hundreds, of places with one, two, or three mechanics at work at some small industry. . . .

The New York Association for Improving the Condition of the Poor employs a special inspector to visit the houses of the poor. The first put an advertisement in the *Daily News* offering to examine any place having bad smells. But the poor tenant is afraid to make a complaint, even if he sees death staring him in the face, because of the fear of being turned out of his place. And when the inspectors go to these places — and they visit thousands of them frequently — it is with great difficulty that they can get information. People will point to the sink, and say, "There is where the smell is, but don't you mention my name." Some of the letters written by people on this subject are of the most pitiable character. I will read a few extracts from the thirty-eighth annual report of the board of health, in which some of these letters are quoted:

. . . Last spring the following advertisement was inserted in an evening newspaper — one which is read chiefly by the working classes:

"A notice sent to John Browne, secretary of the New York Association for Improving the Condition of the Poor, 79 Fourth Avenue, of any defect in a tenement house, will receive prompt attention. Communications confidential."

The above appeared for six weeks, and was responded to by complaints — chiefly anonymous — relating to upwards of two hundred houses, and indirectly to about one hundred more.

The complaints, in many instances, left the story only half told, generally referring to one particular nuisance, inspection revealing other defects.

A perusal of all the letters received would repay anyone desirous of gaining a knowledge of tenement-house life, and of the struggle against adverse circumstances which render the lives of the poor of New York so pitiable.

The following quotations will serve to reflect truthfully, but only partially, a picture of the condition in which so many of our fellow-beings and near neighbors live:

"The privies of —— Forsyth Street are in a horribly filthy condition."

"Will you please to try and do something to relieve the poor tenants of ——— Tenth Avenue; the stench to-day is beyond everything; it can be traced a block away; you will be doing an everlasting gratitude to the — (Poor People.)" . . .

"The cellar is overrun by water; . . . it seems useless to talk to the agent; you can see through the flooring in the basement, and the children there are always sick with colds. — (A Neighbor, ——— W. Thirty-third Street.)"

"The filth (of the privies) oozes out all over the yard, and the stench is intolerable. . . . The stench that was coming up through the front grating was horrible. — (A Sufferer, ——— W. Fortieth Street.)"

"There is a terrible bad smell from the water-closets, . . . the yard flags are loose and the smell comes up . . . I see in the News you will help us poor men. —(——— E. Thirty-eight Street.)" . . .

". . . Manure is thrown into our yard every day; our children have no other place to play in. — (——— E. Sixteenth Street.)"

"I was glad to see your advertisement. . . . I have reported to the board of health three or four times; . . . the sewer pipe is broken, it is making the people in the house sick. — (——— Roosevelt Street.)"

"The privies are full to overflowing, the flooring is all broken, to give the odors better ventilation. — (——— Third Avenue.)"

"The stink (from the cellar) is enough to knock you down. . . . If you will look after this the whole house will be greatly obliged to you. — (——— E. Seventy-fourth Street.)" . . .

". . . There has been in house No. — several deaths since last January of diphtheria, I myself lost two children this last month, and one death occurred last night in the same house . . . and others are sick in No. — with diphtheria; . . . you will receive the blessings of myself and others. —(——— to ——— Third Avenue.)"

"See to leaky hydrant and water closet that empties its filth into the cellar. . . . The house belongs to Trinity Church. — (——— Washington Street.)"

"We ask the agent for water, and he says we must move out or pay the rent, water or no water. — (——— Third Avenue.)" . . .

"The ceiling is all down and the rain comes in, and the waste-pipe runs through the room, so that when it rains we cannot stand the smell, and the roof and roof-stairs are in a terrible state; the roof had no door on all winter. We spoke to the landlady several times about it, and she paid no attention to it. — (——— Third Avenue.)"

". . . After reading your kind notice . . . visit the defective sinks in tenement house, No. —. The landlord does not seem to care. . . . Please do not say there is complaint made; if the landlord would know I am the person he would have me put out, therefore I will not give my name. — (——— Second Avenue.)" . . .

I have here a report on the tenement-house system of New York by a committee of gentlemen, at the head of which was Rev. Henry C. Potter, D.D., which I wish to submit:

THE TENEMENT-HOUSE SYSTEM IN NEW YORK

. . . The total number of arrests made by the police in 1878 was 76,484, of which 30,373, or 19,538 males and 10,835 females, were for drunkenness, and

15,628 for disorderly conduct, chiefly the effect of drink. About 12,000 of these were made in the three crowded tenement-house wards, the Eleventh, Fourteenth, and Seventeenth. . . .

Mr. Charles L. Brace, of the Children's Aid Society, says: "After twenty-five years' experience among the children of the poor in this city, I can truly say that there is no one cause so fruitful of crime, vagrancy, and bad habits among them as the condition of the tenement houses. How they ever grow up to purity, honesty, and decency is a wonder when one knows how they live. The enormous number of vagrant children in this city, our lodging houses alone reaching some 15,000 different homeless boys and girls in the course of the year, arises from the influence of the tenement houses."

A citizen specially interested in the temperance movement writes: "The discomforts of close, gloomy quarters, and above all the discouragement from the sickness and consequent wretchedness sure to prevail in such dwellings, do more to fill the dram-shops than any other material cause whatever." . . .

Here is a picture from life of three tenement houses of the *worst* class:

No. 1. Down in the basement, a resort for vagrants of the worst class, at midday were nine men and three women, all sodden with stale beer; the passageway was obstructed by a helpless wretch who had been ejected from the adjacent room. A little later this same man, after he had been revived by fresh air, was fiercely assaulted and beaten by a woman. In another room where rags and bones, not devoid of putrid flesh, were being sorted, the air was so vile the visitor could not remain. In this building but four closets were provided for the 182 inmates. An attic room here, lighted by one small window, is occupied by four men and four women, almost certainly not married, at a monthly rent of four dollars. In another room three men and four women live — all rag-pickers. Here was a young girl, who was represented as "stopping for a few days." She looked as if she might be saved, for she was obviously ashamed of herself and her friends. In this entire tenement were 182 persons; of these 122 were men, 37 women, and 23 children.

No. 2. A structure of the poorest class. A basement room was unfurnished except with a stove, a keg of stale beer, and boxes used for seats. Around the former were huddled four men and three women, four others being in the room. Humanity gets no lower than these people are, and they are looked down upon by the other denizens of the place. The proprietor of this room (which is 14½ by 10 feet in extent) takes from eight to twelve lodgers at night. Stale beer is sold at two cents a pint or three cents a quart. Another room, the darkest in the house, is occupied by two Italian men and three women. In only four rooms was there anything like a family organization. The police report the arrests for assault and battery in this house to average one a week. In this house are 14 rooms, occupied by 72 persons; of these 19 are men, 24 women, 12 children, and 17 lodgers.

No. 3. In the court are four closets, used by the 118 inhabitants of the house, all in a sickening state. The water leaks from the roof to the ground below through the two intervening floors. In one of the second-story rooms live one woman, six men, two large boys (18 or 20 years old). The woman is unmarried. On the third story in a small room live three men and three women, all unmarried Irish and Italians; 118 people live in this tenement; of these 87 are men, 18 women, 13 children.

Sen. Pugh: The sole power to remedy these evils is with the city authorities, and it is amazing to me that they have not been remedied. It seems most extraordinary.

The Witness: Let me answer that remark briefly. Our board of health is a good body. They have certain funds. They receive six thousand, or more, complaints in a year from all sorts of buildings, from the best to the worst. They send their inspector to examine the buildings. He comes back and makes a report, and a notice is sent to the landlord of the character of that report and of the difficulty existing at the house, with instructions to remedy the difficulty. The inspector goes there a second time, and reports again, and if the remedy is not applied another notice is sent to the landlord. The same thing is done again and if the third notice is not attended to proceedings will be taken to sue the man. This requires a great deal of labor, and you cannot expect officials to do any more than they can. . . .

Sen. Blair: Why is that? I do not understand that statement. — A. I state it, then, as a fact, that buildings have existed in this city, held up by nothing but the elements, you may say; buildings notoriously unfit for human habitation, and only after months have they been condemned by the board.

Q. Why is it? What is the trouble? Have the people no courage to condemn such a thing, and remedy it? — A. The board of health was stated some years ago to have arbitrary power. It was stated, for example, as a joke, that the Shah of Persia was going to have a board of health like ours, established in his government, to carry on the affairs of his Kingdom. They have ample power, but they cannot rise above public opinion. And, if they find $200,000,000 of capital invested in tenement houses to combat them and only half a dozen men to sustain them, what are they going to do do?

Q. Can they not say that such a building is unfit for habitation? — A. Well, I do not wish to criticize the board of health, but I can take you to buildings which are unfit for human beings to enter, in which you could not cross the halls without having your feet covered with filth.

Q. Does anybody live in those buildings? — A. Yes.

Q. Where are they? — A. In this city.

Q. Where? — A. One in Fifty-fourth Street.

Q. When did you see it? — A. Two of my associates inspected it within thirty days, and reported it to the board of health. There are buildings in this city, of the better class, not tenement houses — where people paying as much rent as I pay myself — bookkeepers and clerks and middle-class of people — in Yorkville and Harlem, "skin buildings," as they are called, without any party wall between the cellars, the houses supported by wooden braces, which are splitting with the weight of the buildings — in which the coping of the roof is built with mortar which has nothing but sand in it, and buildings where the sewer pipe has burst and its contents have come up into the room that a poor washerwoman lives in. These are facts. In fact, this whole city, from a sanitary point of view, is simply rotten.

Q. Do you mean to say that the board of health, knowing these facts, do not state them? — *A.* I mean to say that the board of health, from want of courage, or from some cause that I will not state too explicitly, is either ignorant of them, or has ignored them, or has delayed attending to them. . . .

Sen. Blair: Colonel Clark, the secretary of the board of health, testified about this matter, and said that there were difficulties; but he denied quite emphatically the existence of such facts as you testify to. I am sure those facts cannot be in the possession of the board of health.

The Witness: This very report that I have submitted to you has been in the hands of the board of health for a year or more. It is a notorious fact, which has been published broadcast, that buildings in New York City, which were condemned by the citizens' sanitary committee in 1865, for being in a bad sanitary condition, are in that same condition to-day. . . .

Sen. Pugh: You say that these facts which you have stated are open to the eyes of anybody who will go where they are? — *A.* They are.

Sen. Pugh: Then it seems to me they are physical facts, about which there can be no mistake, and the truth or falsehood of what the witness swears about them can be ascertained by ocular demonstration.

The Witness: That is so.

Sen. Blair: You have seen them? — *A.* I have seen them; I can bring you column after column of description in the New York papers of the last two months — the *Sun,* the *Post,* and the *Tribune* — which are simply duplicates of things that have been published in the same papers every summer within my knowledge, till I got tired of reading them; they are facts. The reporters find them out and state them, and that is all the good it does. For instance, one reporter says, "I find a whole family of Jewish tailors living in a cellar, working ten or twelve hours a day, tumbling off their benches and going to sleep on the floor, and getting up and going to work again — in a cellar condemned by law, and unfit for any human being to live in." Another says he found "a woman who had lived in a cellar for twenty years, with a stable twenty feet away, and she said she was very healthy, and had a large family there." It is a question involving no dispute.

Sen. Pugh: If the board of health had not this information they could easily get it, I suppose, the facts being in existence and open to the discovery of everybody? — *A.* Precisely; in fact, their own records show it.

Q. Well, then, for them to say that they had not the information would seem to be very remarkable, would it not? — *A.* It would. Of course I have my explanation of those things, but it is not proper that

I should give them publicly. I appeal simply to the record. There are the facts, and they can be substantiated publicly, and I can duplicate those pictures in a hundred places in New York. . . .

Testimony of William H. Foster

William H. Foster, a printer, was an important trade union official, secretary of the Federation of Organized Trades and Labor Unions organized in 1881, and soon to be one of the founders of the American Federation of Labor.

Sen. George: How long have you lived in Cincinnati? — A. Since June, 1877. I was there in 1873 and 1874 about eight months.

Q. Are you familiar with the actual condition of the laboring classes of that city? — A. I am.

Q. Have you gone frequently among their houses and the places they live? — A. I have, I think, as much as anybody. I helped the commissioner of labor statistics, as I mentioned a while ago, in collecting data for his report.

Q. Describe the ordinary average dwelling of the laborer in Cincinnati. — A. My landlord works in the same establishment that I do myself; he is a married man. He rents a $25 house. I do not know whether the house would be considered very fine here, but it a five-room house, with a bay window and a cellar; there is no yard, but there is a rather fine paved terrace in front. It is a very convenient place for anybody who has children; they can run up and down on their roller skates and have a good time. It is a five-room house, and I have one of the rooms, and the landlord occupies the rest with his wife and child.

Q. How many stories high is the house? — A. Three.

Q. What is the size of the rooms? — A. I am not a judge of measurement by sight, but the one I occupy is about 20 by 16. That is what I would call about the average residence of the first-class mechanics who are paid good wages.

Q. Now, give us the condition of a second-class. — A. Well, many mechanics, earning about $3 a day, will live in a house that will cost $16 a month — a portion of a large tenement building generally, with three or four rooms to each flat. They may live with comparative comfort in such a building, but the rooms would be too small for me. I want room to swing a pair of clubs if I choose to.

Q. Then the next lower class. — A. The lower-class men — I have seen men so low that they had to shove a family of five or six children and themselves, and perhaps their parents, and do their cooking and all, in one room. They have a little trundle bed to put all the children in, and they shove it under their bed when not in use.

Q. That is not usual, however, I suppose? — A. Well, it is not very common. It is among the working poor, though.

Q. What percentage of the working classes would that statement cover? — A. I should say at least 5 percent.

Q. Is there not an intermediate class of dwellings between that and the houses of the $3-a-day men you have described? — A. Yes; there are men who occupy small $10 cottages out in the suburbs. They get perhaps the same accommodations at a smaller rent, but they put some labor on themselves in walking to and from their work.

Q. Then you have no special complaint against the habitations of the workingmen in Cincinnati except those of this 5 percent class? — A. Yes, sir; there is more than that. I would not live in those small rooms that some people occupy. I think they are too small all around.

Q. Are the people healthy that live in these small rooms? — A. I know that when the smallpox ran through the city, the greatest proportion of people died out among those tenement buildings. Whether crowding into small rooms makes the people negligent of their personal cleanliness or not, I do not know, but I think it has that effect. I think also it has a tendency to make men who are forced to live under those conditions inclined to be intemperate in their habits. They find no comfort at home, living in one room, and if they can get a few cents they go and spend it in the saloon.

Q. That is the worst class; but I am speaking of the class just above that, who still live in small rooms. — A. Well, even their comforts are not what they ought to be. A man ought to have a room where he could go and sit down and read without his children climbing all over him and making a nuisance of the house. . . .

Testimony of Joseph Medill

Joseph Medill grew up in Ohio, where he purchased a small local newspaper in 1849. He moved to Chicago in 1859 and bought a part interest in the Chicago Tribune. *He supported Abraham Lincoln in his bid for the Republican presidential nomination in 1860 and during the Civil War figured prominently in the radical wing of the Republican party. He was elected mayor of Chicago after the great fire of 1871 and won a considerable reputation as a civic reformer. In 1874 he obtained control of the* Tribune *and thereafter dominated the editorial policy of that extremely influential paper.*

The Witness: Perhaps next to liquor drinking the worst ill that afflicts the tenant-wage classes is wretched domiciles — overcrowded, badly ventilated, poisoned by sewer-gas and excessively rented. Thousands of such structures in this (New York) and other large cities, including Chicago, where I reside, should be demolished by municipal authority as nuisances, injurious to the public health. It is a dreadful fact that in this naturally salubrious city the annual mortality exceeds the births by upwards of ten thousand, as shown by the sanitary statistics of the municipality, proving that were it not for the in-flowing stream the population of New York would become extinct and the city uninhabited. . . .

Reform is necessary, not only here, but in all the other cities of this country, in the character of the abodes rented to the industrial classes. The rents exacted are twice or thrice too high, as a rule, and most of the houses are unfit for human habitation. And this is one of the bitterest causes of discontent among the wage workers — unhealthy and over-rented tenements. The rents of artisans' dwellings in England average about a dollar a week, as I ascertained last summer when I was there, after careful inquiry of intelligent men in several of the principal cities. Their sanitary condition is far better attended to than it is in this country, which in part accounts for the smaller rates of mortality in English as compared with the cities of America. All over England badly constructed and unhealthy tenements are being torn down as nuisances, by corporate authority, under an act of parliament, and building companies are replacing them by a better class of houses for the working population, to be let at very low rentals. If private capital is unwilling in this country to provide decent and healthy abodes at moderate rents for the industrial classes of our cities, it may become necessary for municipal corporations to do it, and lease or sell the same to the wage-workers at a rate that would repay interest or cost. As good a public reason for this course exists as for providing schoolhouses, poorhouses, water, gas, fire engines, etc., at public expense for the benefit of the people. I cannot see any good reason why the one may not be done if the other may. . . .

Testimony of Joseph A. Chevalier

Joseph A. Chevalier was a Catholic priest of French-Canadian extraction. In 1883 he had been serving as pastor of a church in a working-class parish in Manchester, New Hampshire, for twelve years.

Sen. Blair: What are the personal habits and actual condition of these people [French-Canadians] in their houses, and in daily life as to attention to sanitary conditions, neatness, thrift, economy, cleanliness, and the like? — A. In their houses they are generally clean people; but the tenements for them in the city are bad; their sanitary condition is awfully bad, I guess, in some places in the city.

Q. Some that you have inspected yourself? — A. Yes.

Q. In what condition did you find the tenements themselves? — A. They are too small; then they do not repair them at all for many years; and all around those tenements in the back streets all kinds of dirty things are allowed to stand. In many cases I have seen that myself. When they have good houses they live well, and their health is good; but in many places they get sick on account of the bad condition of the houses.

Q. How large a proportion of them live in houses that are in that condition? — A. Well, you might say at least one-third of them live in those tenements on the back streets.

Q. Can you give an idea of the size of the rooms — these are families, are they — large families? — A. Yes.

Q. How many children may there be in a family? — A. They do not generally have more than three or four rooms for one family — or four or five rooms; as a rule they are very small rooms.

Q. Can you give an idea as to the size of the rooms; how do they compare with this room? — A. They do not have as much room as this.

Q. The rooms are not so large? — A. No; perhaps about as large as half of this room.

Q. And some three or four or five rooms usually make a tenement? — A. Yes.

Q. How many persons in the family? — A. You might say seven or eight.

Q. The two parents, and then the children? — A. Yes. The bedrooms are very small; generally 6 feet wide by 10 feet long; and some smaller than that; but as a rule I guess the bedrooms are about 6 or 7 feet wide and 10 or 12 feet long.

Q. How do these compare with the houses that they came from in Canada? — A. They have good houses in Canada, large houses. . . .

Q. What number [of French-Canadians] are there in Lowell, or Fall River, or both? — A. There are about 12,000.

Q. In Lowell? — A. In Lowell and Fall River, too; the same in both.

Q. Have you visited among them in either of these cities? — A. No.

Q. As compared with other working people in the mills, do you know any reason why they are not as industrious and as desirable as any? — A. I think they are. As a rule, they are sober people. Of course there are some that are not, but they like to work, and they stick to it.

Q. Does any suggestion occur to you of what you would like to see done — what you think ought to be done to make them more comfortable, prosperous, and happy? — A. I think that the tenement houses ought to be kept in better condition.

Q. The tenements themselves ought to be made better? — A. Yes;

then I suppose the wages are rather low; they do not get enough, I guess, to pay their expenses. Groceries are very high.

Q. What prices do they pay for groceries, so far as you know? You may be able to state something about that. — *A.* I believe they are very high; butter, eggs, etc.

Q. Are you able to give the range of prices; I suppose they buy as other people buy in the market. Do you know any reason why they do not get their groceries as cheaply as any other class do? — *A.* Well, I suppose they have to pay a little more because they can only pay for their groceries every month; and I guess grocers sell more if the customers take a book than if they pay cash down.

Q. I suppose, from the way you state it, that you think they ought to be paid oftener than once a month? — *A.* It would be better; if they have money to buy groceries they would get their groceries cheaper, I think; anything that they can buy for cash down they would be apt to get cheaper.

Q. At the end of a month they are paid four times as much as they would be paid at the end of a week. Do you think they are more likely to spend money for other uses if they get it in larger sums? — *A.* No; I think not.

Q. You think they would be more likely to save money if paid weekly? — *A.* They could save a little more money if they wanted to save it.

Q. You think there is a tendency, having it all together in a lump, to waste more of it? — *A.* No; I do not think they waste more of it; but if they buy their groceries for cash they get them cheaper.

Q. But why do they not buy for cash when they receive cash every month? — *A.* They do not have money ahead. Every month they spend all the money they get.

Q. Could they not, by an effort, contrive to get a month ahead, and then be in advance? — *A.* They could, certainly, if they would; but as long as they have money they want to enjoy it.

Q. They are about like the rest of us in that respect, I suppose? — *A.* Yes.

Q. It seems a little hard to hold working people to rules that we do not obey ourselves, and ask them to exhibit virtues that others do not exhibit. — *A.* I think, too, that the wages are rather low.

Q. Does any other suggestion occur to you that might be made to help in the improvement of these people? — *A.* No; I do not think of anything else.

Q. Do you encourage them; do their leaders and clergymen and others that have influence with them encourage them in the idea of remaining and being permanent citizens here? — *A.* Certainly. . . .

Testimony of Timothy D. Stow *

The Witness: Now, in regard to the tenements in which they live. Some of the corporations have very fair tenements. I would mention, as one instance, the Weetamoe corporation. The King Philip corporation, I think, has pretty fair tenements for its operatives, although many of those tenements are neglected. Whether this is because the manufacturers, or their agents, think that it is almost impossible to keep up with the destructive propensities of their tenants or not, or whether it is from sheer neglect I cannot say, but I know the defective condition of these tenements seems to be from sheer neglect in many cases.

For instance, the Slade buildings are very badly located. The tenements were very hastily constructed, and are poorly constructed, so that the average amount of fuel which the operative has to use has to be increased — indeed, has to be nearly doubled — in order to heat these houses during the winter. The access to these houses is in many instances very bad. They are very near a swamp where the drainage is very bad; and through the summertime water and mire are steadily upon the ground within a few rods of the building. It is a noisome, disgusting place. I have noticed, on going in and out of these buildings many times, that the steps were out of repair for long periods. There were some rows of the Slade buildings where the boards of the steps were out and the children and the tenants themselves were likely to break their limbs and injure themselves seriously while going up and down those steps in the darkness of the night by falling through the loose steps. Nothing is done about it through the sheer neglect and the penuriousness of the managers of the mill. There are some corporations at Fall River that are notable exceptions in this respect, though they have not done everything that could be done, by any means. . . .

I want to say a few words further relative to the Slade-Mill tenements and the condition of the operatives in those tenements, and the conveniences offered by the company. They are such today, so far as I am cognizant of them, as to demand that something be said about them. I have not axes to grind. I drive along quietly in my profession; but when it is necessary for me as a citizen to state what I think is right in defense of justice I do it without fear or favor.

This corporation, I said, neglects the welfare of its operatives. I will give you an illustration: I have spoken of the drainage and ventilation and the bad location of the buildings.

But in regard to the water we have in Fall River, it is probably as ex-

* See above, page 30.

cellent water as can be found in the country, and the city has been to great expense in providing it. There is a single source of water there, and that is outdoor. The women who do the work for the families are obliged, summer and winter, to go out of the building and go up one of the streets between the buildings and take the water from a single pen-stock or from a single faucet which has a caliber of seven-eighths of an inch. If they have young children they leave them, of course, in the house while they go out. They are subjected to the changes of temperature which they have to meet on passing from a warm atmosphere to a cold, and quite a number of accidents have taken place in those tenements (that is, within the time the corporation has been in existence) from scaldings and burning of children on stoves and, in one way and another, during the absence of their mothers in looking after these things. . . .

4   LABOR UNIONS

Testimony of Robert D. Layton *

Sen. Blair: Without asking you to go into any matters which you may think proper not to mention here, I will ask you to give us, if you please, a general idea of the objects, purposes, and extent of the organization known as the Knights of Labor of North America. Make the statement in your own way, and as fully as you see fit. — A. Perhaps I can give it to you more fully and more accurately by referring to a pamphlet which I have here, which sets forth our aims and objects and what we hope ultimately to achieve.

Sen. George: Is that an authoritative statement?

The Witness: Yes, sir; I will read the preamble. Our objects are, as stated in this —

Preamble:

I. To bring within the folds of organization every department of productive industry, making knowledge a standpoint for action, and industrial, moral worth, not wealth, the true standard of individual and national greatness.

II. To secure to the toilers a proper share of the wealth that they create; more of the leisure that rightfully belongs to them; more society advantages; more of the benefits, privileges, and emoluments of the world; in a word, all those rights and privileges necessary to make them capable of enjoying, appreciating, defending, and perpetuating the blessings of good government.

III. To arrive at the true condition of the producing masses in their educational, moral, and financial condition by demanding from the various Governments the establishment of Bureaus of labor statistics.

IV. The establishment of co-operative institutions, productive and distributive.

V. The reserving of the public lands — the heritage of the people — for the actual settler; not another acre for railroads or speculators.

VI. The abrogation of all laws that do not bear equally upon capital and labor; the removal of unjust technicalities, delays, and discrimination in the administration of justice; and the adopting of measures providing for the health and safety of those engaged in mining, manufacturing, or building pursuits.

VII. The enactment of laws to compel chartered corporations to pay their employés weekly, in full, for labor performed during the preceding week, in the lawful money of the country.

VIII. The enactment of laws giving mechanics and laborers a first lien on their work for their full wages.

* See above, page 1.

IX. The abolishment of the contract system on national, State, and municipal work.

X. The substitution of arbitration for strikes, whenever and wherever employers and employés are willing to meet on equitable grounds.

XI. The prohibition of the employment of children in workshops, mines, factories, &c., before attaining their fourteenth year.

XII. To abolish the system of letting out by contract the labor of convicts in our prisons and reformatory institutions.

XIII. To secure for both sexes equal pay for equal work.

XIV. The reduction of the hours of labor to eight per day, so that the laborers may have more time for social enjoyment and intellectual improvement, and be enabled to reap the advantages conferred by the labor-saving machinery which their brains have created.

XV. To prevail upon Governments to establish a purely national circulating medium, issued directly to the people, without the intervention of any system of banking corporations, which money shall be legal tender in payment of all debts, public and private.

Sen. Blair: Is that a secret organization? — A. It is.

Q. How long has it existed? — A. Thirteen years.

Q. Is it original in this country, or is it an offshoot from a like institution elsewhere? — A. It is original in this country.

Q. Where was it organized? — A. In Philadelphia, Pa.

Q. Please state whether there are sub-organizations in the different states, and go on and describe the organization fully, as my original question contemplated. — A. The organization originated in Philadelphia, and at its beginning the various trades formed a Trade Union, and then formed a district. Five local assemblies — we call lodges local assemblies — are entitled to a charter. They then become a district assembly. The limits of a district assembly have not been yet clearly defined, as to how much of territory each assembly shall embrace. Local assemblies can determine for themselves whether they are able to bear the expense of sending their delegates to where the district assembly is held, and that consideration has heretofore determined the amount of territory to be included in a district. There has been no definite number of local assemblies fixed upon to be attached to a district; as many as find it convenient can belong to it, or there can be more than one district in a city. All that has to be determined by circumstances. Isolated assemblies which cannot join a district are attached directly to my office or to the general assembly. Once a year we have a meeting, entitled a grand assembly, in which the laws and regulations for the year are made. Delegates are sent from the district assemblies to the general assembly.

Q. From all parts of the country? — A. From all parts of the country.

Q. At what time does that general assembly meet? — A. It meets on the first Tuesday in September of every year.

Q. Where does it meet? — A. At any place that may be designated by the officers of the general assembly. The organization embraces all trades and callings excepting lawyers, bankers, and rum-sellers.

Sen. George: You mean whisky dealers? — A. Yes, sir; those are the only three classes that are excluded from the organization. Manufacturers can belong to it.

Sen. Blair: What is the number of your membership, approximately? — A. Our reports, as far as they were in at the time when I last attempted to ascertain our numbers definitely, showed that we had a membership of 67,000. . . .

Q. You have mentioned the classes that are excluded from your organization; do you admit men and women alike to membership? — A. Yes; we have women in our lodges.

Q. Is there any qualification as to age? — A. A person must be eighteen years of age to be admitted.

Q. There is no restriction in the matter of wealth, I suppose — no property qualification? — A. No, sir; if a person has been a wage-worker at any time in his life, he is entitled to be admitted.

Sen. George: But he must be a wage-worker? — A. Yes, he must be, or must have been at some time, a wage-worker.

Sen. Blair: As a matter of fact, what classes are most numerous in your order — agricultural laborers or those engaged in manufactures? — A. Those engaged in manufactures, if you include the coal miner under that head.

Sen. George: By the "coal miner" you mean the man who digs the coal out of the earth? — A. Yes, sir; the ore miners on the Pacific Coast belong to the same class.

Sen. Blair: Where is the real power of your organization — with what class of men? Who control the organization? — A. It would be pretty hard for me to determine where the strongest power would come in. I cannot answer that question definitely. It might possibly be with the telegraphers, or the miners, or the printers — I could not tell with certainty.

Q. Those several occupations, however, do not act in your meeting as separate classes, one vetoing the other, but each man acts as an individual, without reference to the class he belongs to, and casts his vote independently? — A. Oh, certainly. The fact of your calling being different from mine would not have anything to do with the question.

Q. Please tell us, as far as you feel at liberty to do so, the control or discipline which, as an organization, you exercise over your individual members, and what direction, if any, you, as an organization, give to the industrial conduct or the freedom of action of individual workingmen in their relations with other indvidual workingmen. Is it simply advisory, or is a man put under an obligation to respect and perhaps to comply actually with the general or the specific requirements of the order? — A. He is expected to comply with the specific requirements of the order, under an obligation that he assumes when he becomes a member. So far as discipline is concerned, we have not perhaps been quite as rigid in that respect as we might have been under the circumstances. This action is chiefly advisory; although, if a man assumes a position and then, without any good cause or provocation, so far as we can see or learn, deserts it in a cowardly manner and causes others to be victimized, we undoubtedly bring as much moral pressure to bear upon him as we can — that is, we ostracize him; we have nothing to do with him in the works, do not speak to him, nor render him any assistance more than is absolutely necessary. We do not consider a man of that kind to be a man.

Q. Are some of your members employers of labor? — A. We have a large number of employers among us.

Q. Some, I suppose, who might be classed as capitalists as well as laborers? — A. If they are capitalists, they deny it. They do not assume the position of a capitalist in the sense in which it is generally understood.

Q. Perhaps I used the word in a sense different from that in which you use it. I merely mean by "capitalist" a man who handles capital in the employment of labor. — A. Well, of course, it is necessary if you employ labor, even to the smallest extent, to handle more or less capital, but in the sense in which "capitalist" is generally understood, we have not any capitalists in our organization.

Q. You have no men who are at the head of large establishments? — A. No, sir.

Q. Nor men who are leaders in corporations or anything of that description? — A. Oh, no.

Q. I suppose the main object of the organization is to combine individual laborers in a mass, so that they may be able to protect themselves by the joint strength of the whole against any aggressions of employers or capitalists which might deprive them, or might have a tendency to deprive them, of just compensation for the part which they take in production; that is, of compensation for their labor. — A. That is one of the main objects we have in view while we remain wage-workers; but we are striving toward cooperation, and are trying as rapidly as we can to introduce arbitration as a substitute for strikes whenever that is possible.

Q. What, as you understand it, is meant by cooperation in the sense in which it is contemplated by your order? — A. We aim at collective and distributive cooperation. That is, if we, as members, start a store, and if non-members deal with us, at the end of three months we declare a dividend and give those who have assisted us part of the profits back again, even though they are not members. That is our idea of cooperation. It is not confined exclusively to members of the organization. The idea is to assist others who assist us.

Q. The illustration that you give applies to the procurement of the necessaries of life. I did not know but you meant by "cooperation," that you were aiming to secure a division of the results of the joint investment of capital and labor. — *A.* We do desire that among ourselves, by going into business for ourselves, contributing our own money, and starting a business of our own.

Q. Has that been tried to any extent? — *A.* Yes, sir; many of our lodges own their own buildings, and have stores. We have a cooperative pottery at East Liverpool, Ohio, and there are a number of other cooperative stores. I think there are fifty or sixty underway at the present time in different places.

Q. This pottery is at East Liverpool, Ohio; are there others engaged in the same business in this country? — *A.* No, sir; not any others belonging to the Knights of Labor.

Q. Please state, as fully as they occur to you, all the cooperative institutions of the Knights of Labor in other kinds of business throughout the country. — *A.* The cooperative establishments are principally grocery or drygoods stores and country stores. We have a number of organizations that are building their own lodges with the view of starting stores to supply themselves. At Shawnee, Ohio, we have a finished building, a large opera house, with storerooms, and a lodging-house, and a reading room above. That is, perhaps, the completest building of the kind we have in that line. The cooperative pottery at East Liverpool, Ohio, is perhaps the largest investment that we have.

Q. Give us as definite an idea as you can of the extent of that establishment and its business. — *A.* Well, I have never been down there to see it; I have never visited the works. It has cost the organization, I know, about $50,000. That is the lowest bid I have heard of in connection with it.

Q. That is a place where they manufacture pottery? — *A.* Yes, sir; white-ware — tableware.

Q. How long has that been in operation? — *A.* Since about last September, I think.

Q. Then it has not been at work long enough to show results to any great extent? — *A.* No; but it is starting out with very flattering prospects, owing to the cessation of work in the other potteries there.

Q. Explain as well as you can the organization of that pottery enterprise and the plan of procedure; because I take it that that is probably a good illustration of your general idea of cooperation. — *A.* I have never had the plans submitted to me for examination. They were submitted to the executive board of our order and not to me, and for that reason I cannot tell you just exactly what the mode of operation is; but I understood that the intention was to adopt as nearly as possible the system which has been adopted at Rochdale in England, that is, as nearly as it could be made applicable to this country. Nearly all our stores are adopting that system, or will adopt it when they get going.

Q. Do you expect that that system of combination and cooperation among the laboring men will be extended to other industries in all parts of the country? — A. We hope so. We are working in that direction as fast as we can. . . .

I find in the first place that in nearly every instance the relation existing between employed and employers, with a few honorable exceptions, is not of that cordial nature that should be. I find that the mere idea of organization on the part of the laboring men is repugnant to the manufacturers and employers as a class. As an evidence of that I would state, before going further, that we have had a difficulty at East Liverpool, Ohio, beginning last spring early in May and continuing along, in which not a cent of money entered into the contest at all. The mere fact that the men had joined the Knights of Labor was deemed sufficient reason by the potteries there, and their association, to declare the men discharged and to shut down the works until the men would agree to go back to work, not as members of any labor organization. We have resisted that action on the part of the employers, believing that as American citizens we have a right to join an association for our own defense, our own advancement; we have resented that action of theirs, and the struggle has been a bitter one and is continuing yet. We are slowly gaining a few points, but the struggle, as I have said, has been long and bitter. That probably is the latest and most prominent issue that we have had with the employers in which a large number of men have been engaged, but we have thousands of isolated cases of individuals who have been victimized and driven from their homes and early associations simply because of the fact that they have been members of labor organizations. In many cases no other cause was ever assigned, even after they had done everything possible to discover why they were discharged. And not only this, but in many cases the employers, the coal operators especially, have banded themselves together and put men on what they call the "black list," merely for being members of labor organizations — not the Knights of Labor alone — but other organizations, and have prevented them from going to work at their homes or anywhere within a reasonable distance of their works. I have known one shovel manufacturer to keep two sober, industrious men, with families, from getting work for nearly two years. He followed them from the city of Pittsburgh clear down to Ames's, in Massachusetts, and all the way back again. . . .

Testimony of Samuel Gompers *

The Witness: What I wish to show is the condition of the cigar-makers at that period when there was no organization. When our organization commenced to emerge and reorganize throughout the country, the first year there were seventeen strikes in our trade, of which twelve or thirteen were successful. The rest were either lost or compromised. In the year following we had forty-six strikes, of which thirty-seven, I think, were successful, three lost, and six compromised. In these last two years, since which we have held no convention (we will hold one next year and we will hear the result), I am convinced that we have had over one hundred and sixty or one hundred and seventy strikes, and the strikes have been successful except in, perhaps, twenty instances, where they may have been lost or compromised. The truck system of which I spoke exists no longer in our trade. We have adopted a course of action which our experience has taught us, and that is, in certain periods of the year, when it is generally dull, not to strike for an advance of wages. Formerly, before the organization, men would probably strike for an advance of wages in the dull season, and be content that they were not reduced in the busy season. Our experience has taught us to adopt a different mode of action.

Sen. George: You strike now when business is active? — A. Yes, sir; and then, when we obtain an increase of wages when times are fair, our object is to endeavor to obtain fair wages during the dull season also, and, while we have made provision not to strike for an increase of wages during those periods, we are always in a position to strike against a reduction of wages or the introduction of the truck system, or other obnoxious rules. We have found that, for the purpose of accomplishing this object, it is entirely valueless to organize a union during a strike, and that it is little better than valueless to organize just immediately before a strike. We have found that if we are desirous of gaining anything in a strike, we must prepare in peace for the turbulent time which may come. And the Cigar-makers' International Union, of which I now speak especially, is an organization that has in its treasury between $130,000 and $150,000 ready to be concentrated within five days at any time at any given point. I hold in my hand a copy of the constitution of that organization. Of course I am not desirous of making a propaganda for it, but to illustrate what I have been saying I will read from it this provision: "Any union being directed by the executive board to forward money to another local union, and failing to comply within

* See above, page 7.

five days from date of said notice, shall be suspended." That is, in the event of a strike at a given point, the international president of the organization is directed to direct or request the nearest union to immediately send on its whole treasury if that is necessary, and the unions throughout the entire country and Canada to forward their entire treasury if necessary, to be placed at the disposal of the organization that is in trouble. . . .

There is nothing in the labor movement that employers who have had unorganized laborers dread so much as organization; but organization alone will not do much unless the organization provides itself with a good fund, so that the operatives may be in a position, in the event of a struggle with their employers, to hold out. . . .

Modern industry evolves these organizations out of the existing conditions where there are two classes in society, one incessantly striving to obtain the labor of the other class for as little as possible, and to obtain the largest amount or number of hours of labor; and the members of the other class, being as individuals utterly helpless in a contest with their employers, naturally resort to combinations to improve their condition, and, in fact, they are forced by the conditions which surround them to organize for self-protection. Hence trades unions. Trades unions are not barbarous, nor are they the outgrowth of barbarism. On the contrary they are only possible where civilization exists. Trades unions cannot exist in China; they cannot exist in Russia; and in all those semi-barbarous countries they can hardly exist, if indeed they can exist at all. But they have been formed successfully in this country, in Germany, in England, and they are gradually gaining strength in France. In Great Britain they are very strong; they have been forming there for fifty years, and they are still forming, and I think there is a great future for them yet in America. Wherever trades unions have organized and are most firmly organized, there are the right [sic] of the people most respected. A people may be educated, but to me it appears that the greatest amount of intelligence exists in that country or that state where the people are best able to defend their rights, and their liberties as against those who are desirous of undermining them. Trades unions are organizations that instill into men a higher motive-power and give them a higher goal to look to. The hope that is too frequently deadened in their breasts when unorganized is awakened by the trades unions as it can be by nothing else. A man is sometimes reached by influences such as the church may hold out to him, but the conditions that will make him a better citizen and a more independent one are those that are evolved out of the trades union movement. That makes him a better citizen and a better man in every particular. There are only a few who can be reached by the church so as to affect their daily walk in life compared with the numbers reached by these organizations.

Sen. Blair: The outside public, I think, very largely confound the conditions out of which the trades union grows or is formed, with the, to the general public mind, somewhat revolutionary ideas that are embraced under the names of socialism and communism. Before you get through, won't you let us understand to what extent the trades union is an outgrowth or an evolution of those ideas, and to what extent it stands apart from them and is based on different principles? — A. The trades unions are by no means an outgrowth of socialistic or communistic ideas or principles, but the socialistic and communistic notions are evolved from some of the trades unions' movements. As to the question of the principles of communism or socialism prevailing in trades unions, there are a number of men who connect themselves as workingmen with the trades unions who may have socialistic convictions, yet who never gave them currency; who say, "Whatever ideas we may have as to the future state of society, regardless of what the end of the labor movement as a movement between classes may be, they must remain in the background, and we must subordinate our convictions, and our views and our acts to the general good that the trades-union movement brings to the laborer." A large number of them think and act in that way. On the other hand, there are men — not so numerous now as they have been in the past — who are endeavoring to conquer the trades-union movement and subordinate it to those doctrines, and in a measure, in a few such organizations that condition of things exists, but by no means does it exist in the largest, most powerful, and best organized trades unions. There the view of which I spoke just now, the desire to improve the condition of the workingmen by and through the efforts of the trades union, is fully lived up to. I do not know whether I have covered the entire ground of the question.

Sen. George: You state, then, that the trades unions generally are not propagandists of socialistic views? — A. They are not. On the contrary, the endeavors of which I have spoken, made by certain persons to conquer the trades unions in certain cases, are resisted by the trades unionists; in the first place for the trades unions' sake, and even persons who have these convictions perhaps equally as strong as the others will yet subordinate them entirely to the good to be received directly through the trades unions. These last help those who have not such convictions to resist those who seek to use the trades unions to propagate their socialistic ideas.

Q. Do you think the trades unions have impeded or advanced the spread of socialistic views? — A. I believe that the existence of the trades-union movement, more especially where the unionists are better organized, has evoked a spirit and a demand for reform, but has held in check the more radical elements in society. . . .

Testimony of William H. Foster *

Sen. Call: Please state your connection with the Federation of Trades Unions. — A. I am general secretary of the Federation of Trades Unions. I was chosen to that office at the first annual convention, held in Pittsburgh in November, 1881.

Q. Give us in your own way, as succinctly as you can, a statement of the objects of those organizations and the means by which they propose to attain their ends, and also of the condition of the laboring people connected with them, which has led to the forming of the unions. — A. The objects are to elevate and improve the physical, moral, and material well-being of the laboring classes. That is as succinctly as I can state the objects without going into small details.

Q. I suppose there are benevolent organizations also? — A. Yes, there are benevolent features attached to the trades unions.

Q. As well as special means for protecting the members in their compensation? — A. Yes, sir; they defend their scale of wages, and they endeavor to prevent the employment of young children in competition with grown people; with the object, also, of seeing that those children get the education that is necessary to make them good citizens.

Q. They have a double object, then, in what they do with regard to child labor; one to prevent its competition with adult labor, and the other to promote the welfare of the children? — A. Yes, sir; because they think that the welfare of the country will depend upon the intelligence and character of its future citizens.

Q. What specific means do you adopt for attaining those ends? — A. We aim to reduce the hours of labor to a maximum of eight hours per day, so that working people may have more leisure for mental improvement and for acquiring a proper knowledge of their relations to legitimate capital. By legitimate capital I mean, of course, capital invested in productive industry, as opposed to speculative gambling.

Q. One means is reducing the hours of labor to eight hours daily? — A. Yes, sir.

Q. What other means do you favor? — A. We wish a legalization of trades unions with authority to pursue our legitimate business.

Q. How do you propose to have that done? — A. We think the Congress should enact a law which would legalize trades unions, the same as other corporations.

Sen. Pugh: What power do you propose to give the corporation or trades union? — A. All the power that is given to any other corporation, to sue and to be sued, and protection in its legitimate business.

* See above, page 72.

Q. Power to make contracts, to sue and be sued, and so on? — A. Yes, sir.

Q. Don't the state laws already give you that power in every state? — A. No. In some states they do. In Ohio we have that power at very slight cost. A great many of our trades unions are legalized in Ohio, but if we had a national legalization we think it would be better, because it would make us equal to other corporations that can do business in any state.

Q. You understand that it is within the power of the federal government to create a corporation in any state, do you? — A. That is my understanding of it.

Q. Now, by what means is it proposed that the trades unions, when legalized, shall bring about this condition of things which you desire — reduced hours of labor and just compensation? — A. Well, we are of opinion that Congress ought to enforce the eight-hour law as it stands in all government works and in everything in which the government employs labor. That would be a good example. We think, then, that the various states would be induced to enact similar laws, from the example of the federal government.

Q. Laws prescribing only eight hours of labor daily for laborers in all the different trades and crafts? — A. Yes, sir.

Q. You speak of incorporating trades unions, and giving them certain chartered powers; how do you understand that that would aid in attaining your object of decreasing the hours of labor? — A. Because now there are various obstructions to the free operation of trades unionism. We have not got recognition on the same level as our employers in the discussion of the questions that come up. The average newspaper, even, will not recognize us as having any legitimate rights at all; they think that we ought to be suppressed, in fact; that we have no right to have an organization at all.

Q. Is there any specific remedy for that provided in your organizations? — A. The gradual absorption into our organizations, by a knowledge of their benefits, of the employees in the various industries would, if we were legalized, gradually accomplish most of the good that we claim can be accomplished by trades unions.

Q. Well, suppose that everybody now in the different trades and manufactures belonged to trades unions; what would the trades union do to bring about that result? Suppose the trades unions should say that the wages of labor are insufficient (as they undoubtedly are), what sort of power would be in the union to remedy that? — A. Well, for instance, if we had arbitration legalized, when a question of dispute arose between the employers and the employed, instead of having it as now, when the one often refuses to even acknowledge or discuss the question with the other, if they were required to submit the question to arbitration, or to meet on the same level before an impartial tribunal, there is no doubt but what the result would be more in our favor than it is now, when very often public opinion cannot hear our case. . . .

Testimony of John Jarrett

John Jarrett was president of the Amalgamated Association of Iron and Steel Workers of the United States, a powerful trade union.

The Witness: For some twenty-five years I have given the matter of the manufacture of iron and steel a close study, particularly in relation to the labor employed in that manufacture. The Amalgamated Association of Iron and Steel Workers consists, in other words, of the men that work in our rolling-mills. We take into the association hardly anything but skilled labor. The objects of our association are the improvement of our members, morally, socially, mentally, and financially. We seek to bring about that condition of circumstances between labor and capital, that is, between the employers and the employees in our rolling-mills, whereby the rights of the workingmen shall be properly recognized, and a fair day's wages for a fair day's work will be realized by them. To enter into the history of labor for the period that I have just referred to would take up too much time. I will, however, simply say that in such mills as are controlled by our organization (I mean the Amalgamated Association) a far better condition of things exists than in such mills as are not controlled by the association, and which are known as non-union mills. Better wages are paid. The condition of the men, as a rule, is much better. There is less intemperance among them, and they are better educated. There has been a great deal talked in our organization about adopting new measures whereby the employer and the employed could be brought closer together, especially on the wages question.

At the present time our system is to meet annually with our employers and draft what we term scales of prices, based on the market or selling price of the commodities that we manufacture, iron and steel. These scales are enforced for one year. In our iron mills they operate from the 1st of June to the 31st of May of the following year, inclusive. In our steel mills they operate from the 1st of June to the 31st of December, inclusive. No questions ever arise in our mills during the year once the scales are got established. There are no strikes; there can be no strikes. There may be incidental questions arising, which are generally settled by consultation, that is, by the coming together of the manufacturers and a committee of the men, and talking over the matter, hearing the details of the grievances or difficulty or whatever it may be, and considering it in all its bearings, and as a rule we generally arrange a settlement.

The wages paid the iron and steel workers (I refer to those who are connected with our organization) are on the whole tolerably fair. I claim that this condition is simply the result of organization among the workingmen; in other words, that were there no organization, wages would not be so high as they are. When I say that the men are tolerably fairly paid, I mean as compared with labor in any other country. Perhaps among the manufacturing operatives we are nearly the best paid as compared with similar labor in any other country. It has taken us several years, of course, to bring about this condition of things. We have had many severe struggles, but the result is satisfactory to all concerned. Now, I want to call the attention of the committee to the fact that as a rule in such mills as are not controlled by our organization lower wages are paid than in those that are controlled by us. Of course, there are all sorts of arguments used by the manufacturers, the owners of those mills. They claim that they are paying what they can afford to pay. They claim that the medium, or the controlling influence, whereby wages are governed in this country as compared with other countries is the tariff, and they say they pay all that the tariff guarantees to them. Another significant fact in these mills is that the owners will not permit their men under any circumstances to connect themselves with our organization. They are deadly opposed to it. . . .

There has been a great deal of talk throughout the country of the strike at Bethlehem, Pa. The Bethlehem Iron Company is a large concern, and has a large Bessemer-steel plant. They have also, in connection with their present works, the iron works which they controlled while they were known only as the Bethlehem Iron Company. Now, that strike was brought about in a very singular manner. We instituted a lodge there in Bethlehem somewhere about August, 1882. The manager of the mill had some very strong objections to our organization, and about the commencement of November he sent for a committee of the men and asked them if they had affiliated themselves with the Amalgamated Association of Iron and Steel Workers. They said they had. He told them very quietly that he was very much opposed to that, but he thought he could get along with them very well, and as the time when the adjustment of wages would take place was drawing near, he thought they could easier arrange their matters outside of the organization than in it. The men consulted me on the subject. Seeing so much opposition, and it being the rule of our organization not to be too aggressive, I gave those men the advice that if they thought best to withdraw from the organization they had better do it peacefully. They did so. They withdrew in the month of December. Early in January, when the adjustment of wages took place, those men were not consulted at all, and their wages were reduced in some instances, as much as 48 percent. . . .

Sen. Blair: Do you think that the fact that those men had severed their connection with the Union and were not likely to be supported by the union in a strike had anything to do with the extent of the reduction in that case? — A. That I could not tell, any further than that I believe that the company believed that those men were entirely in their hands, and they could reduce them to any figure they saw proper. That is apparent from the fact that the foreman or superintendent afterwards told the men that he believed they could save them at least 10 percent of the reduction, provided they kept themselves entirely apart from the organization. That came about in this manner: Shortly after the reduction took place the men changed their minds about joining the organization, and he found it out, and told them they were making a mistake, and that if they would keep away from the organization he could probably save them 10 percent of the reduction. He admitted that the reduction was unjust. The men, however, connected themselves with the organization. . . .

After these men organized themselves in that way a little row took place between two men, or rather between the wife of one man and another man who was working in the mill, and this woman abused the child of this other person — a common occurrence among some people — and the father of the child sued the woman and she was fined and had to pay the costs of the case. Her husband then reported the matter to the assistant superintendent, and he, with the general superintendent, decided that the man who had prosecuted this woman had overstepped his limits a little bit, that he had no right to prosecute her without first consulting them in the matter, and they said that unless he would pay the costs of the affair himself he could consider himself discharged. Now, that was really the basis of the strike in Bethlehem. Then the men attempted to negotiate with the manager, but he would not recognize them. He asked them if they were not members of some kind of an association and they said they were. Then said he, "You get out of this office." Next day I happened to be in Bethlehem and I sent in word to the manager that I would like to see him. He said he would not see me as the president of the association, but he would as a gentleman. The men began to hint something to him, that they would do something, would make some trouble in the mill, and they brought back this report to me, and I was surprised to hear within twenty minutes after this that he had issued the order to close down. It has been stated that that mill was closed down by the Amalgamated Association of Iron and Steel Workers. That is false. It was not closed by the Amalgamated Association. It was closed in the way I have been telling you. I was considering the best means of avoiding all trouble there, because I considered this fact, that where the workingmen in this country have not been organized, or even where they are organized, until they have been for some time in the organization and educated in it, they are inclined to be aggressive; they are radical; they do not understand our rules, and they want to strike at once, and every little thing becomes a grievance which they think justifies a strike.

Now, on the other hand, the settled policy of our organization is to try to improve the condition of the men *gradually*. Were it not for these feelings among those men who have just newly joined our organization, several of the strikes that have taken place might have been avoided. Where the organization has been established for years you very rarely hear of strikes, but where it is newly established, then, from the fact that the manufacturers are so deadly opposed to it, and from the fact also that the men are not well versed in these rules and principles, strikes are very apt to take place, and it is under such conditions that the majority of them do take place. When our organization is firmly established, strikes are very rarely known. Again, strikes very often take place outside the organization. In such cases there is no system; there can be no system. Sometimes even the organization will commit a mistake, and in one case our organization did commit the mistake of allowing a strike for wages at a time when the condition of the market really did not justify it; but the men were not well informed on the subject. It takes some time to instruct them in regard to prices, markets, and so on. The conservative portion of the men soon saw that we had made a mistake in that case and admitted it, and soon after we withdrew our claim. Hence that strike was closed, as it was said, with a defeat of the organization; but in fact it was closed simply because our organization had so well educated the men that they saw it was wrong to continue the strike. . . .

Q. You made a statement awhile ago that certain laborers in this country get three times as much pay as the corresponding class in England; who are those laborers? — A. I was referring then to our iron mills. The organization that I represent is one that has control of the wages in our iron mills in particular.

Q. Now, is that statement which you made on that subject a statement which should be unaccompanied with an explanation? If it should stand in that way it would of course be a very strong invitation to like laborers aboard to come here and take their chances of employment — A. There is one trouble that we have had in this connection. The manufacturers have adopted a system of importing men to take the place of our men when they are on strike. The class of common labor that largely predominates in the mills (you must remember that I have been speaking of the steel works), with the exception of the Edgar Thomson Mills, are foreigners—Hungarians, Poles, Italians, Bohemians, men that really don't know the difference.

Q. What difference? — A. The difference between light work and heavy work, or between good wages and bad wages. They simply look at the amount they may get. If you show them that they get twice as much as they got at home in their own country, they think that it is a good thing, and they never know the difference when they are working twice as hard as they did there.

Q. And paying twice as much for what they have to buy? — A. Yes, sir. In investigating these matters I have been disgusted to find that those people can live where I think decent men would die; they can live on almost any kind of food, food that other men would not touch, and in houses that other men could not live in at all.

Q. That is about equivalent to Chinese cheap labor, it is not? — A. Almost as bad, in my estimation.

Q. Do you think those men know as much as the Chinamen? — A. I could not tell that. I never had any conversation or connection with Chinamen. All I know about these men is that I have been astonished and astounded at the little they do know, and when you go to talk with them they are fairly afraid to speak with you.

Q. Why? — A. I cannot tell, unless it is that they are demoralized and afraid of each other. I will give you the reason that a gentleman in Bethlehem gave me. I got hold of one of these Bohemians aside one day with a gentleman who understood the language, and I had a little talk with him about this condition of things. He wanted to tell me that he did better in Hungary than he did in this country. I asked him then, through the interpreter, why he came here. He said it was because he was misled. I wanted to know how he was misled. He became confused. I then asked him if he would not talk with the other men and try to get them interested, so as to do a fair day's work and receive a reasonable day's wages, but he turned round and said that if he did his life would be in danger.

Q. Why? — A. I put that question right there, and he said he was afraid.

Q. Afraid of whom? — A. Of his fellow countrymen. It was as though he would be trying to lead them astray into some net laid for him and them by a sharp competitor. That is the view I took of it. . . .

Testimony of Thomas M. Miller *

Sen. Blair: You have heard the account given by these gentlemen of the relations between employers and employed there, and how they get on under the system they have described. Won't you give us the benefit of your observation and experience of the matter, from your standpoint? —

* See above, page 51.

A. Well, I have not had experience directly in the manufacture of bar iron or steel for some time, though formerly I was proprietor of a large rolling-mill. I think the association of the men together for the improvement of their condition is a very good scheme in many respects, though in others it may not be quite so good. In the matter of making an arbitrary demand for wages, while the manufacturers generally concede to such demand, and as a rule would rather treat with the association than with individuals, still it seems to me to tend to the detriment of manufacture to some extent. I think that as a rule the manufacturers like to pay their men good wages if the state of the trade justifies it; though in some instances of course they do not. They are like other men in that respect, for human nature is about the same on the whole, and some of the manufacturers are liberal while some others of them are close. The liberal men get the best labor, pay the best prices for it. Some of the employers are continually disputing with their men, while others submit to their demands immediately on presentation. In our department of the business we are governed by the association of molders and machinists; they have an association of their own, and as a general rule we let them do as they please. We don't have much trouble, except that we sometimes cannot get our work into the eastern market, to where labor is cheaper; we have to do without that market, and therefore the men have sometimes to do without work — go idle. The prices they demand do not seem to be extortionate as a rule. They seem to want to meet the market generally, but they do not know as the manufacturers know just what the state of the trade is, and how it is going, though they do seek to know it. I think the sympathy of the manufacturers is largely with their men all through the country, particularly in the iron and steel industries, and that they would like to see the men improve their condition by any legitimate means they can adopt, either by legislation or association, or any other way whereby they can do better for themselves and their families.

But the law of supply and demand is the great law that governs the whole business, and in the end all have to bow in obedience to it.

Q. If these unions were more general I suppose it would produce a uniformity in the wages demanded by the men in the same branches of trade, and that, I suppose, would be better for the manufacturers? — A. If the wages were uniform all over the country in any particular branch of business, that branch would be more prosperous for the men employed in it. Whether the people as a whole would be better served it would be difficult to say; but, at any rate, in order to be of any advantage to the manufacturers the rule ought to be universal.

Q. That is the point that I wish to have your opinion about — whether, if trades unions exist at all, it is better or worse for the manufacturers that they should be general throughout the country? — A. Oh, undoubtedly it would be better that they should be general.

Q. Finding them existing in your locality and in your business, you would prefer, if they must continue to exist there, that they should spread and become general? — A. It would be better for us if they were general. I have just come from Washington, where I went to bid upon a government contract, but the work came east because labor is cheaper in the East. It is not necessarily dearer with us on account of the union, but it is dearer because labor becomes scarcer as you go west and prices are better.

Q. In what way, then, would the extension of the trades unions eastward be better for you as manufacturers? — A. If the men could arbitrarily, by association, make the prices in the East the same as in the West, it would be better for us.

Q. And you believe they would do that if the association were extended to the East? — A. They would try to do it, but whether they would succeed or not I don't know. I think they would fail, because labor is so much more abundant in the East in proportion to the demand for it than in the West. . . .

Q. I suppose that your situation as the general manager of a manufacturing establishment gives you opportunities to know a good deal about the relations between the workingmen and their employers, and to judge whether they are generally friendly or otherwise. — A. I don't think they have been so friendly since the unions have been established as they were before. The employers are inclined to treat the men as an organization and not as individuals. They do not have that personal sympathy that they had before with each individual workingman. That is my idea.

Q. Do you think that change has been the effect partially of the organization of the men, or do you attribute it wholly to that? — A. I think that has been the cause. The employers deal with the men now as a whole.

Q. Have you any doubt that the existence of these organizations of the workingmen gives them some advantage in fixing the prices which they shall receive for their labor? — A. There is no doubt of that, and I think it is proper that they should do all they can for the improvement of their condition, and should get as high wages as they can. Whether that is the best way of doing it, whether that plan will ultimately accomplish it, or whether the question will be determined by the law of supply and demand, I am not certain. The manufacturers don't find fault with the men on account of their organization. They only find fault with them when they cannot meet the market. . . .

Q. Take those men that work at seventy-five cents a day, for instance, what occurs to you as a measure that might be adopted to increase the wages of that class of labor? — A. I don't think anything could be done in that way. The lowest class of labor will get the lowest pay inevitably. The law of the "survival of the fittest" governs that. Where labor is very scarce that same kind of labor will sometimes get $2.00 a day, as it does in some places in the West; but where it is superabundant it will have to accept seventy-five cents a day, or less. I don't think any kind of legislation will apply to such cases. The best thing that kind of labor can do is to go west, where there is need and demand for it.

Q. If those laborers were organized and in a position to say whether they would or would not work for a given price how would that operate? — A. Then the people must pay more for the products of their labor, and in return must charge more for what they sell. The great mass of the people of the country are laboring men, you know. They can only get a certain amount of food to eat. If crops are poor they will have to subsist on short rations; if crops are abundant it will be otherwise.

Q. But, over and above it all, the country accumulates from year to year, and what is accumulated is. invested in business. Now if this lower grade of labor got better pay, and all grades above that at the same time were elevated in proportion, might not the result be that the accumulation of capital would be distributed at the time instead of being saved up for the future? — A. It might be; but the result of the accumulation of capital is new and further developments of industry. Mr. Vanderbilt is building a new road through our state from Harrisburg to Pittsburgh, to which he has subscribed $25,000,000. That capital, which has been accumulated, will give employment to a large number of people, and be redistributed among them, no matter what percent the capitalist gets. It might be better if capital got a less percent and the balance went directly to the people, but I don't know how that could be accomplished by legislation.

Q. I don't know that it could be done by legislation, but let it be done by whatever means might be found practicable. . . . Do you think that an increase in the wages of the common laborer would necessarily imply an increase in the wages of the classes above him? — A. Unless it were taken off the classes above, which would have to be done in order to benefit the lower classes, I think it could result in nothing, except increased prices.

Q. But might not some of that increase of wages come from the proportion which capital takes of the joint product, thus lessening the accumulation of capital for the future and distributing it immediately, so as to satisfy the wants of the wage-laborers? — A. If that could be done it would be better. If the parties controlling capital were employed simply as superintendents, simply to distribute the product of labor, it would be better, and probably would be right. But you must have some incentive to action, and unless capital can get a remuneration of 4, or 6, or 10, or 20, or 100 percent, as the case may be, we shall not have any industrial progress.

Q. No; but don't you think that if the laborers, without whom capital would not be employed at all, were able to make a general demand for more wages and to refuse to work unless the demand was complied with, the result would be that capital would be just as eager for investment at 6 percent as it is now at 8; that is, when it was once satisfied that it could do nothing unless it agreed to pay the increased wages? — A. It might be so; but I think the result of the accumulation of capital is industrial development. . . .

Q. Then will not the result be that, of the price realized for the joint production of labor and capital combined, labor will be able to take a larger share than it now gets; thus lessening, it may be, the accumulation of capital? — A. Yes, that is true; but they would have to put it in the savings bank. Or else, if the government debt was paid off, it would have to be invested in development in some way.

Q. I grant you that, if it was accumulated in banks; but I am only thinking of wages increased to such an extent as to be expended in the improvement of the condition of the laborers themselves, giving them better homes, better food, better clothing, and better conditions generally. It would seem that there are vast numbers of laborers who are not able to provide from their wages the comforts or even the necessaries of life. — A. That is true. The fact is that the common laborers of the land are the sufferers from all these organizations of skilled labor. The puddler gets $3.50 a day, whereas the man who works under him gets only $1.25. There is no tendency whatever in the unions to advance the condition of those men. The unions are combinations among certain classes of the workingmen to advance their own peculiar interests and wages, and the result is disaster to those laborers who are not so able to combine. . . .

Testimony of George Storm

George Storm was a member of the firm of Straiton and Storm of New York, probably the largest cigar-manufacturing concern in the United States. The company employed over 2,000 workers and produced about 250,000 cigars a day.

Sen Blair: I notice that the cigar-makers' union is a powerful organization among the trades unions. Are any of your working people members of that organization? — A. I believe the majority of our working people belong to one trades union or another; I believe there are several in our trade.

Q. Do you have any difficulty with them? — A. Not at all.

Q. So far as you know, they probably favor your adjustment of the difficulties, or do they interfere with it? — A. Well, I do not know that they do. I do not know that the trades unions, or leaders thereof, favor the adjustment as it is made in our establishment. But all men are alike in one respect, they like power, and as we have the largest establishment of its kind, naturally trades unions would like to use it as a lever, and they would like to come and interfere in our business probably if they could.

When I speak of trades unions, I speak of those who have control of trades unions, and I draw a line between the people who belong to those organizations and those who pretend to speak for them. So far as we are concerned, it matters little to me if a man belongs to ten organizations; but those organizations, whatever they may be, can exercise no influence directly in the adjustment of anything that may occur between ourselves and our men. We reserve to ourselves, according to compact with them, and as long as it exists, the right to adjust our difficulties in our own way.

Q. You say you "reserve" it. What do you mean? When you employ a man do you say to him ————? — *A.* We say nothing to him; it is a mental reservation — in other words, we should not permit people who are not in our establishment and who have no knowledge of our business or the interests that enter into it — to dictate to us what we should or should not do. . . .

As I regard the trades unions, they are simply combinations of those engaged in labor for the purpose of accomplishing something which they propose to accomplish by the union of their forces. I do not think that anyone will claim that the formation of such societies is wrong, or that they overstep the line of propriety, because, in this country, at the present time, everything seems to be done by combination.

But, aside from that fact, they have a perfect right to associate themselves for the purpose of studying out how best to solve this great problem of wages, and of existence, and of the comforts which they propose to derive from their wages.

As to the mistakes that they make, and I have thought over them repeatedly, I cannot but come to the conclusion that they are largely due to the influence of operators from the other side — from Europe — who come here with notions and ideas based on institutions as they exist there. They fail to shake off that feeling when they come here; they do not recognize that the circumstances here are different. . . .

Now, I recognize the fact that every immigrant who comes here with the determination to work is an acquisition to the country, but I am unwilling to believe that it is just that we should depend upon that supply constantly, and have this particular species of work reserved for them, and that our own youths here should be prohibited from acquiring the knowledge of it; because in that matter, the trades unions certainly exhibit an amount of selfishness that they would not like to have applied to themselves. They drive the surplus population who could acquire a knowledge of a trade into a mass of unskilled labor that floats about the country.

These unskilled laborers are certainly also human beings. And if the trades unions have such a great care over those who are not capitalists, they ought not to ignore this class of unskilled labor, although they do ignore it altogether. That, I think, is all wrong. . . .

Therefore, I think that, so far as the trades unions are concerned, when they undertake to regulate that portion of the mechanical arts, they overstep the laws of propriety and of common sense, and show an entire disregard for the welfare of their fellow-beings, who are in a like position with themselves, and probably worse.

Then again, I think that when they propose to dictate to an individual of their own class who, in order to be permitted to work, and with the results of his labor to maintain his family, when they say that he must comply with certain requirements of their own, they trespass upon the dearest rights that a man has, and I would blush to know a man that would put up with a thing of that kind.

It is these things that make trades unions so extremely odious to many minds. People do not even care to touch or come in contact with men that are so unreasonable, and I have reason to believe that the great majority of those who constitute trades unions are not in sympathy with this idea.

Men will naturally say, "If this is so, why should it be tolerated?" For the simple reason that a species of terrorism is exercised to get people into trades unions. Once there, the quiet, hardheaded man who wishes to get along quietly in the world, pays little attention to it. He simply pays his dues. The agitators, who desire to aggrandize themselves at the expense of their fellow workmen, make themselves popular, they run the machine, they make the laws, and they enforce them.

If the trades unions were to get rid of these nonsensical provisions that grate upon the sensibilities of the community, they could be made to serve a most excellent purpose in the amelioration of the condition of working people of this country. And they do deserve a great deal of consideration.

But it is a great species of tyranny when a corporation or association, or even one man, will demand of working people, as a condition of employment, that they shall pledge themselves not to belong to any association. . . .

Testimony of Charles Siedler

Charles Siedler was a member of the firm of P. Lorillard and Company, manufacturers of pipe tobacco, chewing tobacco, and snuff. The company employed about 4,000 workers.

The Witness: Labor questions have not given us a great deal of trouble in connection with our works. While we employ a very large number of people, yet peace and quietness exists with us from one end of the year to the other, usually. . . . Those who are the most diligent, the most energetic, and the most skillful receive the largest wages. Then we endeavor, in all our intercourse with our work-people, to treat them as human beings — with kindness; and consequently it is very seldom indeed that we ever have any labor disturbances. The latest instance of the kind happened about one year ago, when in one of the departments one morning I found that the girls refused to work. Upon investigating the cause I found that the superintendent of the factory had dismissed an incompetent foreman, who proved, however, to have been a great favorite with the working girls — perhaps because he was lax for his employer's interest — and in consequence of his removal the girls concluded that they would go on strike and insist on his being reinstated. I told the superintendent to go and talk to the girls and state the case to them plainly, and endeavor to reason with them. It was useless, however. They insisted on calling for their late foreman, and they would not have anybody else. I waited a little while, thinking that time would bring them to their senses, but finding that they did not resume work, I called them together in the factory and spoke with them myself; told them that if they had any grievances at any time we were always prepared to listen to them, and to remedy them if they were just. They appointed a committee, but that committee, before they waited upon us, had received an ultimatum from their numbers that they would not have anyone to preside over them except their favorite foreman. Finding that they were obstinate and obdurate, I immediately set about to accomplish their work without their help. That I did by telegraphing instructions to the far West to have the work performed there. As soon as that information leaked out, they were very glad to come back into the factory and resume their places.

On one or two other occasions we have had slight irregularities in certain of the departments, but they were quickly overcome by our substitution of new workmen. In one particular branch the men struck in a body, because the superintendent endeavored to carry out what he considered fair treatment towards the workmen in another department by shifting the labor from one place to another. The men in charge of department No. 1 were receiving, in the opinion of the superintendent, too large an amount of money for weekly wages, while those in No. 2 were not earning quite as much, and the work was about the same. He endeavored to equalize matters by shifting the men. One department of the men struck in a body and refused to work and threatened to waylay all those who would not do as they did. We telegraphed to Virginia for a large number of men to take their places, and as they came up in a body and strikers did not molest them.

A few years ago we had a number of foreign workmen, they were chiefly Bohemians, Russians, Austrians, and Polish Jews, who had been engaged to make cigarettes. They were very fractious and unruly and would not submit to discipline; they insisted on doing their work in their own way and according to their own wishes, coming and going as they pleased, and we told them that they had to submit to our orders, otherwise their places would be vacant. The result was that they went out; and having mentioned that case, I think I have named about all the strikes that we have encountered.

As a rule we have no trouble with our working people; the firm treats them, as I stated before, with kindness and forbearance. . . .

Testimony of Jay Gould *

Sen. Blair: Do you think the labor unions of the country are an injury or a benefit to the laborers and the country generally? — A. Well, I cannot say about that. I have not paid much attention to those unions. I think that anything that tends to elevate the working classes or to educate them, or that provides for those who are in want, provides a fund for the widows and orphans in any particular business, I think anything of that kind is the legitimate object of such societies. But when they get beyond that I think they get into a broad sea that they cannot control, because labor, like everything else, is regulated by the law of supply and demand. "You can lead a horse to water, but you cannot make him drink."

Q. You think that intelligent labor can command a higher price, however, than uneducated labor, do you not? — A. Well, yes, it can command a higher price; that is, it can seek other fields of labor where the compensation may be higher. There is no reason why young men should not be educated to do more than one thing, so that if they do not succeed in one avocation they can try their hands at another. . . .

Testimony of William Steinway †

The Witness: The relations between ourselves and our men have always been very good until lately disturbed by the entrance of the socialistic and the communistic element in the labor unions. I myself think that labor ought to organize, as it has organized. I am not opposed to

---

* See above, page 47.
† See above, page 48.

labor unions, and any labor union that is carried on in a sensible way can do a great deal, not only toward bettering their own condition in the way of wages, but also in equalizing wages in the various cities, and in resisting in times of depression the great deterioration and fall of wages. We have gone through very hard strikes. We have been singled out. Our house being the strongest and largest, has been made the target of strikes. It is just about a year ago now that one of the most senseless strikes was inaugurated during my absence in Europe by the socialistic and communistic element inducing our men to strike against an honest, faithful bookkeeper, against whom they were unable to allege the slightest grievance, except that they did not want him, and that their union had so ordered. They were unsuccessful, however. The strike lasted over nine weeks, and inflicted a loss upon us of $75,000. Furthermore, of late years the labor union, especially the pianoforte maker's union, which claims three thousand members, in order to induce everybody to join strikes ordered by them, exercise over them a terror of the idea that unless they go with them they will be treated as "scabs" and be driven out of every shop in the city of New York, or in the United States. Many of our older men, who have been with us twenty and twenty-five years, and quite a number of whom own houses, both in Astoria and New York, have come to me personally or written me letters about this terrorism exercised by members of the trades unions; but, as I said, with the exception of that, I am not opposed to labor unions; but on the contrary will here give it as my opinion that strikes are a necessity and should not be legislated against, and cannot be legislated against. The fierce competition of manufacturers, and especially in our trade, makes it impossible that any manufacturer could arbitrarily raise his price unless he is forced to do so by a strike for higher wages. It would be simply impossible for him, and he would be laughed at by his customers if he attempted to do so. . . .

Testimony of Timothy D. Stow *

Sen. Blair: I would like to know your idea about this: Many people say that these labor agitators are a set of men who are looking for their personal aggrandizement. — A. I do not believe that that is so, sir.

Q. What would you say about that — I mean the men who are agitating the labor question? — A. I do not know any agitator in Fall River who has anything at heart except the good of his fellowmen. I think the statements of those who stigmatize them as discreditable are entirely at variance with the truth and with the fact.

* See above, page 30.

Q. You have some acquaintance with them, I take it? — A. Yes.

Q. What about their intellectual qualities? — A. Well, I do not know of more than half a dozen who may be called agitators in Fall River, and, indeed, I think that number may be reduced. The most prominent man there now among the laborers, that is, a man connected with the organization of laborers, is Mr. [Robert S.] Howard. He is a man of intelligence, and has devoted much time and study to this labor question. He is of a very nervous temperament. So far as his ideas are concerned — his wish to benefit his fellows — they are all right; but he may have some ideas that are far in advance of his fellows.

Sen. Pugh: I do not understand that the class of men that are condemned as agitators, mischief-makers, and organizers, are actual workers, but men on the "make," who appeal to the prejudices of their class for their own selfish uses in some outside matter. It is not the actual workers that agitate. I do not understand that that term covers the workers. — A. Well, that class may not do very much of that sort of work, but they think and aid the others.

Sen. Pugh: Mr. Howard, I regard as a man of intelligence. I have heard him testify. He seems to be familiar with this whole question, and to have devoted a great deal of thought to it, and I think he thoroughly understands the relation of labor and capital, and the responsibilities and failures of each.

Sen. Blair: We called Mr. Howard before us, and we have had other just such representative men as he from all parts of the country. The congress of the Federation of Labor from all parts of the country had a meeting in New York while we were there, and we called many of their men to testify; but they were denounced as cranks and agitators. I do not know who were referred to unless those were the men. We have had no such men as Senator Pugh has been describing — outside men who stir up strife among others for their own benefit. Do you know of any such men in Fall River? — A. No, sir; I do not.

Q. If you know any such I would like to have that distinction made. — A. I know that among the manufacturers there, men of that kind are branded as agitators, and that they have some desire for their own advancement.

Q. Is Mr. Howard sometimes called an agitator? — A. He is regarded so.

Q. Do you know of any other man except Mr. Howard and his associates who are stigmatized as agitators down there? — A. Well, I am stigmatized myself to some extent on account of my radical views there. I am always ready when I see injustice to talk against it. That is a part of my democracy.

Q. You use the word "democracy" in its broad sense? — A. Yes; not in a political sense. . . .

Testimony of R. Heber Newton *

The Witness: Trades unions represent the one effective form of combination won by American labor. Trades unions need no timid apologists. Their vindication is in the historic tale of the successful advances which they have won for workingmen. . . . Doubtless they have committed plenty of follies, and are still capable of stupid tyrannies that only succeed in handicapping labor, in alienating capital, and in checking productivity — that is, in lessening the sum total of divisible wealth. Such actions are inevitable in the early stages of combination on the part of uneducated men, feeling a new sense of power, and striking blindly out in angry retaliation for real or fancied injuries.

Trades unions are gradually, however, outgrowing their crude methods. The attempts, such as we have seen lately, of great corporations to break them up, is a piece of despotism which ought to receive an indignant rebuke from the people at large. Labor must combine, just as capital has combined, in forming these very corporations. Labor's only way of defending its interests as a class is through combination. It is the abuse and not the use of trades unions against which resistance should be made.

The chief abuse of our trades unions has been their concentration of attention upon the organization of strikes.

Strikes seem to me in our present stage of the "free-contract" system entirely justifiable when they are really necessary. Workingmen have the right to combine in affixing a price at which they wish to work. The supply of labor and the demand for goods, in the absence of higher considerations, will settle the question as to whether they can get the increase. The trying features of this method of reaching a result are incidental to our immature industrial system. Strikes have had their part to play in the development of that system. We note their failures and forget their successes; but they have had their signal success, and have won substantial advantages for labor. Their chief service, however, has been in teaching combination, and in showing labor the need of a better weapon by which to act than the strike itself. . . .

Labor ought to have found out that a stunning blow between the eyes is not the best method of inducing a kindly feeling and a just judgment on the part of capital. It ought to have found out that the strike is a boomerang whose hardest blows are often dealt backward on the striker.

Trades unions in this country seem to me to be gravely at fault in clinging to such an obsolete weapon. They should have turned their attention to our modern improvements upon this bludgeon.

* See above, page 37.

Arbitration is a far cheaper and more effective instrument of adjusting differences between capital and labor — a far more likely means of securing a fair increase of wages. It places both sides to the controversy in an amicable mood, and is an appeal to the reason and conscience — not wholly dead in the most soulless corporations. . . .

Trades unions ought, among us, to emulate the wisdom of European workingmen, and use their mechanism to organize forms of association which should look not alone to winning higher wages but to making the most of existing wages, and ultimately to leading the wage system into a higher development. . . .

Now, of this effort at cooperation I find scarcely any trace in the trade organizations of our workingmen. Trades unions have until very lately passed the whole subject by in utter silence. What has been done by workingmen in this country in the line of cooperation has been done outside of the great trade associations, which form the natural instrumentalities for organizing such combination. They offer the mechanism, the mutual knowledge, the preliminary training in habits of combination, which together should form the proper conditions for the development of cooperation. Is it not a singular thing, considering the manifold benefits that would come to labor from such a development, that the attention of these great and powerful organizations has not heretofore been seriously called to this matter? It is a hopeful sign that two of our later trade organizations avow distinctively in their platforms the principle of cooperation. The Central Labor Union of this city and the Knights of Labor both profess to seek the development of cooperation. It remains to be seen whether there will be anything more than the profession.

Out of our trades unions, by combination among them, there might be already developed on our soil a power representing the labor element of the country which, with universal franchise, would be practically omnipotent. Could our trades unions enter the field of politics with reference to measures in the interests of their own classes, measures justifiable, necessary, and on which reasonable minds could be readily convinced, not many elections would be held in our various states before these reforms would be accomplished. Is there not a certain aspect of childishness on the part of so vast and powerful a body of men as is represented by those trades unions in their pitiful appeals to government for the help which they have it already in their power to force from government? . . .

5　STRIKES

Testimony of Samuel Gompers *

The Witness: While I am in the labor movement and take a stand
opposed to strikes whenever they can be avoided, I have no sympathy
with, nor can I indorse or echo, the statements of many men who are too
ready to condemn strikes. Strikes have their evils, but they have their
good points also, and with proper management, with proper organization,
strikes do generally result to the advantage of labor, and in very few
instances do they result in injury to the workingmen, whether organized
or unorganized.

Sen. George: You mean ultimate injury? — A. Ultimate injury. Strikes
ought to be, and in well-organized trades unions they are, the last means
which workingmen resort to to protect themselves against the almost
never satisfied greed of the employers. Besides this, the strike is, in many
instances, the only remedy within our reach as long as legislation is entirely indifferent to the interests of labor. . . .

My opinion is that the first few strikes that workingmen generally
indulge in are lost, from the fact that their employers are unable to com-
prehend the idea that labor has certain rights which they ought to respect; second, because they are really unaware that the laborers who are
on a strike are capable of inflicting an injury upon them; and third, that
when they are once in a strike and hold out for a considerable period
they do not like to weaken and accede to the terms of their employees,
but prefer to make large sacrifices from their wealth or capital rather
than to accede to those demands. . . .

As to this general outcry among employers (and sometimes the press
will echo the cry), about the men on strike being turbulent, about their
being destroyers of property and violators of the public peace, the truth
is that where these offenses are committed they are very seldom the work
of the men on strike, nor are they countenanced by the men on strike,
but that they are not committed by overzealous friends I will not say.

Even in such instances, however, the organizations of labor are the
conservators of the public peace; for when strikes occur among men
who are unorganized, often acting upon illy-considered plans, hastily
adopted, acting upon passion, and sometimes not knowing what they
have gone on strike for, except possibly some fancied grievance, and

---

* See above, page 7.

hardly knowing by what means they can or may remedy their grievances, each acts upon his own account without the restraint of organization, and feels that he serves the cause of the strike best when he
does something that just occurs to him; while the man who belongs
to a trades union that is of some years' standing is, by the very fact
of his membership of the organization and his experience there, taught
to abide by the decision of the majority. Therefore when anything
of that kind I have mentioned occurs or is heard of in the organizations that are of long standing, it is condemned in the most strenuous
terms and action is taken to prevent the accomplishment of any such
purpose, or if it is accomplished to prevent the recurrence of it. The
members of our organization are made to well understand that such
a mode of warfare in strikes is not tolerated in any well-regulated or
well-organized trades union. So high an authority as the Duke of Argyle,
in his work, *The Reign of Law*, states that "combinations of workingmen
for the protection of their labor are recommended alike by reason and
experience." When we strike as organized workingmen, we generally win,
and that is the reason of the trouble that our employers go to when they
try to show that strikes are failures, but you will notice that they generally
or always point to unorganized workers. That is one reason also why when
the employers know that the workingmen are organized and have got a
good treasury strikes are very frequently avoided. There are fewer strikes
among organized workingmen, but when they do strike they are able to
hold out much longer than the others, and they generally win. The
trades unions are not what too many men have been led to believe they
are, importations from Europe, if they are imported, then, as has been
said, they were landed at Plymouth Rock from the Mayflower. . . .

Testimony of L. G. Pettyjohn, D. H. Lloyd, and Daniel Daniel

*While the committee was holding hearings in Birmingham, Ala-
bama, in November 1883, a number of striking members of the
Amalgamated Association of Iron and Steel Workers aired their
grievances.*

L. G. Pettyjohn: I am a puddler by trade, I work in the Birmingham
Rolling-Mill. . . .
Sen. Blair: If you have in mind anything that you wish to state to the
committee you may go on and make your statement in your own way. —
A. Well, I would like to speak more in behalf of trades unions than

anything else, as they are something new in the South, comparatively speaking. . . .

The object of our association is to educate mechanics who work at the business up to a standard of morality and temperance, so that they will respect their employer's interest as much as their own, and I think we are succeeding so far. We have gained the respect, I think, of the people of Birmingham. . . .

We propose to mete out justice to our employers by giving them a fair share, or even giving them an extra fair share, of the profits on their capital invested, by establishing a basis, a sliding scale, for the government of wages, and our scale here begins generally on the 1st of June and terminates on the 31st of May of every year.

But we were unfortunate down here in not getting our scale signed the first of last June, so we have been on strike ever since the 1st of July. We worked on through the month of June on condition that the scale would be signed as soon as it was presented, but it was delayed by some means or other so that it didn't get here by the 1st of June, but we understood from the superintendent that it would be signed. It was presented sometime in June, but after giving his word that he would sign it, the superintendent said that the authority was not vested in him to sign it, and that he would have to wait until Mr. Caldwell, the president of the concern, came down. Mr. Caldwell had a sick child, and said he couldn't come, and he did not come. So we worked on until the 1st of July. Then they were going to stop through the month of July for repairs to the machinery, and Mr. Caldwell hadn't yet turned up; so we sent a committee from our lodge to Louisville to see him to get him to sign the scale, for we thought like this, that if he did intend to sign the scale we would be out of our $4.00 a week as long as we did not present it. So we sent a committee to him, and he refused to sign the scale, and consequently the strike began from the day he refused to sign. Since then we have had the president of our association down here. He was here in the early part of this week to try to make a compromise with the company by offering for us to work at Wheeling prices. They have been in the habit of getting half a dollar a day above Pittsburgh prices at this place. That was the inducement offered when the mill first started, that they would pay the highest price paid east of the Mississippi River; in other words, that they would pay the highest price paid in the country. . . .

Q. How many men are there in this mill? — A. When the mill is running a single turn there are between 250 and 300 men.

Q. How many belong to your lodge? — A. We have between 125 and 130. I am confident the number is over 120.

Q. Are they all white men? — A. All white. As I said before, this was the inducement offered to mechanics to come down here, the high prices that they would get, because Birmingham being a new place they would naturally expect to have to pay pretty high for everything that they bought. Very few of the men that came down here at first brought their families, but afterwards they sent for them.

Q. Where did the men come from mostly? — A. Well, they are from every state in the Union almost.

Q. You speak of its being held out as an inducement to you that you were to have half a dollar more, or something more than the Pittsburgh rates? — A. Yes, sir. As I have said, they paid the highest price paid in the country, and that was half a dollar above Pittsburgh rates. Pittsburgh at the two and a half cents rate would amount to $5.50 a ton, but we were to get $6.00 a ton for boiling. We were offered these inducements to come here, but trade is a little depressed now, and our employers seem to be trying to take advantage of the depression in the trade to get part of that half dollar a ton, if not all; they want all of it. We have offered to split the difference with them. After the president of our association came down we offered a compromise to work at Wheeling prices, $5.75 for boiling; but Mr. Caldwell, the president of the Birmingham Rolling Company, says he will agree to nothing but Pittsburgh prices flat; that is $5.50 for boiling, and seventy cents in the finishing department for heating. So it seems no matter how honorably trades unions conduct themselves there is [*sic*] times when parties will try to take advantage of the men. Now we have tried to mete out justice to our employers in that mill the same as in every other mill here and at the North. If a man neglects his work through drink, or anything of that sort, we don't wait for the company to discharge him; the company will be told that such and such is the case, and then it is with them whether they will put him off or not; but if they do discharge him on the spur of the moment, he does not have an advocate in us, because we feel that he has neglected his work by getting under the influence of liquor, and we do not try to save him. In other words, by acting in that way he has cut himself loose from the association, because the association does not recognize or countenance anything of that sort. The main object of the Amalgamated Association of Iron and Steel Workers is to educate the mechanics of that association up to a standard of morality and temperance, and good workmanship. A man has to be known as a good workman before he can get into the association. We think that if employers would recognize us as a body of workingmen trying to build up their business as much as their own, it would be a benefit to both parties, both employers and workingmen.

So far as regards strikes, the witness who was here a little while ago said that the men generally came out "at the little end of the horn." We admit that they generally lose, but strikes are very often forced upon them. If we were to accept every reduction put upon us, the consequence would be that today one-half the tradesmen of the United States would not get more wages than for ordinary labor — after serving an apprenticeship to learn a trade, a man couldn't command any more pay than if he had never learned his trade. It is an old saying that a good man will always command good wages, but that does not hold true in every case — at least in my estimation. . . .

D. H. Lloyd: Well, we expected, as it is generally the case, to have our scale signed for the year, and we expected that it would be signed at the same prices that had been paid heretofore. That was the general understanding of our committee when they went before the manager and the president. They anticipated trouble, and they gave us to understand that if we worked through June they would pay the prices we demanded, in proportion to what they had paid heretofore. If Pittsburgh was reduced we expected a reduction in proportion; but if Pittsburgh was not reduced we expected to be paid in the same proportion as before that time. But, after getting us to work through the month of June, we endeavored to have our scale signed in the beginning of July, and they refused to sign it. . . .

Sen. Blair: How many of you are there that refused to work? — A. The whole of the members of our organization.

Q. Did that take away all the help in the mill? — A. It took away the skilled work, and a great deal of the labor besides.

Q. About how many men? — A. In the vicinity of 130.

Q. Has the mill been idle ever since? — A. It has.

Q. What is the prospect of its starting up? — A. I hardly know. We sent for the president of our association lately, and he came here and endeavored to make a settlement by accepting a reduction of twenty-five cents per ton in what we term the puddling or boiling department, and a reduction of 5 percent in the finishing department. Our committee went down and stated to the mill people what we proposed to do; but they would listen to nothing but Pittsburgh prices.

Q. Was there a reduction of Pittsburgh prices last June? — A. There was not.

Q. And the point with your employers is that they refuse now to pay any more than Pittsburgh prices? — A. Yes.

Q. This addition of 10 percent they declined to pay? — A. Yes.

Q. And the offer you made them by way of a compromise was to take what percent advance on Pittsburgh prices? — A. We offered to accept 5 percent where we had been getting 10 percent heretofore.

Q. You offered, as the common saying is, to split the difference with them? — A. Exactly.

Q. And you say they refused to confer with you at all about it? — A. We had a conference, to be sure, but that was the end of it. They would concede nothing, whereas we had conceded one-half of our claim.

Q. What do you think is the prospect of the mill starting up again? If you should not come to an agreement with them will they get other help? — A. I hardly think they will be able to do so. I do not think they would be satisfied with the help they could get. They have spoken about resorting to non-union men, as they are termed — hiring men that do not belong to our association; but I hardly think they could get such men that would suit them. I am satisfied in my own mind that they could not, because that has been tried elsewhere.

Q. The skilled workingmen are with you in your union? — A. They are.

Q. How are you getting along during all this time when you are out of employment in your regular trade? — A. Well, we are not making much money, but we can very easily live by sacrificing some little luxuries. . . .

Q. With reference to the future, how do the working people of your acquaintance regard the prospects of Birmingham as a business place and a good place for working people? — A. Well, the natural advantages of Birmingham for manufacturing many things are great, and that is one reason why we think that we should be paid a little more wages here than elsewhere. The same product, pig iron, for instance, in our business, I think, is better here than it is up North.

Q. Better how; better in quality? — A. I don't know that it is of a better quality, because they manufacture as good pig iron in Pittsburgh as anywhere.

Q. Then what do you mean by saying that it is better here? — A. I mean that it is cheaper.

Q. And you think you ought to have a share in that advantage which Birmingham has? — A. I think so. I would state just here that I called the attention of the president of our company to that matter; I told him that we labored under disadvantages here, and pointed out to him that the company had advantages. He wanted to know wherein. I told him on account of the material necessary to produce iron, coal and everything being cheaper. He told me that was none of my business. I told him I thought it was — that whereas we labored here under disadvantages, and they had advantages over other sections, I thought there ought to be a division. . . .

Daniel Daniel: I think the best thing that could be done for the advancement of the laboring men in the South would be for Congress to appropriate money to start mills that could be run by skilled workmen on a fair percentage of interest to the government. If the government would appropriate money to the men as a loan, we would show them that we have got talent enough to work a rolling-mill at less cost than these capitalists claim is required. We claim that they are eating up the profits with percentages and big salaries, and that they want to cheat us out of our hard-earned money to pay these big salaries and to put us in a position so that we cannot educate our children or ever have more than enough to keep body and soul together, so that we can never get out into society in any respectability. I claim that by the government doing that it would fetch good citizens to the State of Alabama and help to develop these natural resources that are in the ground. Here is coal, for instance; we have to pay for the coal that we use in this town from $3.00 to $5.00 a ton, although it is got right out of the mines around us; that is, we have to pay that retail price for that coal, while the manufacturers get it at $1.00 or $1.50 a ton. . . . We claim that they can buy iron in this town from this blast furnace for $13.50 a ton, but they insist on taking Pittsburgh prices, although they don't get their pig iron from Pittsburgh; they get it right at home. Now, if the Pittsburgh people have to get iron from Alabama to manufacture, and have to pay freight on it from here to Pittsburgh and then back again, when it goes to the southern markets — to New Orleans, for instance — I should think that these people here could afford to pay a little higher wages than Pittsburgh pays, as they promised to do. I was the first man that ever heated a piece of iron here, and they said at that time that they would pay the biggest prices in the country, and we are not asking them to do that today.

Sen. Blair: Do you consider that they have broken their faith with you? — A. We consider that they have broken their word, if their word amounts to anything, but I suppose they don't care much about their word if they can make the money.

Q. Is the feeling which you have now expressed the feeling generally among the men that are on strike here? — A. Yes, sir; this the general feeling.

. Q. Do these mill people deny that they promised that they would give you this extra percentage of pay? — A. No, sir; they do not deny it, but they won't pay it any more.

Q. They take the ground, I suppose, that they said that to get you here? — A. Yes, sir; and they have got us here now, and they think they have got some new men broke in; but they have tried that when we men have left here on different occasions but they had to get back the old hands.

Q. Which side are the people here generally for, for the company or for the workingmen? — A. The people are for us in the main. This company does not spend a dollar in this town and we spend all we make. . . .

Testimony of Norvin Green

Norvin Green was a Kentucky physician and state legislator who became interested in the fledgling telegraph business in 1853. Grasping the importance of coordinating and centralizing the telegraph network, he rose rapidly. In 1857 he organized the North American Telegraph Company. When Western Union, the first coast-to-coast telegraph company, was founded in 1866, Green was named vice-president. In 1878 he became president of Western Union.

Sen. Blair: There has been testimony before the committee in reference to the general feeling or state of mind which exists throughout the country between the capitalists or employers on the one hand and the employed on the other — their personal relations and the feeling that exists between them as two classes (if they can be spoken of in that way). What is your observation in regard to that, or can you say anything about it that you think may be serviceable in bringing about a better state of things than now exists? — A. That is a very difficult problem. It is a difficult thing to determine what is best to be done in regard to that. My sympathies are with the laboring people. I would like to see them prosper. I like the institutions under which a man may be anything and everything which his capacities fit him for. But as far as my observation extends — and I have studied the subject somewhat (I have in this portfolio here a paper on this general subject which was prepared in my office under my direction) — as far as my observation extends, strikes have proved a failure.

Q. Is that a paper that you would be willing to submit to the committee? — A. With some revision I would be willing to submit the paper. It goes a little farther than I can go; that is all the objection I have to it. The data which it contains were gathered and arranged by others, and some of the logic of the paper goes farther than I am disposed to indorse. Still, the data here collected, which I have examined, establish to my mind the fact that both in this country and in the old countries strikes have proved a failure. I think that organizations of labor, with a view of absolutely controlling its reward, have proved failures. There is not one strike in twenty that has occurred in this country or in England that has even partially succeeded in accomplishing the objects in view. On the other hand, there is the great fact that those employees are most likely to receive increased compensation and promotion who are most loyal to their employers and least loyal to these organizations. That is a general fact. The employees that stand by their employers in times of trouble are, of course, most likely to be promoted; and generally employees who are deeply concerned for the interests of their employers, and who go beyond what may be considered their routine duties to look after and advise as to those interests are most apt to be promoted, both in salary and position, so that whilst there is no question at all of the right of laborers to organize, no question in the world of their right to hold meetings and discuss what is best for their own interests and act upon such discussions if they choose, no question of their right to quit work whenever they choose, either individually or in a body, yet the experience of the last fifteen years — I believe the first organization of the Knights of Labor was about 1868 — the experience of the last fifteen years has proved that such organizations are a failure for the attainment of the objects they have in view. I do not think anybody can recall five instances where strikes have been even partially successful. On the other hand, these organizations have produced a feeling of distrust between capital and labor. They have cultivated distrust on the part of laborers, and a feeling that capital does not propose or intend to do them justice, while, on the other side, they have produced a distrust on the part of capital of these laborers or employees that are at the head of the organizations. I think, on the whole, that such organizations have done more harm than good. I do not see but that they must necessarily do more harm than good — organizations of that kind. I do not think they are calculated to promote the interests of the workingman. I think that organizations are right. I think that not only has nobody any right to object to them, but I go farther and believe that for many purposes organizations of workingmen are good for their members; but whenever they assume to dictate the terms of their employment, just to the extent that they do that they react upon their members, and do them harm, as a general thing, instead of good.

Q. It is claimed that they do not undertake to do that; but that, finding themselves, as they consider it, badly paid, they fix their price, ask it, and if it is not paid, simply quit work! — *A.* Well, that process has not succeeded. I think it may be pronounced a failure as a general rule, though they clearly have a right to do it; there is no question about that.

Q. May not this often be the case that the strike itself proves a failure, but that the fact that dissatisfaction has existed to such an extent as to result in a strike and an interruption of business, oftentimes induces the employer to make concessions, as you have done in this instance; and oftentimes to see the approach of trouble, and anticipating a strike, may not the employer be influenced to make concessions before the trouble results in an actual strike? — *A.* It may have that effect, and may be successful in that way to some extent, but the spirit of our people is that nobody likes to negotiate about anything under a menace. Our people can be led, but they don't drive worth a cuss; and the moment you attempt to treat with them under a menace they get stubborn and nothing can be done. . . .

Q. But here is your corporation, and here are other great corporations, which, as you say, are conducted, not for the public good, but for the benefit of the stockholders. That is the principle you enunciate here as the one upon which your corporation is administered. You are responsible to your stockholders and not to the public, and you do the best you can for the stockholders, and in so doing endeavor to get your help as cheap as you can, and we know that all the other corporations do the same. Now, you, the employers, have all the capital of the country; you have something that you can live on for a year or two to say the least in case of any difficulty with your labor, but the workingman has nothing of the kind. Under such circumstances what chance has the workingman or the laborer of any kind to get any increase of pay for his labor, even though he may be worthy of it, if he does not combine so as to be able to do you more damage by refusing to work than you will do yourself by agreeing to pay what he asks? Is it not evident that, the two parties being in such relative positions, labor can get nothing except by organization? — A. I have no objection to the organization of labor, and no doubt of its right to organize, but I think that if anyone will study the history of all the strikes that have taken place in this country he will find that they have left the strikers in a worse condition generally than they were when they began.

Q. That has no doubt been so in many instances, but that is not an answer to my question. — A. When I announce to you that we manage our property for the benefit of the stockholders, I say to you at the same time that corporations, like individuals, are capable of doing a great many things that are not merely just but also generous. For instance, there is no earthly obligation on us to pay a man's widow anything after he dies in our service, and yet we are doing that continually for a limited period, paying the widow, one, two or three months' salary, as the case may be.

Q. There is no legal obligation to do that? — A. There is no legal obligation and no moral obligation that I know of. The man was just as anxious to get employment as we were to employ him. But we had one man, an operator, dying of consumption, who had a family with no other means of support; he was constantly expecting to be able to return to duty, but we knew that he never would be able to return, yet we paid him half salary for nine or ten months and paid the widow the salary for two or three months after he died. We knew he would never come back, but he had been in our employ a number of years, twelve or fifteen, and had been a very faithful man, and so we thought it right to treat him generously. Therefore, while the general rule of our action is to do the best we can to promote the interest of our stockholders consistently with fulfilling our obligations to the public, we realize that there are certain public obligations that we are expected to fulfill by reason of the franchise given us to do business, and we try to fulfill them. I say that whilst our governing principle of administration is to promote as best we can the interests of our shareholders, having due regard to these public obligations, yet we are not insensible to the appeals of our employees in deserving cases, but, on the contrary, we respond to them in the manner I have indicated.

Q. I do not doubt that at all; but we were both of us speaking rather with reference to general systems than to the particular acts of your corporation. — A. Well, the way in which you put the question seemed to hold me up before the public as alleging that the only motive influencing us in the administration of our corporation was the interest of the stockholders, and therefore I thought it necessary to make this qualification of that statement; that was all.

Q. I had not arraigned your company in any way; I had reference to the relations of capital and labor generally. Capital generally acts upon the principle which you enunciated in dealing with labor, does it not? — A. Yes, sir.

Q. The capitalist employer gets his labor just as he gets his flour, as cheaply as he can, as a general rule, does he not? — A. That is true as a general rule.

Q. The wage-workers of the country have been estimated as high as 15,000,000 of our population. I do not know how many wage-workers there actually are in the country, but certainly they constitute a very large proportion of our people. Now, single-handed, what one of them can obtain a raise in wages which affects, not only himself, but all of his class? How can any single wage-worker hope to obtain such a raise from your corporation or from any railroad corporation or from any large employer? He cannot appeal to your generosity, because a concession to him carries with it a concession of millions before you get all the way round, as you have got to do for every other man of the same class what is done for him. This being so, if it comes to be a fact that as a whole the workingmen, being the creators and the original producers of all this wealth, if it comes to be a fact that they are not getting a sufficient proportion of the wealth which they produce in the way of wages, what remedy have they but in organization, which gives them, to some extent, strength corresponding to that of capital, and enables them to enforce attention to their demands? — A. I said awhile ago that that was a very difficult problem, and one that requires the attention of the best minds in the country, but that the method which had been adopted of trying to coerce higher salaries had not been a success generally, in my judgment. Now, I have said in regard to our company what I think is true in respect to all these organizations — that one of the faults of an organization is that it will almost certainly make every conceivable effort to better the condition of its members and to increase their wages, *whatever those wages may be*. I believe that, with the conviction in the minds of our operators that they had power to dictate terms to our corporation, the strike would just as likely have been made had the wages been 50 percent higher than they were.

Q. That may be true as to individuals, but do you think that the great mass of your employees would act in that way? — A. If you give a man $100 a month he wants $150, and when you give him $150 he wants $200. Now, I am not saying that in disparagement of the laborer. I am speaking of the instincts of humanity generally. . . .

Testimony of John Roach

In 1883 John Roach was the largest, best-known, and most controversial shipbuilder in the United States. Irish by birth, he had come to America in 1842 as a poor immigrant. Originally an ironworker, he prospered, and after the Civil War began to specialize in constructing iron ships. In the 1870's he became an important contractor for the Navy. Roach's critics claimed that he had obtained many government contracts because of his heavy contributions to the Republican party and that he had defrauded the government in carrying out the work. The awarding of contracts to his firm in 1883 for all four of the Navy's first "modern" warships when his friend William E. Chandler was Secretary of the Navy caused a great furor.

The Witness: It must not be understood here that I am opposed to trade unions. The true way to convince any man is to let him have his own way, after you have reasoned with him. I am going to make a statement now, and if any man can contradict it, I wish him to do so. That statement is that no one has ever heard me ask a man what his politics or what his religion was; and not only that, but there is a standing order in my shops that any foreman who may become the tool of any political party, and who undertakes to use his influence with the men to help any political party, will be discharged when proper complaint is made of such action on his part and proper proof offered. I am quite willing to open my shop to the trades union men, and I have done it. I say to the men, "you may enjoy yourselves with your unions just as you do with your religion or your politics, but while you are in my workshop you must conform to my rules." Now, what are those rules? One rule is that every man has got to speak for himself. I say to the men, "When you came to seek employment of me, you came in your own individual capacity, you presented yourself on your own individual merits, and it was upon that condition that I hired you. Now, if you have any complaint to make, make it for yourself. I will hear it, and try to treat you fairly; but you must not attempt to take the control of my workshop out of my hands." I do not care how many union men come into my shop. No man shall be denied employment by me simply because he is a union man, I am satisfied that wherever coercive measures have been used to make men do this or that — for instance, to vote this ticket or that ticket — not one percent of them could be relied upon to vote as they were required or as they might have promised. . . .

Now, with regard to strikes, there is probably no employer in the country who has had less trouble with his labor in that respect than I have had. I take a great deal of pains to encourage and reason with my workmen. I will give you an illustration of that. Very often I have a man come to see me about his wages. Three or four months ago a very enterprising man, a good talker, came to me and said, "Mr. Roach, I want more wages." "Well," said I, "why do you want more wages? You know I am paying you double what you got on the other side of the water" (the man is a foreigner). "Well," said he, "but it costs me double the amount to live here that it cost me there, so I am no better off." Said I, "Do you get no more for the amount you pay here than you got for what you paid there?" "Oh, yes," said he, "I do." "Then," said I, "why don't you do with less expense here and save more?" The principal difficulty with this man was his rent; and, by the way, this rent question is a very sore one in New York. I asked the man, "What wages do you get?" Said he, "I get $15.00 a week, $60.00 a month, if I work every day, and I pay $12.50, or nearly 20 percent of my whole income, for the bare walls of the place I live in; 20 percent of all my toil goes for a place to shelter my family." "Well," I said, "what kind of a place is that? How much did you pay for your house on the other side?" "Oh," said he, "a great deal less than that." "What accommodations did you have there?" I asked him. He said that the accommodations were poor, and he went on to describe them. "Well," said I, "there are plenty of those places where the Chinese live down town in New York that you can rent for the same price that you paid on the other side of the water; now why don't you go down there and get rooms?" "Oh," said he, "what position would I occupy in your shop among the other mechanics if I did that? And besides, my family don't want to live there. My landlord is" (to use the man's own language) "a damned hog."

Now, I am not a landlord, and I have no interest as a landlord, but I have some workmen who are landlords, and I said to this man, "Well, we have some men that are landlords, you know, here among ourselves. There are Jim Brown and Tom Burns; they are just as gentle and kind men as I ever saw; their children go to Sunday school, and they are very nice men, and you can't call such men as they are hogs." He scratched his head.

I thought I would bring him face to face with one of these landlords, and I sent for Tom Burns, and I said, "Here, Tom, is one of your fellow workmen. He says that out of regard for you as a fellow workman he won't call *you* a hog; but he does call everybody else that is a landlord a hog; what have you got to say about this matter, and how came you to own a house?" "Well," said Tom, "I had a little money in the savings bank, where I was getting 5 or 6 percent interest on it, and I took it out and I bought a house, and I mortgaged the house and I pay 7 percent interest on the mortgage [that was the legal rate of interest at that time], and when I pay that interest and pay my taxes and keep the house in repair, and take into account the time that it is empty occasionally, and also sometimes when the tenant is sick and does not work and cannot pay the rent — when I sum these things all up, why I wish I had never seen the house. It is not very profitable to me as it is." . . .

Now, if we are to have cheaper rents we can only have them by reducing the price of American capital or else reducing the wages of labor. The workingmen cry out about the high rents, but when you call together the carpenter and the mason and the plumber and the man who makes the brick and ask them, "Are you willing to hold up your hands for a policy that will reduce your wages, so as to enable Tom Burns to afford to rent his house cheap?" they will answer you, "No!" There seems to be a strong disposition nowadays to excite discontent among working people, and the worst enemies of the workingman are those who try to deceive him, for political purposes or in the interest of foreign competition, who try to make the poor man believe that he is injured because he pays so much for his coat, and tell him that that coat could be bought on the other side of the water so much cheaper if this tariff were taken off. The proper way to settle that question is to ask the tailor what he gets for making that coat here, and to compare that price with what the tailor gets in Europe. That tells the tale. And why do those people come here and never go back to stay again where clothes and rent are cheap? It is a small and petty thing to be arraying one class of labor against another, and trying to excite discontent in the mind of the American workingman, upon the ground that he could get his coat or his boots or something else a little cheaper only for what is called "protection." My observation and my experience lead me to the conviction that there is no country in the world in which the people are so well off or so happy as they are here. When you look back at the condition of this nation at the close of the Civil War, without credit, buried in debt, not one among the nations of the earth believing that within the lifetime of any man then living it would be able to restore its credit; when you look back at that condition of things and then look at this nation today, feeding not only itself but also helping to feed the rest of the world; when you see our population at the same time enjoying comforts which no other population existing on God's earth enjoy; and when you see still further that we have now a credit inferior to that of no nation in the world, everybody must admit that we have certainly been making mighty strides. There never was, in my opinion, a better opportunity for the workingman than there is in this country today. . . .

There is a great outcry among certain classes of workingmen for higher wages and for uniform wages for men engaged in the same kinds of work; but how can you harmonize, how can you average men in that way? Take my own case, for instance. I am content to put myself down as a man who is willing to get as much out of labor as can be got out of it fairly, but I am paying one man nearly double the wages I pay to another, though they both belong to the same trade and are working side by side. I do not say that the difference in all cases results entirely from the superiority as a workman of the one who gets the higher wages, but as a general rule it does result from that to a great extent. One man is more wasteful than another, or is less regular at his work than another, or something of that kind; and of course there are many other reasons in many cases why we pay one man more than we do another in the same occupation. I have men in my employ who have worked for me for thirty-five years. Of two men in the same trade and working in the same shop one will be a moral man, a good man, a faithful man, who does not require to be watched; he will be faithful no matter whether the boss is present or not; whenever the bell rings he will be at the shop ready to go to work. Or, to take another illustration, one man is more careful and economical than another; and the man who cannot be faithful and economical for the boss will seldom be so for himself. A careful man sees a piece of timber, for example, and he thinks of some place that that will fit, and he takes it up carefully and uses it for that purpose, while the other fellow throws it away and goes and gets a board and puts a saw into it and saws out a portion and spoils the board, when he might just as well have taken that loose piece of timber. Then, again, some men are very good workmen when they are at work, but they are never to be relied upon. Such a man is often absent from the shop. Perhaps he drinks, or perhaps he spends his time on excursions, or gunning, or something of that kind. I have no sympathy with that man in his demand for higher wages, because I have come to the conclusion that the more money he gets the worse he is off; and when such a man makes big wages one week, generally he will not work the next week. I think he would be better off if he had to work all the time, and I have no sympathy with him. Now, this being the state of the case as we know it actually to exist, how are you going, by any legislation, or by any trades-union organizations, to force an employer to pay men of this latter class as much as he pays good, trustworthy men?

I will give you an illustration of how that thing works sometimes, and how it is met. I had a strike about a year ago at the Chester shipyard, the first in a long time; for, as I have said, I am about as little troubled in that way as any man. A deputation of seven men came from the wooden shipbuilders to represent them and confer with me. I said to them, "I cannot hear you as a deputation; you must come in your individual capacity if I am to deal with you." "That will take too much time," they said. "Very well," said I, "I will give you the time; I will be at the loss of time." I would not recognize them as a deputation, and they said they had to go back to see whether my suggestion was in accordance with the will of the organization, and to consult as to how they should act. I said to them, "I have got no time now. Be kind enough to postpone this matter until next Saturday." In the meantime I called the foreman (sometimes a great deal of the difficulty in these cases exists with the foreman himself), and I said to him before I went away, "Have for me on next Saturday the names of all the men that this deputation came to represent, the wages that each is receiving, and the time that each is making with reference to regularity of work, and so forth. Find out for me, if you can, how many of these men send their children to church or to school, how their families are clothed, how many of the men are drunkards; classify them as fully as you can."

He classified them into three classes, and when I came down the next Saturday I notified these men that I would give them half a day out of my own time and I would talk to them in regular order, but that I insisted that each man must represent himself without reference to what his neighbor had to say. When they came I had them separated into these three classes, and they stood there classified in that way. There were about one-fifth of them who were really very valuable men, and to whom it was a pleasure to pay money, because they made a good use of it, and you knew when the money went into their hands that it was going to be used to make their homes happy and give their families the comforts of life. When this class of men came up I asked them what they wanted. "Well," said the first man, "I want more wages." I asked him, "How much more do you want?" Said he, "I want so much." I said, "Timekeeper, mark these men down with that increase of wages, to go to work." Then the next class came up, and of course the best talker, the man who could make the most noise and talk the loudest, stepped up first. He began to talk, and the next man began to talk, and the next man began to talk, but I said to them, "I will not give you one dollar more. You are getting more money now than you are entitled to. You are getting more than is good for you. There is not a man in this line who is in the habit of making a full week's pay. My shop and my tools are standing there idle while you are off hunting, or something else, and the capital that I have invested in these tools is idle and the plant is suffering while you are idling in that way. I will not give you one cent advance." Then the next class came up, and the spokesman began to talk. To that class I said, "I do not want you at all; you are only wanted here when there is a surplus of work. Some of you men, as I am informed, do not pay your board, nor do you pay your landlords; the widows that some of you board with have to come here and ask that your pay be stopped to pay for your board. I do not want you at all. There may come a time that I may want you, but I do not want you now at all." Now when these men separated, the question was put by the inferior men to the men of the better class, "Are you going to desert us?" And there was quite a tussle over that question, and a delegation of the first-class men came to me and said, "Mr. Roach, can you not do so and so?" I said, "I have no change to make. There are some of those men who are as good workmen as you are, and when they do as you do I will leave instructions here to have their wages advanced." And in fact I have now in my workshops men who are receiving certain wages upon condition that if they shall make full time and continue sober, at the end of a certain time they shall be paid the advance. There is one man in my employ, an excellent man, moral in every other way except that he will drink liquor, a man that I am paying $2,500 a year to, a man whose services are invaluable, but he has this fault, he will drink; and if you were to know of the thousand and one means I have resorted to to cure that good man they would astonish you. The last plan I attempted with that man was this: I said to him, "I will not cast upon you the odious reputation of having been discharged because you are a drunkard. I will not bring that disgrace upon your family. I will not discharge you. If it is done you have got to do it yourself." I wrote a letter for him, addressed to myself, running about in this way: "Mr. John Roach: I hereby hand you my resignation. I prefer to be a drunkard rather than to be a sober man and to retain your respect and confidence." "Now," said I, "when you want to take the next glass of liquor, just sign that letter and hand it to me." That was several months ago, and I have not got the letter yet. So you see, as I said before, that if I appear to have better luck in dealing with my men than other employers have, it is because I take a great deal of pains to talk with them and reason with them. Now, when you ask me whether the workingmen are as well off in other employments as they are in mine, I can only say I do not know. I do not pay any more wages than others pay; in fact, I am charged with paying less; but there is a reason for that. However, I exact as much from my men as other employers do, and I do not see why every other employer cannot produce a record equal to that of myself and my workmen. . . .

Testimony of Jay Gould *

Sen. Blair: You have had considerable practical experience with labor, have you not? — A. Yes, sir; I have been all my life either a laborer or a hirer of labor.

Q. What is your observation and opinion in regard to strikes, their causes, and their results? — A. Strikes, of course, come from various causes, but they generally come from a class of dissatisfied men — the

* See above, page 47.

poorest part of your labor generally are at the bottom of a strike. Your best men do not care how many hours they work, or anything of that kind; they are looking to get higher up; either to own a business of their own and control it, or to get higher up in the ranks.

Q. But from the necessity of the case only a very small number can expect that. — A. Well, there are a great many who have places in view all the time. Of course there are only so many places to be filled, but there are a great many that are looking after those places. There may be only one place to be filled, but there may be five hundred nice, industrious fellows who are all working for it.

Q. That keeps them quiet? — A. Yes, sir.

Q. And may they not, for that very reason, be willing to put up with hardships and insufficient compensation for the time being? — A. They may.

Q. So the fact that these men were contented, or, at all events, were quiet, might be no reason for believing that the mass of the laborers were receiving fair pay. Now, don't you think, when you come to treat of the labor of the country in that broad way, and to consider that most of the laborers must always necessarily be in the ranks, so to speak — privates — and can never reasonably expect to become officers or to be promoted, do you not think their dissatisfaction may oftentimes be based on the fact that they do not receive compensation enough to keep them from suffering? — A. Is it not true that they get better pay here than in any other country? That is why they come here, I believe.

Q. I believe so. — A. And is it not true also that capital, if it gets better remuneration in some other country than it gets here, will go there? You cannot transfer your house, but you can transfer your money; and if labor is put up too high here, all the manufacturing will be done abroad, because the capitalists will go where they can get cheaper labor. So that when you sit down and try to get a panacea for a particular evil you run against a great many obstacles that come in the way of putting it in practice, and my observation has been that capital and labor, if let alone, generally come together and mutually regulate their relations to each other. There are some of these people who think they can regulate the whole of mankind, but they generally get wrong ideas into the minds of the public.

Q. Notwithstanding the fact that labor is better paid in this country than elsewhere, capital is also very much better paid in this country, and is likely to be so, at least for the present, and capital, like labor, is coming here from the older countries; and yet we find labor here dissatisfied to a great extent. Is not that so? — A. I think not. I think there is a far greater satisfaction here among the workingmen generally than anywhere else in the world, far greater than among the laboring classes that I have seen abroad. I only speak of what I have seen myself. . . .

Q. Yet there seem to be numerous strikes in the country this present season. For some reason labor is restless, uneasy, and to some extent unemployed. — A. Well, there is a little overplus of labor. In the first place, we have been importing an enormous amount of new material in the way of immigration; all those people had to be placed. Then we were building railroads too rapidly, and now we have stopped. That leaves a surplus of labor. The manufacturers, too, have been going on and manufacturing more than the consumption of the country required, and they are reducing their production. This, with the fact that we have stopped building railroads, has left a surplus of labor here for the time being which has got to place itself. . . .

Testimony of John W. Britton *

The Witness: I should like to say a few words on the subject of strikes. My observation proves that strikes originate generally in large shops and among large bodies of workmen. The question that naturally suggests itself is, why? I have looked into that subject and my answer is, that the man who employs twenty-five or fifty men becomes personally acquainted with them, and if a man in his employ has a grievance he comes to the employer directly and states his grievance. In large shops one man doesn't count, so the men organize a committee, and the committee come to the office. I went through this eight-hour strike in 1872. I was treasurer then of the only employers' association that I ever joined, and the last; and I had an opportunity of getting a pretty thorough knowledge of the workingmen, as well as of the "bosses." And when Anna Dickenson came to me and said, "I want to talk to you about this strike, and you can talk to me freely, because I am on the side of the employers," I simply told her, "Well, I am on the side of the men." I saw the utmost selfishness displayed by the employers in that strike, and I saw workingmen in it that made the greatest of sacrifices for their fellows; and whether they were right or wrong, we must admire the spirit of sacrifice. We burnt gas for six weeks and issued documents by the barrel, and brought leading manufacturers to this end of the country; we had men come in there who used our gas, our paper, and our printing material, and when we assessed them $20.00 apiece I had to give a man $3.50 a day to collect the money. I was treasurer. Each member of the association was assessed $20.00 to pay expenses; some of them represented millions of money, and I came short of the collections about $200, which I had to pay out of my own pocket. Yet, another man collected $2,500 to prosecute the strikers. I don't believe that employers, taken as a class, are any better than mechanics.

* See above, page 50.

I have learned to respect working people, because I have seen so much in them which the people who only look at their dirty clothes do not see at all. I come in contact with the people. I do not hestitate to say to my men, as I did say to them last October, "We have never had but one strike in this shop and we will never have another. I would rather suffer any loss than have a strike. You may make demands on me that are unjust. If I cannot talk you out of them, show you that you are working in the wrong direction, and are killing the goose that lays the golden egg, I will yield rather than have a strike. I won't embitter the shop against the office for the sake of a few thousand dollars." I have a rule in my shop to the effect that if a man has a grievance he comes in and tells me of it, and I do not receive him as if I were the biggest Indian in the world and as if hc were of no earthly account. The moment you take away a man's self-respect, he is hard to deal with. You will succeed very much better if you treat him as a man and an equal. In this country all men are equal before the law, and if a man comes to you about your own business, or any other business, for that matter, even if he is a little dirty, he is entitled to fair treatment. I am not in politics, and am not giving the working people any "taffy." I have practiced what I preach.

I can give you an instance of how things should be between employer and employee. Two years ago we were working all piecework, and we were debating about the future, and so failed to give out the work, and some of the men were waiting for it a month or six weeks. The first thing I knew, we heard that the shop was agitated; that this delay was considered a plan to bring about a reduction of wages. I considered that a great misfortune. Perhaps some employers would say, "That is a good thing; they ought to be frightened once in awhile." I went right up to my men and said, "I have heard the rumor that is about, and I feel very much aggrieved by it. I supposed that the relation between the office and the shop was such that you would not think we would descend to a trick in order to lower wages. When we want to lower wages we will come to you and tell you the reason why we ask for the reduction. Don't ever believe that we are trying to fix things in the office so as to deceive our men." You must always carry out your promise to men; even if you are foolish enough to make a threat, carry it out; but you must give your men confidence in your honor and integrity; you must have proper relations with them. When there is one man on one side of the fence and five hundred on the other, and the one man has all the money and the others little or none, there is no use going around in grand style, making a loud noise, and getting their ill will. In the first place it is not right, and in the second place it is not profitable. I am not afraid to say publicly here, that I am not afraid of my men, nor afraid of ever having a strike in my shop. I believe in the justice of the workingmen if they are shown that their employer is not going to take any advantage of them. . . .

I tell my men I don't object to their joining trades unions. I do not believe in trades unions; I do not believe in giving up to any irresponsible man my right of private judgment. That is the reason I belong to no association. I would not join an employers' association under any conditions. If any among them is fool enough to quarrel with his men I am not going to help him. Let every tub stand on its own bottom. I say to a man that he can join any trade union or association or church or school that he pleases. It is his business. . . .

In a strike that took place in 1872, an employer in the brown-stone business stood up in a meeting of the employers and told what indignities he had suffered from his men — and they certainly were great indignities. He and his partner were themselves practical stonecutters. They had a contract which they were obliged to have completed by a certain day, and they could not get skill enough, in their estimation, to complete the contract in time; so one of the employers took his coat off and went to work with his own hands. Every man in the yard stopped work at once. They said it was taking the bread out of the poor men's mouths. It is hard for an employer to stand that. Another man at this meeting stood up and said that it was a terrible state of affairs, but that it was the employer's own fault to allow that sort of tyranny to grow up in his place. "If a man comes to my office," he said, "and says, 'I want twenty-five cents more a day,' I tell him, 'The first thing you do is to take off your hat,' he takes it off. The next thing I tell him is, 'Now, you leave; I don't propose to have any man talk to me like that.' " That, to my notion, is the kind of employer that causes strikes. I can show you some of the best employers in New York City who have had strikes in their establishments, but it is owing to the influence of other employers who have oppressed their men and forced them to combine. The just employers have had to pay the penalty of the bad work done by others.

One of the practical difficulties which I have seen in my intercourse with men is, that the business between the workshop and the office is generally done by a committee. That is a most unfortunate thing. The shop has a grievance; the men hold a meeting; it is all debated and rehearsed; a committee is appointed to wait on the "bosses" and protest against it and ask for a change of program. This committtee is naturally selected from among those who believe with the men and favor them. They go down to the office and it is debated there, *pro* and *con.*

Now, I do not care how correct and just the position of that employer may be, when that committee returns and reports to the full meeting what has been done in the interview with the employer, the committee have to garble the account. If they take up the side of the employer, there is a suspicion that they have been bought, and the question perhaps is asked, "How much did you get?" They have got to distort the argument of the boss, whatever it may be. They cannot, and dare not, tell the whole truth. There is no man bold enough to stand up in a shop of 500 men and be under the suspicion of selling out the interest of his fellow men. That is a position that I have never seen any man bold enough to stand. And they are very careful that such a suspicion shall not be aroused. They would rather lie than be supposed to be false to the interests of their fellow men. When we had the strike of 1872, and saw the results. I made up my mind that I would never under any circumstances, make a reply to a committee on any important subject. If it were a question of general advance of wages, or of shorter hours, or of any question of similar supreme importance to both the men and ourselves, I should weigh every word of argument presented by the committee, and I should give it fair consideration, and then I should report direct to the men themselves, so that my position should be thoroughly understood, and not garbled. . . .

Testimony of Joseph Medill *

The Witness: There is an almost universal impression prevailing among the trades-union people — those engaged, I mean, in labor combinations for mutual defense. I am not making any attack on them at all. I recognize a great deal of good and usefulness in those unions; but there is a universal impression prevailing among them that the employers in the United States could afford to pay much larger wages than they do if they wanted to without increasing the prices of their goods, and that they do not out of pure selfishness. I think the dissipation, if it were possible, of that fallacy would be the most useful thing that could be done. I think that if the laboring classes of the United States — the mechanics especially — could be brought to see that under the fixed laws of trade, of supply and demand, the employer has really little more control over prices where not protected by patents than over the winds and the weather, the largest possible good would be done; for if the mechanics saw that they are really, as a whole, paid about as much as it is possible to pay them they would then yield to the inevitable and seek other ways of improving their condition, and the feeling that they were being systematically cheated all the time would die out. In my newspaper, and in personal discussions, I have tried in my small way to get them to see that in a country where competition in trade has free play and full

* See above, page 73.

operation, it really fixes the maximum price on the whole for wages, and I have tried by iteration to get this idea before them: never to strike for higher wages on a falling market on the line of goods you are working on, for if you do you will inevitably be defeated, as your employer in that case can always make more money by locking up his shop than by paying the increased wages demanded while the prices of his goods are declining. I have tried to get this further idea into their minds: that no man is carrying on manufacturing from motives of benevolence purely. He has behind his motive gain, and if he does not see a reasonable prospect of making a satisfactory profit on his investment he will quit the business and not risk its dangers and losses, and that the time to strike is on a rising market, and that is the time that they do not often need to strike, because, under the law of active demand, the employers searching for new workmen bid one against the other, and it does not require much combination to get better wages on a rising market. And when the market is bad or sluggish or standing on a poise, the men had better arbitrate, and they had better arbitrate anyway in all cases than to strike. I have tried to teach those lessons, and I have endeavored to show that every strike, even if successful, costs more than it is worth; and if unsuccessful, the loss chiefly falls on the workmen, and nobody gains. It is a species of civil war every time. Now, if any method could be devised by the legislatures to stop strikes it would save millions upon millions of dollars of earnings to the classes who live by their hands in the United States and to the men that hire them. . . .

6 THE DEFENSE OF THE STATUS QUO

Testimony of Jay Gould *

Sen. Blair: I did not think of getting to this point so early, but we are there from the course which the examination has taken. Won't you please give us, therefore, as fully as you see fit (and as you suggested a little while ago, I do not see anything to be kept back in a public matter like this), your idea in regard to the establishment of a postal telegraph for the purpose of supplanting or rivaling the existing telegraphic systems of the country now controlled by private ownership? — A. Well, I think that control by the government in such things is contrary to our institutions. A telegraph system, of all businesses in the world, wants to be managed by skilled experts. Our government is founded on a political idea; that is, that the party in power shall control the patronage; and if the government controlled the telegraph, the heads of the general managers and the superintendents would come off every four years, if there was a change in politics — at least as often as that — and you would not have any such efficient service as you have now. The very dividend of the Western Union depends upon the company doing the business well, keeping her customers, and developing the business. But if the government controlled it — why if the Democrats were in power it would be a Democratic telegraph, and if the Republicans came into power it would be a Republican telegraph, and if the great Reformers came in I don't know what they would do with it. I think they would ——

Sen. Blair: [Interposing.] It will not be very important to decide that until they come in.

The Witness: No, sir.

Q. You think the telegraph would be made a political machine? — A. I think that would be one of the dangers.

I would be perfectly willing, as far as I am concerned, to let the government try it — to sell them out our property and let them take it and try it; but it would be very unjust on the part of our government, if it should go into the telegraph business, to take away the property of its own citizens and make it valueless. Why, even Mexico would not do a thing like that. . . .

* See above, page 47.

Q. Have you an idea as to what the government ought to pay for that property? — A. I think it ought to pay what the property is worth; no more. I think the method of ascertaining the value that was provided in the act is a very just one — the method of appraisal.

Q. And I understand you to say that if the government cares to try the experiment of conducting the business of telegraphy in this country, you would be willing that it should take that property at such an appraisal? — A. Perfectly willing. At the same time, I think, as I said before, that it is contrary to the genius of our institutions. I think it would be better today if they would take the post office and have it run as an individual private institution.

Q. That is a subject in regard to which I should like to hear your views and reasons. — A. I think that, because individual enterprise can do things more economically and more efficiently than the government can. . . .

Q. Would you regard a corporate property like that of the Western Union, which is based upon a franchise to which the public are a party, as standing upon the same ground with reference to its right to create an increase of earning power that a piece of private property stands upon where there is no franchise obtained from the public? — A. I look upon corporate property in this way. I make a great difference between corporate property and private property. Corporate property is clothed with public rights and has duties to the public, and I regard those duties as paramount, really, to the rights of the stockholders. A corporation has first to perform its public obligations and the business that it was created to do; but when you have gone to that extent, then beyond that, I put it upon the same ground as private property. I judge of its value by its net earning power, the same as I judge of any private property; because I have faith in the government — I have faith in the republican institutions under which we live.

Q. Right upon that point, is one of those public rights of which you speak — the right to exercise the power of reducing, regulating, or controlling the charges which the corporation may make for the services which it renders to the public and for which the public pays. — A. They can regulate those charges within the limits of legislative direction. For instance, if the legislature should come in and fix a limit, that becomes the law of the corporation. The legislature can regulate the rates to be imposed. That is the great hold of the public upon corporations. If unreasonable rates are established or unreasonable regulations made by a corporation, the legislature can come in and control them, and its directions are paramount. For instance, if there was a great clamor that the Western Union Company was charging unreasonable rates, it would be perfectly fair for the legislature to come in and examine into that question, and if they found the rates or regulations unreasonable, to control them by legislative action. Their control is paramount to every other control. But that would be a very different thing from the government going into the business of telegraphing and destroying the property of her own citizens.

Q. I do not think that any Granger ever stated any more strongly than you do the right of the legislative power to control corporations or to regulate their charges to the public. — A. In the management of our corporations I have always sought to carry the people living along our roads with us, to let them see that we were building them up at the same time we were building up our properties; and we have succeeded very well in that. There is no clamor along our roads. . . .

Q. Do you think there would be any opposition made to a general national law regulating the fares and freight charges upon interstate commerce? — A. Well, I don't know about that. I think the freer you allow things to be the better. They regulate themselves. The laws of supply and demand, production and consumption, enter into and settle those matters. . . .

I know that some years ago, when I was connected with the Chicago and Northwestern road, the states of Wisconsin and some of the other states passed what were called the "Granger laws"; but they repealed them afterwards, because they found on practical investigation that that legislation was tending to frighten capital away from those states, and to retard their development. Finding that to be so, in order to bring back confidence they repealed the laws and left the roads free to work out their own success. The best evidence of the correctness of what I say about the effect of competition is to take the rates and see how they are coming down. Take the rates for a series of years and you will find a gradual reduction of the charges to the public. . . .

A corporation is only another name for the means which we have discovered of allowing a poor man to invest his income in a great enterprise. In other words, instead of one man owning any of these great properties in bulk, they are divided into small shares, so that the man who has got only $200 or $500 or $5,000, or whatever it may be, can own an interest in proportion to his capital. That is what a corporation means.

Q. Then, in your opinion, the natural operation of the laws of descent as they exist in this country is to guard the community against any danger from the perpetuation of associated corporate wealth, or of great individual fortunes in the future? — A. Yes, sir; I do not think there is any need to be afraid of capital; capital is scary. What you have got to fear is large, ignorant masses of population; I don't think the liberties of the people have anything to fear from capital. Capital is conservative and scary; but what you have to fear in a republican government like ours, where there is no military control, is large masses of uneducated, ignorant people.

Q. Do you think there is any danger to this country in that direction? — A. I think we are accumulating great masses of such people from abroad. Whether we have a system that will educate them up rapidly enough I do not know.

Q. If there was to be any legislation in any direction on this general question, don't you think that it might as well be in the direction of educating the people as in any other? — A. I think that is what we should do — educate the masses, elevate their moral standards. I think that is the only protection we can have for a long period in the future. When the people are educated and intelligent you have nothing to fear from them.

Q. Do you think that to do that would accomplish more for labor than anything else we could do? — A. Yes, sir; because education fits a man so that if he does not like one field of labor he can go to another. Business is constantly changing, and where there is an excess of one class of labor there is very likely to be a lack of another class, and if a man is properly educated he can turn his hand to a great many different things. . . .

Q. Do you think that the large employers of labor, the manufacturing corporations, the transportation companies, the telegraph companies, and so on, and also individuals who employ help in large masses and who necessarily classify their help, paying them different rates of wages, according to classes rather than according to their individual merits — do you think that they might profitably ingraft upon their business some system of assurance, or some method by which a portion of the earnings of the laborers should be contributed to a fund, and perhaps a proportion of the profit of capital also, to secure the working people against want in seasons of nonemployment, and against the disabilities resulting from accident, sickness, or old age? Could something of that kind be introduced which would be of benefit to the laboring people? — A. The trouble about that is that the drones would get control of the money and spend it, in nine cases out of ten. It is a good thing in theory, but I fear it would not work well in practice. . . .

Testimony of Joseph Medill *

The Witness: The chief cause of the impecunious condition of millions of the wage classes of this country is due to their own improvidence and misdirected efforts. Too many are trying to live without labor — that is, industrial or productive labor, and too many squander their earnings on intoxicating drinks, cigars, and amusements, who cannot afford it. While they continue to spend their surplus earnings on these things they

* See above, page 73.

will not get on in the world and will fail to accumulate property. The possession of property among the masses is really due more to saving than to earning; on small earnings a man may still save something, while no amount of earnings will improve his bank account without economy. The power of waste is vastly greater than the power of production. The wisest politician and the most original thinker on social subjects which this country has yet produced, laid it down as an axiom that "a penny saved is better than two pennies earned." It was the habit of saving which he inculcated as absolutely essential to success in life. I refer, of course, to Dr. Benjamin Franklin. It was to the working classes that he addressed his wise maxims, his suggestions, and advice. I have rarely known a steady, sober, industrious man, who saved his surplus earnings and prudently invested them but attained independence before old age.

And I have never known a workman, no matter what might be his wages, who freely indulged his appetite for liquor and nicotine, that ever made much headway. And that observation covers a good many thousand workmen with whom I have come in contact during my life — of all classes. This sort of people always remain poor and dissatisfied — complain of their "bad luck," denounce the tyranny of capital, and allege that they are cheated in the division of the profits produced by capital and labor.

Those who have closely investigated the subject estimate that the money spent by the wage classes of our cities and towns on intoxicating drinks exceeds $400,000,000 per annum. Of course, the total consumption of liquors is a great deal more, taking in the remainder of the population, which I do not include under this head; and to this enormous sum must be added at least $100,000,000 for cigars, and $100,000,000 for useless amusement, and gambling, making a total of $600,000,000 a year absolutely squandered by the discontented employee classes of this country. I have understated the waste of wages on those injurious indulgences in order to be safe in my estimate. The money thrown away on liquor by the wage-workers for the last ten years would have provided each family with a comfortable home free of rent, thereby emancipating all of them from servitude to landlords. If that squandered money has been loaned out at interest it would now amount to the enormous sum of $5,000,000,000 — at a moderate rate of interest, say 5 percent — multiplied into the last ten years. And if invested in railroad stocks and bonds during that period, it would have transferred the ownership of every mile of railway in the United States to the possession of the laboring classes who have wasted their wages in drink. Drink is the evil progenitor of most of the ills which the poor man encounters and is the cause of the "bad luck" which keeps him in poverty. I have used that term "bad luck" several times because it is a stereotyped phrase in every household that has a hard struggle in life.

The wage classes cannot support in idleness a quarter of a million saloon-keepers, and their bartenders and families, and pay the rent of their dram-shops, and at the same time hope to prosper themselves. No trade-union combinations, or Knights of Labor "strikes," to force up wages or shorten the hours of work will enable them to do it; and no relief that political legislation can give will essentially improve their condition in the absence of the virtues of temperance and economy, the cornerstones of prosperity and independence. . . .

It is a standard belief in trades-union lodges that the ills of labor would be relieved in great degree by shortening the day's work to six or eight hours, as it would cut down production per man 25 or 40 percent, thus creating a great demand for extra labor, which, in turn, would force up wages to a high point, say, twelve hours' pay for eight hours' work or fourteen hours' pay for six hours' work. And it is alleged and contended that nothing stands in the way of the adoption of this scheme of long pay for short work except the unfeeling selfishness of employing capitalists. In my opinion, this idea to get a "corner" on the labor market would prove delusive, and fail utterly, if tried; and for these reasons: increased wages for short work would instantly attract to this country countless multitudes of foreign workmen. They would rush hither as fast as fleets of steamers could bring them, and quickly swamp the demand for extra labor caused by short work. In a little while they would be soliciting employment at reduced wages, and offering to work for ten hours a day for probably half the pay that had at first been demanded for six hours' work, and this by reason of the oversupply of labor. But the panacea would fail to cure from the operation of another cause. It is an axiom that "dear labor makes dear goods." The effect of large wages and small work would be to greatly increase the cost of production and the price of manufactures in proportion to the enhancement of labor prices; the demand for such goods would necessarily decline, because the remainder of the community cannot afford to buy as large a quantity of artificially dear fabrics. Rents, too, would advance to the same degree that the cost of building houses increased, and the number of new structures would greatly decline, and that would cut off labor. Merchants would refuse to buy the excessively dear domestic goods produced under these circumstances, but would import what merchandise they needed, and if the trades unionists undertook to double up the tariff in order to prohibit importation, the great agricultural masses would sternly resist being thus fleeced for the benefit of any city class of producers. . . .

Sen. Blair: We are required to inquire into the relations between labor and capital, and we have construed that as implying that we should try to learn something of the personal feelings that exist between laborers, as a body, and the employing class, and have taken some testimony in that direction. Now, as you have observed it, what attitude or feeling do you think these two classes occupy with reference to each other? — A. Well, I suppose a feeling generally of distrust and disatisfaction. They are not amicable, as a general thing.

Q. Is that feeling that you refer to on the increase or decrease in this country? — A. I think it is on the increase steadily.

Q. Do you think it of a character sufficiently serious to occasion any alarm or require attention? — A. Well, it is a serious question. Yes, sir; it is a growing dissatisfaction. The trades unions of this country are feeling more and more dissatisfied with their position, and they are developing more of what might be called a communistic feeling — a tendency or desire to resort to what may be called revolutionary and chaotic methods of rectifying things. They are not satisfied with their division of the profits of business, and they look at the enormous and sudden acquirement of fortunes by a few speculators with feelings of dissatisfaction and anger. I think that expression is not too strong. . . .

Testimony of Norvin Green *

Sen. George: Has not the company substantially the power to dictate the wages of the employees? If not, why not? — A. Because all employment, all forms of labor, are governed by the laws of supply and demand. Our operators (who have for the most part learned their business in our office) have had time to learn a good many other things, and they are a very intelligent class of men. They are competent to do other kinds of business. We are constantly losing valuable operators, who find employment on railroads. I remember going south at one time and finding that the conductors on the New Orleans and Jackson Railroad, the ticket agents, and in fact all the staff of that grade had been taken from our lines — they had all been operators. They can find employment in other services for which they are quite competent, and, therefore, we have to pay them wages corresponding to what men of like capacity obtain in other employments, or else we could not keep them. As to a large class of our employees, however, I have no doubt that we could get them for less than we are paying. I refer to the female operators. There is a large number of female operators unemployed in the city today, and there is great pressure among them for places — 200 or 300 applicants.

Q. I think you misapprehend my question. I am asking simply as to

* See above, page 113.

the *power* of the company, not as to the fact of what it does. — A. I think I am answering that question. I have answered as to this latter class of our operators that I think the company has the power to reduce their salaries very materially, and could supply their places at cheaper rates; but as to the main staff of our operators, as to that largest of all classes, as appears by the table which I have presented, the class to whom we pay $80 a month, I think that if we tried to reduce their pay we should not be able to retain them, because that class of men can get employment in many other pursuits. . . .

Testimony of John Roach *

The Witness: The labor question I consider to be the foremost question of the time. What I may have to say about the business in which I am engaged, and the relations that exist between myself and the workingmen whom I employ will cover many classes of labor, because I employ some 3,000 men, in Chester and New York, and these men are engaged in some twenty-five different branches of mechanism. They work up materials of every kind that enter into a modern iron ship, from the ore in the mine and the timber in the forest into the forms necessary to produce the final result — the finished ship.

Being a workingman myself, and having occupied some forty-five years ago as humble a position as that of any man now in my employ, I can speak from experience on this subject. When I started out for myself I laid down a certain course of action based upon certain principles which seemed to me to be sound. I believed as a basis that *labor applied to natural resources was the foundation of all wealth.*

All our rich prairies, our boundless forests, our wealth-yielding mines, our vast coal beds, our great waterfalls — all these were here before the white man set his foot on the soil. For countless years they had remained in the undeveloped condition in which they were found; I need not say how small was the wealth of the country then. The Indian had all these natural advantages thrown open to him, yet was as though they did not exist. When he traded at all he was a free trader indeed. He would sell his valuable skins for a pouch of tobacco, a bottle of firewater, or a string of beads, giving dollars' worth for penny's worth, and he grew poor while the white trader grew rich.

The natural resources, the material of wealth, were all here. When did this country begin to accumulate wealth? When the white man began to apply labor to cultivate the soil, to fell the forests, to dig into

* See above, page 118.

the bowels of the earth, to make nature serve him — in a word, when he began to use the materials God had given him.

Taking this view of it, I held that the government is under one supreme obligation to its citizens. It has one duty of legislation in behalf of labor. That duty is to apply legislation practically and intelligently so that it shall aid labor in the development of the natural resources of the country. To do this, the legislators must find out what the natural resources are, what the needs of the people are, and how far it is within our control to satisfy these needs from our own resources. The condition of labor at home must be compared with the condition of labor abroad. The legislation applied must be such as will make the terms of competition equal, while favoring the elevation of labor. The end to be sought is a policy that will enable our people to develop the natural resources of our own land, to develop the natural talents of the workingmen, and to supply our own wants within ourselves. This legislation should not be in the interest of any one man, sect, or section of the country, but as broad as God's law, giving an equal chance to all. The road to heaven is open to all, and the road to this great wealth buried in the soil should be as free as that, by the system of legislation instituted. We do not want class legislation, nor laws to help the profligate at the expense of the proficient man. The question is then whether our legislators have studied these things; whether they have intelligently applied legislation to labor. Where they have not, labor remains almost dead; where they have, labor rises up and becomes successful. Now, it seems to me that with one exception legislation ought to cease with this. There is legislation free to all, but then the poor have got to be taken care of, the schoolhouses at all cost have to be kept open, and the poorest man wants such a system to exist that his child can receive as good an education as that of the man of means. . . .

I propose to give you my own experience, the experience of a man who probably employs more workmen, engaged in a greater variety of labor, than any other employer in the country. My payrolls this last year amounted to $1,587,000. For forty years of my life I have scarcely had a holiday. My business demands my whole attention. I am conversant with the employments and the work of all these men and with all their movements. Over fifty of them served their time in the same workshop with me. When I started in business four men of us walked together out of the Allaire Works with $400 capital, and began business. We made a little money in that business, but none of the other three men seemed to want the establishment to grow beyond that size where it gave employment to us four and a few assistants. That was the extent of the idea and of the ambition of those three men to make progress. When the first thousand dollars was saved they each drew out $250, and put the money into beginning to build a little house. They drew out, preferring not to risk anything in the business, and to work for me by the day. My own idea of the capacities of the business was different, and the result is that I have got some of those men in my employ at the present time. . . .

In the month of June last there were employed in my shipyard at Chester 1,540 men. The pay of those men, including apprentices and laborers, all told, amounted to about $2.19 a day, counting lost time and all. Now, as an evidence of what workingmen can do for themselves, I will give you some facts which cannot be contradicted. Among that number of men and boys, all told, employed in those shops, there are 287 owners of houses; that is, a house to every five persons including boys and all working in the establishments. . . . Now, I have carefully watched those men that owned houses, and other men that did not own houses, and still others who did not own houses, but who had their little savings laid by in a manner which I will explain to you hereafter. Some of the men have put their savings into houses, and others have invested them in other ways; and of course there are still others who receive the same pay, but who do not own houses or anything else, and never will. Those men do not work the regular hours; they are off drinking or at something else, and the probability is that in most cases there is not the same harmony and economy at home in the families of those men that there is among those who own their own houses. Now, to talk of trying to make all these different kinds of men equal by legislation is, it seems to me, about the most foolish thing that ever was thought of; there are so many elements that go to make up the differences between these several classes of men, in condition, character, and everything else. . . .

I went into my workshop one morning and I saw a quarter of a million dollars' worth of tools and machinery standing idle. There was no more productive power in them than there was in so many tombstones. The idea struck me most forcibly, "Where did all this wealth come from, and what are all these tools and machinery worth without labor?" I went out of the shop with my head down, and I looked around the corner of the street and I saw from 500 to 600 men sitting down. They might as well be the corpses buried under the tombstones, for they were not producing anything. There was the chasm — labor and capital at war, neither producing anything. It has been stated that I said labor must not antagonize capital. I say labor must not antagonize capital, and capital must not dare antagonize labor; each must have that right which belongs to it. I called a few of the leading men together. The issue was not wages; it was who had a right to rule; whether these men were to work for me ten hours or whether they were to work eight. I said, "I will adapt myself to suit your condition for an experiment." I found that the only way to get along with labor was to be kind and gentle and to discuss subjects without feeling or passion; discuss them with the idea that they might be right, and were certainly going to have fair play. "I shall, then, for an experiment, ring the bell for quitting work twice a day for the future. Go back to your work. I shall ring it at eight hours, so that you can quit at eight hours, and I shall ring it at ten hours, to give every man his choice who wishes to quit at the end of ten hours, but I shall pay by the hour. I shall give eight hours' pay to the eight-hour men and ten hours' pay to the ten-hour men." They would not accept that proposition; they must have the ten hours' pay for the eight hours' work. I explained to them, "You are only selling two hours of leisure time to increase the cost of your living 20 percent; you are only asking me to concede to you two hours more leisure time and adopt a policy that would make you pay 20 percent more for all your living." "How is that?" I took up a paper similar to that I showed you here, giving a statement of what was imported into this country — it was true fifteen years ago as it is now — and I pointed out to them the hundreds of millions of dollars' worth of foreign manufactured goods, such as I and other manufacturers were making, that were coming into this country at that time under the then existing law. "If," said I, "by your eight-hour law you add 20 percent more to the cost of the home production, how much more will come in? The very idea of that eight-hour law, unless our revenue laws were changed, would close every factory in the land. It could not be otherwise. It would add to the cost of the article, and if you institute this eight-hour system, you must call for another law that will give you protection against the increased cost of what you are producing. If the carpenter, the mason, the laborer, the painter, the plumber, and the gas-fitter who do the work upon your house only work eight hours and demand ten hours' pay, will not your rent increase?" "Yes." "Will not the cost of the clothing on your back increase?" "Yes." "While you are talking of the wonderful improvements made by machinery, take into consideration that the farmer's man has as much of a right of this law as you. Can such a law be made expressly for a minority of labor, or shall it be made for all labor? Then suppose you demand that the man who cultivates and works on a farm shall be reduced to the eight-hour system, simply because the mowing machine, the thrashing machine, and the reaping machine have done the work of lots of men, will not that increase the price of your food?" "Yes."

The question was left an open question with them, and after the matter was explained I had no more trouble of that kind, and have had none since. The men went to work and they preferred working ten hours, and the better class of them are very anxious to work twelve hours, if they can get twelve hours' pay for twelve hours' work. . . .

A great deal of the troubles that are complained of come from idleness and want of economy; and if you were to go among these men who make those complaints you speak of you would find out that there is one little extravagance and another little extravagance that ought not to exist. I will illustrate that by two boys, common shoeblacks, coming across on the ferryboat from Long Island. I met a little boy, a shoeblack. Of course he came up to seek employment. Said he, "Boss, a shine." I put out my foot and he laid down the traps that he had. He had a cigarette in his mouth smoking. While he was shining I asked him, "How old are you?" "Thirteen years of age." "Have you been to school?" "Yes, I was at school till I was twelve." I pulled out of my side pocket a large white envelope and pencil, and said I, "How far have you advanced in your education?" Said he, "I have learned to figure." "Well, I want to put some questions to you; answer the questions." The boy thought he was losing too much time on that one shine, and so I said, "I will pay you and make it as profitable as any work you have done for a long time. Now, how many cigarettes do you smoke in a day?" "I smoke four." "What do you give for each cigarette?" "One cent." "Multiply that by four and that is four cents. Now, how many days are there in a week?" "Seven." "And you smoke Sundays too?" "Yes." "Multiply that by seven and that is twenty-eight cents. Now, how many weeks are there in a month?" "There are four weeks in a month." "That is $1.12 cents. How much are all the clothes you have got on your back worth? You are the poorest dressed boy almost I ever saw." He said, "Not over a dollar," hanging his head. "Then you smoke out a whole suit of clothes every four weeks?" "Yes." "Now," said I, "I want to enter into a contract with you." This is not the way with all the shoeblacks; there are other clear-headed shoeblacks, but I said to this one, "I want to enter into a contract with you," and I put my hand into my pocket and I fortunately had a big round dollar. I gave him the dollar and said, "Now, this is the condition, that you will smoke no more cigarettes. If you do not keep your contract I will see if there is not a law to put you in jail." He grabbed the dollar and went. Next morning I came along and I will show you what he learned, as young as he was. Next morning when I came on the boat again I saw him. While I was at one end of the boat he was at the other, but he had a cigarette in his mouth. I went to him and took him by the shoulder and said "I am going to look for an officer to send you to jail; you have committed a crime; you entered into a contract which you have not kept." "Well," said he, "I had some left." "Then I will let you go if you will promise me you will not buy any more." He went off. Next day I caught him again, and then I was determined to frighten him. Said he, "I do not know what to say." "Well," said I, "give me my dollar." "I have not got it; it is gone." "What did you do with it? If you made good use of it I do not know that I shall be very hard on you." Said he, "I went down to the minstrels and took two other boys, and I spent fifty cents, and gave the other fifty cents to my mother." "Then," said I, "I will only inflict one-half the punishment on you. Give me half a dollar and I will let you go." Of course he went. I have come over on that boat every morning regularly, and I asked the man on the boat if the boy was there as he had been before generally as a shoe-black. He said he had been all the summer, but now he had deserted the boat and gone away and sought another boat rather than face me or give up the cigarette. If he only has the constitution to stand it he is going to be a wonderful complainer about legislation after awhile.

Then, crossing the Jersey City ferry a year ago, to go down to the shipyard where I go every week, I met a shoe-black there, an intelligent, bright-looking lad about sixteen years of age. He wanted a job to shine my boots. Of course I gave it to him, and he went to blacking them. While he was at work I asked, "How old are you?" Such an age. "You look better clothed than the most of shoe-blacks. Have you been to school?" "Yes." "Why do you follow this occupation?" "Because I can make more money out of this than I can out of anything else." "Why do you want this money?" "I have a poor mother and a little sister." "Well, how much do you make in a week?" "I average a dollar a day, and I cannot get a dollar a day at anything else, but I do not intend to stick to this all my life." "Now, tell me what your stock in trade is worth. This is a wonderfully profitable business, a dollar a day for a boy of your size. I want to see what capital you have invested in your stock." He sat down and put down his box, and gave me the price he paid for the box, and the price that he paid for his brush, and the price that he paid for blacking. I asked him then how many shines he made out of one box. He told me, and it showed the sharpness with which that boy watched the business he was engaged in. I am going to watch him. I am going to see him occupy a different position during life. . . .

Here were two boys in the same business in life. One was able to tell a lie and gave up the boat he was working on and went off somewhere else to avoid facing me. The other made a careful investigation of facts, studied out what he was making, knew all about the business he was in. Will you tell me that without any advantage on earth, with only a fair chance, that one boy will not get along, and will you tell me whether, with all the advantages you can pile up, this other boy is not going to be found in the very reverse condition, and at some future time be found calling for legislation and demanding a fair division of the profits? . . .

Testimony of Francis A. Walker

Francis A. Walker was one of the most influential economists of the Gilded Age. He was best known for his work as Superintendent of the 1870 and 1880 censuses, and greatly improved and expanded the work of the Bureau of the Census. From 1873 to 1881 he was professor of political economy at Yale. At the time of his testimony before the committee, he was president of the Massachusetts Institute of Technology. Although his testimony suggests his essentially conservative position, he was actually a moderate by the standards of the day, For example, he believed that wages were related to productivity and he favored reducing the hours of labor. In other words, while he was an advocate of free competition, he was nonetheless aware that complete laissez faire *was a practical impossibility in an industrial society.*

The Witness: I believe that all the governmental action which it is desirable to take in the interest of labor is comprised within two heads: Factory acts and sanitary regulations; and governmental action in both those directions, in my judgment, can, under our form of government in the United States, be better done by the legislature or government of each state for itself than by the government of the United States acting one for all.

I say all the government *action*, for I heartily believe in the government of the United States obtaining and diffusing information in regard to the condition of labor, and in regard, generally, to the industries and the trade of the country to the very largest possible degree. I believe in that, rather, because I think the diffusion of information is the best means of reducing to a minimum governmental action. I believe in general that that government is best which governs least, and that interference with trade or manufactures is very undesirable. Yet I recognize the fact that evils may and do exist which require correction by the force of law. I think government will reduce its function to the desired minimum best by diffusing information and spreading light, rather than by interfering positively by commands and prohibitions. Therefore I believe in governmental collection and diffusion of information in the highest degree, mainly because in that way I believe government may reduce to the lowest terms its own active interference with trade and industry.

I believe, as I have said, that the action necessary to be taken in regard to the interests of labor, namely, factory acts, in the usual acceptation of that term, and sanitary regulations in the usual interpretation of that term . . . can be best taken by the governments of the several states, each for itself.

My reasons for holding that opinion are two. The first reason is common to a large class of governmental measures, which base, or should base themselves upon sociological principles, in which class I should include the pauper system of any community, the educational system, treatment of the insane, of the deaf, dumb, and blind, and of prisoners, as well as the factory acts and sanitary regulations of which I speak. All those have this in common, that they should be based upon the results of experience or direct experiment bearing upon the best system to be adopted in one or the other class of public exigencies.

The ground of my belief in thinking that in those cases it is better that each state for itself should determine its policy is, that social science, or sociology, is at present in a very primitive condition. It has made very little progress, and much of the progress which we seem to have made at times we find has not been made. We are not yet advanced in the science of society, especially as concerns the matters I have mentioned — the care of paupers, the deaf, the dumb, the blind, the insane, the idiots, and the criminals, and although we have made some progress in regard to elementary or popular education, we have yet much to learn.

In this matter of factory acts and sanitary regulations, we have still very much to do, and for that purpose our state-rights system is admirably disposed to the development of sociological principles. We have here a great number of states, many of them having populations closely like each other in their character and experience, others very widely unlike. We have these states, each for itself, trying experiments now. That has been so in regard to public elementary education; that is, the system of one state differs more or less from that of every other. Each state is trying a system of poor relief for itself; each is dealing with convicted criminals on a more or less individual system. Those experiments are going on side by side, and as the result of those experiments we shall in time undoubtedly reach a rather positive conclusion that one system is better than others, or than all. . . .

My second reason . . . is found in this consideration (to take one of those classes by itself). Factory acts are only needful and not positively harmful in societies which have reached a certain stage of development. For example, in regard to the employment of women and children and the operations of machinery, if such a body of legislation were to be imposed upon a community where manufacturing industry was just making its beginning it not only would do very much less good but infinitely more harm than by being imposed upon a community like Massachusetts or Rhode Island. As to the lack of reason for such regulations being uniform over a country like the United States, if a factory were being set up in a county in Iowa containing a population almost exclusively agricultural of, say, 20,000 people, a factory population of 200 would not require protection by law to anything like the extent that a factory population here in the East would require it, because there there could be recourse to the land; and if the conditions became unfavorable the farming population could absorb the others, who could go on the land. If the factory operatives were ground down by their employers they would resort to the land. . . .

Sen. Pugh: Have you given any thought to the subject of the power or agency of the federal or state governments over the question of wages for skilled labor employed in those manufacturing industries over the mere question of the amount, more or less, of pay? What power or agency can be exercised by the federal government or by the state governments upon that subject? If there is any, what is it — taxational, educational or otherwise? — A. . . . The state must enforce all contracts for labor as well as other things, therefore it is proper for the state to require that the contract shall be such as to be capable of enforcement. A contract for the payment of wages in kind is not capable of enforcement, as for the payment of wages "in flour," for one kind of flour is worth one sum and another kind of flour another sum. It is perfectly right, therefore, that the state should prescribe that labor shall be paid for in money. . . .

Q. Is there anything else that you think would be of value to suggest upon those questions? — A. I think the government of the United States may do a great deal of good, as, in my judgment, it has in the past done a great deal of harm, to the working classes of the country, by maintaining a sound currency. There is no evil against which it is so hopeless for the workmen to fight as bad money. . . .

7   CRITICS AND REFORMERS

Testimony of John S. McClelland *

The Witness: The whole system of production at the present time is based, not upon the wants of the people, but upon the avarice and greed of those who are engaged in the administration of the industries that produce. The productive capacity of the country is much greater than its consuming capacity, and as a consequence the working people, by the aid of labor-saving machinery in the hands of capitalists, are enabled to produce this enormous quantity of products in a very short time, and are then to a great extent forced to be idle during a large part of each year while the surplus products are being consumed. While the capitalist is receiving the benefit of that surplus production the laborer remains in enforced idleness, and he has only received wages for the three or four months that it was necessary for him to work in order to produce enough to last the employer and supply the market the whole year through.

Sen. Blair: I agree that labor does not gets its just share and that it ought to have more; but we live in a practical world, and are subject to an existing order of things which is based upon conditions which we cannot change, at least not radically or essentially. We cannot change the nature of the human animal very much, certainly not without the lapse of very great periods of time. Now, is there anything which you can suggest, short of a radical and distant revolution in the nature of society, which will give us some practical remedy — anything which will improve things *now*, while you and I are alive, or within some reasonable period that our posterity can look forward to, without changing the system of individual ownership of property? — A. You say that no change in this existing order of things can be made. Now ——

Q. [Interposing.] No, I say the existing order may be modified or improved, but I understand that you propose an entirely different system, by which the government shall take charge of the administration of all business. You do not say so distinctly, but the logical outcome of your premises is that the government shall become the entire people, transacting all public and all private business. That is the result of your theory practically carried out. Now it seems to me very difficult to go far in that direction with any practical benefit, at least at present. — A. Not at all, sir. My idea is that, taking the telegraph system as a starting point, the government might make a start there, and from that the

* See above, page 18.

146

plan could be extended. If the government should say to the telegrapher's organization as it is at present constituted, embracing all the talent and skill necessary to conduct a system of telegraphing from the highest to the lowest branches of it — if the government should say to this body of men (first incorporating them into a legalized organization), "We will advance you sufficient capital to enable you to start at once in the telegraph business"; that is, "We will take your labor and skill, which we know you possess, as sufficient security — as sufficient basis for credit, and we will advance you the necessary capital to carry on the business," it seems to me that would be entirely practicable. Because it is upon the labor of the employees of capital that the capitalist obtains his credit now, and why should not the same system be extended by the government to such an organization of workingmen?

Q. I do not mean to combat your idea of the government taking charge of that industry, which, from its peculiar nature, seems to be capable of being conducted in that way; but ——

The Witness: [Interrupting.] Well, I was going on to say that a starting point could be made there, and from that the system could be extended to other kinds of business.

Q. You think, then, I suppose, that ultimately the government could do all the farming in the country, for example? — A. The government would not be doing any of the work. These organizations of different industries would be the recognized contractors for the performance of their several kinds of work. They would then carry on the different branches of trade only to the extent that was found necessary.

Q. And all the profits of each avocation would be distributed, I suppose, among those engaged in it? — A. Certainly.

Q. Well, even in that view, might there not come to be oppression of one avocation by another, because all the while it is the individual consumer who makes the market for everything produced, and might not one avocation prey upon another under such a system, as one competing power now does upon another? — A. The reason why these corporations prey upon one another now is explained by the motive that prompts them in this business. That motive would be done away with. . . .

Sen. George: Are you familiar with the sentiments of the laborers generally connected with the labor organizations? — A. Yes, sir.

Q. What is their feeling generally towards capital? — A. There is a generally unfriendly feeling, brought about by the conditions which have been enforced upon them by capital. They are beginning to think more and more that they are entitled to a larger share, a fair share, of the fruits of their own labor.

Q. And that it is unjustly withheld from them by capital? — A. Undoubtedly.

Q. That, you say, seems to be the general opinion of labor in this country? — A. As far as I understand it.

_Q_. Is there any unfriendliness on the part of the laborers to the existence of capital as capital? — A. Nothing more than is brought about by the education, as I may call it, of the laboring classes, in the course of which they are led to see that capital as at present organized is absolutely unnecessary.

_Q_. Do the laborers generally recognize the necessity of capital in production? — A. They do. They have not any antagonism to legitimate capital itself, but they have an antagonism to the system which gives capital the power it has now and to the uses made of it.

_Q_. There is no general desire, then, among the laborers of the country to destroy capital? — A. Only through cooperative effort on the part of themselves to become, in turn, what may be called small capitalists; that is, to engage in cooperative industry and do away with the necessity of capital as it exists at present. . . .

_Q_. Is there any general disposition among the laboring people of the country to divide out by law capital as now accumulated? — A. Do you mean to parcel it out among themselves?

_Q_. Yes. — A. Not that I know of.

_Q_. Then there is no feeling among them, so far as you know, which would prevent the protection by law of the property which any man may hold now as his own? — A. I will say this, that there is a considerable undercurrent among the laboring classes of this country, which would require only a certain amount of agitation to set it into practical operation, and there is no telling to what extremes it might go if it was only started. I believe myself, and have believed all along, that the political structure of this country is resting on a sand heap, owing to the degradation of labor. . . .

_Q_. What is the general feeling of the laborers of the country, the wage laborers, toward their employers? What is the relation between laborers and their employers generally? — A. Generally that between slaves and their masters. The different departments of industry have so developed by the introduction of machinery that capital has been to a large extent centralized, and large numbers of men are employed in one institution in nearly every industry, and as a consequence of this, labor has become more and more degraded. We find in many of those large institutions that the men are looked upon as nothing more than parts of the machinery that they work. They are labeled and tagged, as the parts of a machine would be, and are only taken into account as a part of the machinery used for the profit of the manufacturer or employer.

_Q_. There is not, then, in your opinion, a feeling of confidence, harmony, and goodwill existing between the employers and the employed in this country? — A. Certainly not.

_Q_. On the contrary, in your judgment, and from your observation, the fact is directly the reverse, a feeling of suspicion and antagonism? — A.

Directly the reverse. The working people feel that they are under a system of forced slavery. . . .

Q. What intercourse is there between the average employee and the employer? — A. I don't know that there is any at all. The business is conducted generally between the employer and his employees through foremen or superintendents, and the employee is very seldom, if ever, brought in contact with his employer. In a great many cases he does not even know his employer when he sees him.

Q. Well, what is the nature of the intercourse between the superintendent and the employees generally? — A. Generally the superintendent is overbearing — orders on one side and submission on the other. . . .

Testimony of Thomas B. McGuire

Thomas B. McGuire was an example of a man who had come down in the world. Originally a small businessman, he was at the time he testified before the committee a truck driver.

The Witness: I have been in the express business about five years. I embarked something like $300 in the business, thinking that I might become something of a capitalist eventually, but I found competition so great that it was impossible for me to do so; I found that the railroad companies had their regular wagons and their collectors on the trains previous to their reaching the city asking for the privilege of carrying the people's baggage, and by that means they were enabled to get any business of that kind that was to be had. I found also that another company had taken the furniture moving into their hands. A case in point: A gentleman in New Street asked me one time what I would charge him to bring two truckloads from a certain station in Jersey. I told him $75. It was 23 miles out there; the truck was a four-horse truck, and I was to handle everything. He went to the Metropolitan Van Company and had the work done for $60. Now, my profit on that job at the price I asked, had I received the work, would have been somewhere in the neighborhood of $20; but that company did the work with better appliances than I could have furnished and made a great deal more money than I could have made out of it. A man in the express business today owning one or two horses and a wagon cannot even eke out an existence from the business. The competition is too great; that is, the competition from these monopolies. For instance, the Adams Express Company and all those other express companies do local express work also, and by that means they prevent people who go into the business in New York City from ever getting any higher up than barely existing — not living but barely existing. That is my experience. I found that when I lost a horse I was not able to replace him; that is, I could not accumulate enough out of my earnings to do so. I found, moreover, that I was not able to buy feed for my horses even at low prices. Some two years ago I paid $2.10 for eighty pounds of oats, while these corporations could buy the same quantity for $1.60 or $1.80; I paid from $2.50 to $3.00 a set for horseshoeing, while they had theirs done by contract at a price which would not amount to $1.25 or $1.50 for each horse. So that everything is against a man going into the express business in a small way. . . .

Sen. Call: What capital would be required to begin an express business here with a reasonable prospect of success? — A. Ten thousand dollars would give a man a fair opportunity to compete with these large companies, I think.

Q. How was it fifteen or twenty years ago in regard to that? — A. This competition did not exist at that time. Then a man embarking $300 in the business had an excellent chance of becoming a successful expressman and accumulating some money and probably some property.

Q. How is it as to trucking in that respect? — A. Men who embarked in trucking twenty years ago have become wealthy, to my own knowledge, have become the owners of houses and other property, and are doing a vast business, some of them having from fifteen to twenty trucks. They have got employment from different large drygoods dealers, importers, and others, and they have got into the good graces of some of our custom-house officers and got the run of the public stores. . . .

Q. What capital would now be required to begin that business with a fair prospect of success? — A. At the present time, to be able to go into that business with any chance of success, you would have to be somewhat of a ward politician. If you were that, probably with $25,000 you might be able to compete with these other people with a fair chance of success. . . .

Q. Now, supposing you wanted to borrow that money to start your trucking business, how would the case stand? Don't you suppose there are some cases of that kind where deserving men borrow money from the banks and use it to advantage in establishing a business, trucking or any other legitimate business, and don't you think that some of those poor men who have borrowed money in that way have made it efficacious in business and have benefited themselves and the community by it? I am no advocate of the banks, but let us see whether it always happens that the use of this money inures to the oppression of the people —— A. [Interrupting.] It is not the money; it is the system under which it is loaned ——

Q. [Interposing.] Let me ask you this question —— A. [Interrupting.] I will answer two or three at once if you let me. You asked me a question about a bank lending money to a truckman.

Sen. George: Did you ever know of a bank lending money to a truckman? — A. I was going to mention that, but I was going to put my answer in another way to make it lucid. The banks never lend money to the truckmen or anybody else without collateral, and I never had very much of that. But when this money is loaned, it must be loaned at a rate of interest. Now, when there is only $13 per capita for each individual in the United States, and the interest foots up $20 per capita, where are they going to get the other $7? There is the injustice. The moment the money is loaned, that recognizes the fact that there is a debt, and the moment that debt is there, the man is no longer producing for himself but for the other man, the one who lends the money.

Sen. Call: I understand that theory very well, but —— A. [Interrupting.] It is not a theory, it is a bare fact. That is how the banks are favored by this class legislation, and while they have their representatives in Congress to make laws for us, and while our Senators get so well paid at the rate of $8,000 a year ——

Q. [Interposing.] Are you certain that a Senator gets $8,000 a year? — A. I beg pardon. I take that back. I don't know how much they get, but I know it is said that they are bought up very often.

Q. Are you quite sure that you are giving correct testimony? — A. I think I have read in a book called the *Star Almanac* (I am very fond of reading), that a Senator's salary is in the neighborhood of $8,000 a year. If I am mistaken about that it is an error of the head and not of the heart.

Q. Why not have a little more charity? — A. I have given over having any charity for politicians. I saw them today in one of our civil courts dispossessing a poor woman, and the man who did it ——

Q. [Interposing.] You don't condemn us for that, I hope? — A. No; but is it not part of the system of government under which we are living?

Q. Well, we are not responsible for that. We do not make the government. — A. No; but you are a part of it.

Q. What have you to suggest to us by way of a remedy for these evils? — A. Well, I would have you to look into all these things in place of spending your time making magnificent speeches. For instance, I live in a tenement house, three stories up, where the water comes in through the roof, and I cannot better myself. My little children will have to go to work before they are able to work. Why? Simply because this present system under which we are living is all for self, all for the privileged classes, nothing for the man who produces all the wealth.

Q. Let us see about that. You arraign me here as one of the representatives of this corrupt and oppressive system. Now, I have taken my two hands and gone out into the woods and built a house for myself to live in, and I have seen the rain come through and fall on my people, and I have gone into the fields day after day and worked with my own hands to make something to eat for myself and my family. Now it would be the height of folly for me on that account to utter a tirade against you because you had happened to get $10,000 in some way and I had not. There are two sides to this question. You talk about the "politicians" without knowing whether we are politicians or not. You have no knowledge whether I have sought political life or not. However, without indulging in any recriminations (for false accusations never do any good), let us see how the evils that do exist can be remedied. You say that you would have us to look into the social condition of the people. That is all very well; but what power have we to change existing conditions? We are sworn legislators under a constitutional form of government, sworn to exercise no powers but those which that Constitution gives us. You arraign us here because of the case of some poor woman who has been turned out, you say, by some politician in this city. Now, what power have we to prevent that under our form of government? — A. You have got the power to see that every man gets what the Constitution guarantees to him — an opportunity to enjoy life, liberty, and the pursuit of happiness.

Q. Do you understand it to be a fact that we have that power? — A. Yes; the Constitution reads that way.

Q. Is that all there is in the Constitution? — A. That is about as far as I want to go.

Sen. Blair: That is in the Declaration of Independence, is it not? — A. Well, have it the Declaration. When I was thirteen years old I was in the Army of the United States, so I have had but little opportunity for education or study. I merely give you that point because I generally hear it on election day from the gentlemen who say they are "glad to see the horny-handed sons of toil gathering around the banner" under which they vote, and all that sort of thing.

Sen. Call: Why do not "the horny-handed sons of toil" send men of their own choosing to make laws for them? — A. Simply because the entire political system from top to bottom is a system of bribery and corruption.

Q. Then you distrust popular government? — A. I do under the present arrangement. The moment an alderman is elected, some railroad corporation will write to him, saying, "Mr. Reilley, we are glad to see that you have been elected alderman; call upon us immediately, and we will see that you have two or three conductors appointed upon our line."

Q. Are not those very often taken from among the sons of toil? — A. Yes, sir; but the matter is entirely arranged by the idlers who never do any labor. A man who works for his living has to work too long and too hard to be able to find time and opportunity to educate himself in "politics."

Q. You seem to be pretty well educated? — A. Oh, no; I have listened to the politicians somewhat, and being of rather an inquiring turn of mind, I have followed them up a little closer than some of the others do. I heard what they said to the people about election times, and then I tried to see if it would work in practice, but I found it wouldn't.

Q. Don't you think anybody else in the country has done that besides you? — A. Oh, undoubtedly. I am only a drop in the bucket.

Q. Then, how is it that, with so many people looking out for their interests, the workingmen do not get better representative men to make laws for them? — A. Simply because the system of bribery is so complete that it is impossible, and if anybody believes in independent political action and tries to carry it out, he will have the papers of the city of New York hounding him as a "socialist" or a "communist." Whenever a man undertakes to advocate the cause of the working people, the papers come out and denounce what he says as the "ravings of a demagogue," and so on, and for that reason our poor unfortunate, untutored, workingmen are deceived, and are simple enough to believe in the party who promise them that they will do away with the system of convict labor and make the reforms for them.

Q. Do you think you are giving a proper description of the workingmen of this country? — A. I know I am giving a proper description of the workingmen of New York.

Q. What do you call a workingman? — A. Every man that works for a living, every man who produces anything useful.

Q. Well, do you think that you could not find a representative among the workingmen here who could not be bought to betray their interests? — A. Under the present system of politics here, where the appointing power is in individual heads, those parties will always use their power to provide for their own reelection if possible. . . .

Sen. Blair: I don't care to listen to accusations of this kind much longer. This witness evidently looks upon the legislative bodies of this country as made up of a set of rascals, and he cannot expect anything from a committee which is a part of such a body.

The Witness: I did not think that Senator Blair would take the matter that way.

Sen. Blair: No, you don't understand me. I feel like this, my friend, that on an average we human beings are all very much alike. I have never known a single instance of bribery in the House of Representatives or in the Senate of the United States; never a single instance of the kind, and I have been there eight years; and I don't believe that either of the other Senators here present have ever known of an instance. There is a very general and widespread misconception as to the personal character of the legislators of this country. I don't believe that, man for man, the church in the United States, or any other organization in the United

States, averages any better in the matter of personal moral character than do the members of Congress, and you labor under a very serious mistake, and approach the subject from a wrong direction when you come to it with the idea that anybody is here or anybody is there to deal with these great public questions dishonestly. I speak now of the members of Congress generally, and I say that the great majority in either party is composed of honest men. These problems of life are very serious, and I can see how a man in your position, having capacity and ability which, with proper opportunity, would enable you to fill any situation in the country — I can see how you, crowded by circumstances, may come to feel and think as you do, and what I say to you now I do not say reprovingly at all — God knows I do not. But, my friend, you are wrong in your estimate of men. The majority of men are honest men throughout the length and breadth of the world. I do not care to believe in the doctrine of total depravity, for that includes myself, and I don't choose to hold or to admit that I am only fit to be an exemplification hereafter of eternal punishment by fire. I don't believe that men are totally depraved. I believe that men on the whole are good, and that you can safely appeal to their better nature.

The Witness: I did not bring out this discussion myself. It was brought out by the questions of a member of the committee.

Sen. Blair: That is all true. I am not finding fault with you; I am only speaking of the evident condition of your mind on this subject, and I do wish, if I can, to disabuse you and others who feel and think as you do because life has been hard with them, of the idea that knaves are the rule rather than honest men. It is not so, and you are entirely mistaken and very unjust if you think that the legislators of this country, as a class, are the knaves that you represent them to be.

The Witness: Well, if you lived in New York as long as I have lived here, and had lived in the neighborhoods that I have lived in, and if you had looked around you and seen the practices that are going on there among the poorer classes; if you had seen them having to vote themselves slaves every year, I believe you would think as I do. They are trades unionists eleven months in the year and the other month they are worked up by political heat and they go and vote right against their convictions. If you saw these things and if you saw those people send their wives out to scrub other people's floors, and their little children to work as cash-boys and cash-girls in other people's stores, you would have just the same sentiments that I have.

Sen. Blair: I have seen some of the things you speak of, and I believe it is because you have seen so much of them that you feel and think as you do, but you are, nevertheless, in error as to the facts.

Testimony of Conrad Carl *

The Witness: There is another thing which I think very deeply interests the workingmen — taxes. The taxation system is unjust in the United States. It is only indirect taxes, which fall back upon the workingmen. The workingman has to pay taxes in rent, and in provisions, and so on. He is the last one that they can fall back upon, and they get the taxes out of him. It is only the workingman that is the taxpayer, in my opinion, in the United States.

Sen. Blair: You think labor is the packhorse that carries all the burden? — A. Yes. If anybody is to help that, legislation must do it. Who shall do it? Shall the workingmen make a revolution or a rebellion? The workingman is the peacefulest man in the world when he can have his living, but if he goes on strike the whole world cries out that they are a dangerous class; but the workingmen are glad when they can be home by their wives and children making a living. I have my arguments here against indirect taxes, and I will read them: "So long as legislation is unjust to the poor, to tax the poor who have nothing but their daily earnings, to tax them by indirect taxes, there is no way to better the condition of the workingmen. The foundation of all society is based upon injustice, to make the rich richer and the poor poorer. The rich receive donations from the state by legislation; from the laboring men will be taken the last cent, by high rents and high-priced provisions. No wonder the rich become proud and brutal and say, 'Damn the public.' The indirect taxes are a fraud and a crime against the workingmen, and society will have its punishment sooner or later for it. Such legislation creates dangerous men. The millionaire corrupts the courts and legislation. He does not care for the law nor the Constitution. He has neither a duty nor a love for the country; he is proud for himself; a state in the state opposed to the state. The dangerous classes are not to be found in the tenement houses and filthy districts, but in mansions and villas. To make rich people as we have today, means to make them superior to their fellow citizens; to give them power to dictate to their fellow citizens their own will. They deprive the laboring men of their right to protect themselves. When there lies so great a wrong on the bottom of society as to tax the laboring man by indirect taxes, there grows wrong after wrong, and it will grow as high as Babylon's tower if we do not go against it in time." . . .

* See above, page 20.

155

Testimony of Henry George *

Sen. Call: You have been engaged for some years, I believe, in looking into the labor question, the condition of the laboring population, and the relations of labor and capital, have you not? — A. For some time, with a great deal of attention.

Q. We should be glad to have a statement from you in your own way of any facts that may be within your knowledge in regard to the condition of labor in its relations to capital, and any suggestions of remedies which you think would bring about an improved condition of things. — A. As for specific facts I presume you could get them with much more advantage from other persons, from those who are familiar with each locality and the particular facts relating to it. The general fact, however, is that there exists among the laboring classes of the United States a great and growing feeling of dissatisfaction and discontent. As to whether the condition of the laboring classes in the United States is getting any worse, that is a difficult and complex question. I am inclined to think that it is; but whether it is or not, the feeling of dissatisfaction is evidently increasing. It is certainly becoming more and more difficult for a man in any particular occupation to become his own employer. The tendency of business of all kinds, both in production and in exchange, is concentration, to the massing of large capital, and to the massing of men. The inventions and improvements of all kinds that have done so much to change all the aspects of production, and which are still going on, tend to require a greater and greater division of labor, the employment of more and more capital, and to make it more and more difficult for a man who has nothing but his labor to become his own employer, or to rise to a position of independence in his craft or occupation.

Q. Can you state any economic reasons why that is the case? — A. I do not believe that there is any conflict of interest between labor and capital, using those terms in their large sense. I believe the conflict is really between labor and monopoly. Capital is the instrument and tool of labor, and under conditions of freedom there would be as much competition for the employment of capital as for the employment of labor. When men speak of the aggressions of capital and of the conflict between labor and capital I think they generally have in mind *aggregated* capital, and aggregated capital which is in some way or other a monopoly more or less close. The earnings of capital, purely as capital, are always measured by the rate of interest. The return to capital for its

* See above, page 41.

employment, risk being as nearly as possible eliminated, is interest, and interest has certainly, for some time past, been falling, until now it is lower than it ever has been in this country before. The large businesses which yield great returns have in them always, I think, some element of monopoly.

Do you wish me to go right on and give my views generally, or do you desire me to limit myself to answers to your questions?

Q. I wish you would first give us the economic reasons why there are such aggregations of capital. I would like also to have you explain the sense in which you use the term "monopoly" when you speak of these aggregations of capital. — A. I use the term "monopoly" in the sense of a peculiar privilege or power of doing certain things which other persons have not. There are various kinds of monopolies. As, for instance, the monopolies given by the patent laws which give to the inventor or to his assigns the exclusive right to use a particular invention or process. There are certain businesses that are in their nature monopolies. For instance, in a little village if one puts up a hotel which is sufficient to accommodate all the travel there, he will have a virtual monopoly of that business, for the reason that no one else will put up another to compete with him, knowing that it would result in the loss of money; and for that reason our common law recognizes a peculiar obligation on the part of the inn-keeper; he is not allowed to discriminate as between those who come to him for lodging or food. Again, a railroad is in its nature a monopoly. Where one line of road can do the business, no one else is going to build another alongside of it, and, as we see in our railroad system, the competition of railroad companies is only between what they call "competing points" where two or three roads come together, and as to these the tendency is to do away with competition by contract or pooling. The telegraph business is in its nature a monopoly; and so with various others. Then again, there is a certain power of monopoly that comes with the aggregation of large capital in a business. A man who controls a very large amount of capital can succeed by underselling and by other methods, in driving out his smaller competitors and very often in concentrating the business in his own hands.

Q. You see the term in a broader sense then, than that of a monopoly created by law. You include in it any exclusive right, whether created by facts and circumstances or by law? — A. Yes. As I have said, there are businesses which are in their very nature monopolies. The two most striking examples of that are the railroad and the telegraph.

Q. In your opinion, what are the economic reasons why business tends to become concentrated and why all industries have a tendency to aggregation in the hands of a few? — A. I think that is the universal tendency of all progress. It is because larger and larger capitals are required and because labor becomes more and more divided. For instance, when boots and shoes are made by hand the only capital required is a lap-stone and a little kit of tools, and any man who has learned the trade and can get a piece of leather can sit down and make a pair of shoes. He can do it in his own house and can finish his product there and sell it. But when a machine is invented to be used in that business, the shoemaker requires capital enough to purchase that machine, and, as more and more machines are invented, more and more capital is needed, while the skill required becomes less and less. I believe you have it in testimony here that in the process of shoemaking now there are sixty-four different branches, thereby requiring that number of costly machines and differentiating the trade into that number of subdivisions. . . .

Machinery, in my opinion, ought to be an advantage to labor. Its primary effect is simply to increase the product of labor, to add to the power of labor, and enable it to produce more. One would suppose, and in fact it was supposed at the beginning of the era of modern inventions, that the effect of the introduction of machinery would be to very greatly improve the condition of the laboring classes and largely to raise wages. I think it quite certain that its effect has not been that; that, while very many articles have been greatly cheapened in cost and in price, wherever there has been an increase in the wages of labor it can be traced to something else; generally to the efforts of the laborers themselves, by the formation of trades unions and organizations which have wrested from their employers a higher rate of wages, or to improvements in government, or improvements in intelligence, or improvement in morals. I think that whoever will thoroughly examine the facts will come to the conclusion that John Stuart Mill is right when he says that "all the labor-saving machinery that has hitherto been invented has not lessened the toil of a single human being." While, on the other hand, by permitting and requiring this great subdivision of labor and dispensing to a great extent with skill on the part of the laborer, it has reduced him to a far more dependent condition than that which he occupied before. That is illustrated by the case we were speaking of awhile ago. The old-fashioned shoemaker, having learned his trade and purchased his kit of tools, was his own master. If he did not find work in one place he could find it in another place. He had the means of earning a livelihood wherever he could find people who wanted shoes. But now the shoemaker must find a great factory, and an employer with a large amount of capital. Without such an employer he is utterly helpless: he cannot make a shoe; he can only make one-tenth or one sixty-fourth part of a shoe, or whatever the proportion may be. It is the same way with all other trades into which machinery has largely entered. The effect of the introduction of machinery in any trade is to dispense with skill and to make the laborer more helpless. I think you all understand that effect of machinery.

Q. Your idea is that the introduction of machinery in the trades tends to prevent a man from mastering the whole of his trade — that he learns a part of the trade instead of the whole trade? — A. Yes. That in itself might not be a disadvantage; but it is a disadvantage under present conditions; those conditions being that the laborers are driven by competition with each other to seek employment on any terms. They must find it; they cannot wait. Ultimately, I believe the whole trouble to come from the fact that the natural field of employment, the primary source of wealth, the land, has been monopolized and labor is shut off from it. Wages in all occupations have a certain relation to each other; fixed by various circumstances, such as the desirability of the employment; the continuity of the work; the ease or difficulty of learning it; the scarcity of the peculiar powers required, and so on; but in a large sense they must all depend upon the wages in the widest occupation. That occupation in this country is agriculture, and everywhere throughout the world the largest occupations are those which concern themselves directly and primarily with the soil. Where there is free access to the soil, wages in any employment cannot sink lower than that which, upon an average, a man can make by applying himself to the soil — to those natural opportunities of labor which it affords. When the soil is monopolized and free access to it ceases, then wages may be driven to the lowest point on which the laborer can live. The fact that in new countries wages, generally speaking, are higher than they are in old countries, is simply because in those new countries, as we call them, the soil has not yet passed fully into private hands. As access to the land is closed, the competition between laborers for employment from a master becomes more intense, and wages are steadily forced down to the lowest amount on which the laborer can live.

In a state of freedom the introduction of machinery could but add to wages. It would increase the productive power of labor, and the competition with each other of those having such machinery and desiring to employ labor would suffice to give the laborer his full share of the improvement. Where natural opportunities are closed up, however, the advantages resulting from the use of machinery, minus that part retained by monopolies arising from its use, must ultimately go to the owners of land, either in higher rents or higher prices. You can see that very readily if you consider a community in which one person or a small number of persons had full possession of the land. In such a case no one could work upon the land or live upon it save upon their terms. Those who had no land, having no means of employment, would have to compete with each other for the privilege of working for those who had the land, and wages would, of course, steadily sink to the point at which a man could barely live. Now, if you imagine a labor-saving invention introduced there, no matter how much it might add to the productiveness of labor, the landlord could necessarily claim the whole advantage, just as he could claim any advantage arising from increased fertility of the soil. If invention were carried to the farthest imaginable point, so that labor could be entirely dispensed with in the production of wealth, the raw material must still be obtained from the land, and therefore the landowners would have all the wealth that could be produced, and would be absolutely independent of labor. There would be no use for anybody else, save as their servants or as pensioners on their bounty. This point is of course unattainable, but towards it labor-saving inventions tend, and their general effect is to raise the price of land. This is illustrated in the effect of railroads. Railroads very much reduce the cost of transportation, but that does not add anywhere to the wages of labor, nor yet, generally, to the profits of capital. It simply adds to the value of land. Where a railroad comes wages do not increase; interest does not rise; but land goes up in value. All human production in the last analysis is the union of labor with land; the combination, transportation, or modification of materials furnished by nature so as to adapt them for the use of man. Therefore where land is monopolized labor becomes helpless. Where one man owns the land he must necessarily be the master of all the other men that live upon it. Where one class own the land they must necessarily be the ruling class. Those who have not land must work for those who have it. In a ruder state of society, such as that which existed in Poland and in many other countries of the world, the system of serfdom resulted simply from the ownership of the land. The laborer was a serf because he must get his living out of the land which another man owned. In a state of society like ours, where the land is very largely divided up, you do not see this so clearly; but you can see it, on one side, in the large sums which the owners of land are enabled to obtain without doing anything themselves, and on the other, in the conditions which exist among the lowest class of laborers. . . .

Sen. Pugh: We have a large public domain now, subject to settlement and cultivation under the homestead law — millions of acres of land unoccupied.

The Witness: Where is it?

Sen. Pugh: Out in the western states and in the southern states.

The Witness: Practically, that is of but little use to people here. But the extent of our public domain is very much exaggerated. The best part of it has been taken. What is left, the millions of acres that figure in the Land Reports, comprise all the deserts, all the mountain chains, all the poor land. An immense amount of land that is carried on the books of the Interior Department as public land is really now in private hands, consisting of railroad land which has not been surveyed and patented, of land upon which various claims have been filed but not yet perfected, and of land held by the ownership of the water. All through the western part of this continent water is scarce. I know, for instance, of a ranch of a million acres which is for sale in this city. It will probably be taken to London and sold there. Nearly all of that million acres is government land, and it is not the legal title that is for sale, but virtual possession. What the parties have obtained title to by preemption and homestead entry is the banks of two streams. It is impossible to use that land for grazing (the only purpose that it is fit for) without access to the water. The man who commands the access to the water commands this million acres of land just as truly as though it were patented to him. All through the West enormous amounts of land are held in this way. That it is not an easy thing for a man who wishes to go upon government land to get any such land that he can use profitably is proved by the high rents that are paid. Men do not pay largely for what they can get for nothing. You will find that in all our new states arable land already commands a high price.

The rent of land in California, where it is rented on shares, varies from one-fourth to one-half the produce. In the new Northwest the rent is usually one-half. In New Jersey I inquired, the other day, of a farmer in a part of the state where I happened to be, and he told me that the rent there was one-half. That is an enormous rent. Buckle, in his *History of Civilization*, estimates the rent in Ireland as one-fourth of the product — and Ireland has always been supposed to be a very highly rented country.

Sen. Pugh: In the South you can find an abundance of rich land, uncultivated and unoccupied, which can be rented very much under that figure.

The Witness: There may be special reasons, there probably are special reasons, why the stream of immigration has not been directed to the South.

Sen. Pugh: That is very true.

The Witness: All these considerations must be taken into account. But I have seen men who started out to find a piece of the public domain upon which to make a home and who have come back disheartened. The last time I came across the plains I met one family who had sold a farm in the Platte Valley and had gone away to the Pacific Coast and up into Oregon, and who were coming back, the man intending to go to work on a railway. I found a long train of Southwestern men from the Choctaw Nation who had been as far as Washington Territory and Puget Sound and who were coming back. You will find them passing and repassing in that way all the time, and you will find generally that the man who starts out to get himself a homestead on government land will find that the cheapest way to get it is to buy or rent. The speculator keeps just ahead of the settler. Our laws, although intended to secure every man a home, have operated just the other way, just as have the land laws of Australia and New Zealand. A large business has been carried on, and is now being carried on, in the making of entries. A man files a preemption claim or a homestead entry, perfects it, and sells it out to a capitalist, and then goes on to repeat the operation. I noticed the last time I came across the continent that at Council Bluffs there was an advertisement of one of these land-grant railroad companies posted up offering some 2,500 improved farms for sale. I take it that those improved farms were pieces of railroad land on which men had settled, on which they had paid something down, giving a mortgage for the balance, and which they had been obliged to abandon, the land reverting to the railroad company, which was again offering it for sale. A great deal of that land through the West is not fitted by nature for agriculture. There still exists "The Great American Desert," although land-grant agents wipe it out of the maps.

Q. Are not the unemployed classes very much increased in number, and is not the opinion that there is a scarcity of employment encouraged by the fact that the demand for employment is generally for particular kind of employment in a particular place? For instance, take this city or Boston, or Chicago, for an illustration. We find large numbers of people out of employment, and they say there is not a sufficient demand for labor; but when we come to inquire into the fact, we find that what they speak of is a demand for a particular kind of labor in a particular place, to wit, New York or any other of the cities. They could go elsewhere and find employment, but they demand employment in New York or Boston, or Philadelphia or Chicago, and they cannot find it there, although they could find it elsewhere if they were willing to go and seek it. . . . — *A.* All that you say may be true in individual cases, but it is not generally true. You will find today in all the cities unemployed men. . . . If you have any experience in these large cities, you are constantly beset by men who say to you, "I want something to do; I am willing to do anything." Such men are always walking our streets and tramping along our roads; some even in the best of times and when hard times come a great many. There may be at times, a surplus of labor in some branches of industry and not in others. That, under our present industrial system, is constantly likely to occur to some extent; but under a state of freedom it would be quickly relieved. Where too much of one thing was produced relatively to other things the price of that article would fall as compared with the prices of other articles, and capital and labor would naturally be attracted to the production of the others, thus quickly restoring the level. There come times, however, when the supply of labor seems to be in excess of the demand, not in two or three occupations, but in all. In fact, to some extent this is true even in what we consider normal times. We are used to it, but it is really strange that there should ever be a seeming oversupply of labor when you consider that the real demand for labor is labor itself. The two hands are always accompanied by a mouth, and until human wants are satisfied, there must always be need for human labor. When you analyze trade you find that it is the exchange of commodities for other commodities, the exchange of the products of one kind of labor for the products of another kind of labor, so that it is really labor that creates the effective demand for labor. The only explanation of these general depressions is to be found in the fact of the monopoly of the natural opportunities for labor; in the fact that labor is shut off from access to the land, so that it is unable to employ itself. You said awhile ago that all men could not go to farming. It is certainly true that all men would not want to go to farming; but in every trade you will find some men who probably would go to farming if there were profitable opportunity. If you were to open today a large body of agricultural land within convenient distance of these cities, and make it free, you would find a grand rush for it; a rush which would relieve labor in almost every trade, by reducing the number of those competing for work, and which again would increase the demand for labor in these various occupations.

Now, I think these industrial depressions, that seem to spread over the whole civilized world like great waves, can ultimately be traced to the fact that land is not thus open to labor. I think we can see their genesis in this country. For instance, there is an era of stimulation. We go largely into railroad building; business is brisk; there seems to be a good demand for everything. Now, there is one thing, and only one thing, which, during all this time, rises in price, and that is land. Your city lots increase in value; your agricultural lands also. Wherever your railroad goes land jumps up three, four, five, or six hundred, or perhaps a thousand percent. Now, the rise in the price of land means that the man who wants to use the land must pay a greater premium for doing so. The raising of the price of land is the raising of a barrier between labor and its natural opportunities. Then you find that these high prices of land check building, check settlement, check improvement. Thus comes a check to production at the very foundation of the industrial system, the stratum on which all our industries rest; and necessarily this cessation of production causes a cessation or reduction of demand, of demand for other things. That, in other avocations again, checks production, and so the impulse runs through the whole industrial network and produces what seems to be paralysis everywhere, and in all occupations you have men idle who would gladly be at work. . . .

Sen. Blair: Now there is a point that I would like to have you explain. You say as to land, yes; but I do not see how, logically, you can apply that principle to land and not carry it further. That is the difficulty in my mind as to your theory. I do not see any difference between a piece of land unoccupied and a piece of the same land occupied — real estate. I do not see any difference between land as a productive power and the mowing machine or the yoke of oxen or any other form of thing which is material, which is property, and which is made the tool of production. I do not understand why you stop the application of your theory at unoccupied land.

The Witness: I do not stop at unoccupied land, not at all. *Land*, I say, including occupied and unoccupied land.

Sen. Blair: I do not understand why you stop at land.

The Witness: In short, you do not understand the distinction I make between land and such other kinds of property as you have spoken of — the mowing machine, oxen, etc.

Sen. Blair: It looks to me like this, and I would be glad to have it made clear: This division of production, or of the market price realized for production, from which wages and interest and rents are paid, from which all parties and all forces entering into the produced article are compensated. It looks to me as though this matter of division was one, as Mr. Smith said, of higgling in the market, and success in the higgling depends upon the intelligence and power which each higgler has to make his higgling successful. But I do not see how the working man, the wage-worker, unless we first produce the millennium or some entirely new order of things which cannot result until we are all dead and until our children and grandchildren are all dead (and that is too late for the purposes of this investigation) — unless by some such means I do not see any way by which the wage-worker can get any more pay out of it, unless by his intelligence and his personal force or his personal force combined with the forces of others of his own class, he can stand up and say, "I will not work until you give me so much." And he must have accumulated something so that he can live a part of a year, or a year, in order to enforce his demand. Capital cannot live forever. It is the annual production that keeps the world in motion, and when a combination of laborers are able to take care of themselves one year, capitalists and monopolists must agree to a fair distribution or a fair payment of wages, or else submit to destruction. And the destruction of the capitalist in that way, or of his property, continued for a year or for a reasonable length of time, makes him "hungry" and places him upon the same level as the wage-worker, whose personal necessities and sufferings, in the shape of cold and starvation, often compel him to yield.

The Witness: You have asked me questions that involve a great deal, and I shall have to go over a good deal of ground to answer them. You ask me first what distinction I make between land and other species of property — oxen, machinery, etc. There are very essential distinctions. In the first place, the land is a *natural* element; the machine, the house, even the yoke of oxen, are the product of human labor. In the next place, land is something that exists from one generation to another, which each generation in its turn and in its time must apply to for its subsistence.

Sen. Blair: Permit me to ask you if the land in our condition of things is any more necessary to the existence of the man, to his actual existence, I mean, than is the milk which is produced by the cow which feeds upon the land, or the grain which grows from the land? We do not eat the land; we do not wear the land. The land is the primary cause, just the same as the Almighty is, and you might as well say that we must distribute the Almighty *pro rata* among human beings, or that He must become common property, as to say that the land which He has created must become common property. It is the necessity that I feel today for protection against the elements and for the nourishment of my body that is the exacting thing, and I do not think the land is any more necessary to human life than the other elements.

The Witness: You must certainly agree to this, however, that while those other forms of property exist for a little while, land is something that exists from one generation to another.

Sen. Blair: How is that? "Land" is not a definite mathematical term; land is of no use unless improved by human labor. It is only as it can be immediately utilized that land is of any consequence. Land in Africa is of no consequence to us because we cannot use it. Land here is of consequence to us provided we can use it; but even land here is of no account unless we can use it — of no more account than if it was real estate in the moon or the distant stars. It must be improved and utilized by actual immediate occupation in order to be useful to us, and it may be that land which is of some account today will be of no account tomorrow. So that it is not a fact that the same land is a perpetually available element in the matter of human sustenance any more than personal property which perishes in the using.

The Witness: Please let me go on to state the differences between land and other property. There is a difference in the origin; there is a difference in the permanence, and there is a difference as to value. The value of a cow, of a machine, or of a house, depends upon the amount of labor that, upon the average, is required to produce it. The value of a piece of land is not that. Nobody produces land. The value of it is the amount of the produce of labor that the ownership of that land will enable the owner to get from the man who does use it. Take these buildings that we see around here, that big building over there of Mr. Bennett's, for instance; that building represents a certain amount of labor expended in getting the materials, putting them upon the ground, and erecting the structure. That is something that Mr. Bennett has done, or has had done. The value of the land on which that building stands results not from the exertions of Mr. Bennett, but from the fact that there are two million people around this place. It is they, and not Mr. Bennett, who have given that land its value.

Sen. Blair: Now, is it so? Does it not result from the additional fact that Mr. Bennett has obtained raw material and has combined it with the land?

The Witness: Not at all.

Sen. Blair: Until that land is utilized is it of any more account than a piece of somebody's cow pasture?

The Witness: Certainly. Right here near it is another lot which is vacant, with a board fence around it, yet that lot is worth $500,000. What gives that land its value?

Sen. Blair: The fact that it can be combined with human labor, and nothing else.

The Witness: If that land was in the interior of Africa it could be combined with human labor just as well, but it would not have the same value.

Sen Blair: It could not, without an enormous cost for transportation and building up a city around it; and this land is only valuable because it has been utilized; and it is utilized only because you have that city around it. I do not see the distinction in this respect between land in the unoccupied condition you speak of and land in that condition which affords opportunities of transacting business.

The Witness: Take the Astor House across the street. Suppose you go out on the plains and put up a building as good as the Astor House; do you thereby make the ground on which that building stands as valuable as that on which the Astor House stands.

Sen. Blair: No; and why not? Simply because the Astor House in a desert supplies no human wants. It is like property destroyed. And so this vacant lot here is of no value.

The Witness: Until you surround it by a great city.

Sen. Blair: But you leave this lot unoccupied, surrounded as it is by a great city, and it is of no more value than the land in the desert so far as the supply of human wants is concerned. It has a market value now because it is available for such purposes.

The Witness: You were speaking of the *value of the land*.

Sen. Blair: But what is it that sells? It is not the value of the land. It is the availability of the land for use.

The Witness: Unquestionably it arises from the fact that it is here in the center of a great city.

Sen. Blair: And if you do not convert it to use it is not available. Its availability for conversion to use, and the conversion of it in combination with labor and other things, is what makes it valuable.

The Witness: But that vacant land is not so combined. It is still lying to all intents and purposes in a state of nature.

Sen. Blair: But it is not the land in and of itself that is valuable. It is the land plus its situation which makes it available, that gives it value. Until that availability is made use of it does not yield actual valuable results, but it can be so made use of at any time.

The Witness: Precisely. Therefore the value of that land is only the power which the owner has to obtain a revenue from it whenever he wishes to.

Sen. Blair: Precisely.

The Witness: And that revenue must come from the labor of other people.

Sen. Blair: But it is the power to combine that land with human labor and with wood, with brick, with mortar, with various other things, which in combination constitute a building that renders it valuable.

The Witness: The power to erect a house on it?

Sen. Blair: The power to have a house erected upon it; the power to convert it to an available purpose.

The Witness: Not [at] all. If you had a piece of land in the interior of Africa you could erect a house on it?

Sen. Blair: You would not have the power of utilization in that case; you would have only the power of waste. Land has no value until you can utilize it.

The Witness: But you can utilize it. You will find in small towns large edifices as good as many in Paris or New York, but you do not find the erection of those edifices gives equal value to the land underneath. What gives value to the lot is that its owner has the power to command a large revenue from it. No matter how rich land may be, no matter how well situated it may be, or how available it may be, it is worth absolutely nothing until somebody is willing to pay a premium for its use. That constitutes the value of land. Now the value of a horse, or of clothes, or of anything else comes from the human labor expended in producing it, in creating it, to speak metaphorically; but no human labor created the land. It existed before we came into the world and it will exist after we are gone. It is the field of our exertion. That is the difference between land and other kinds of property. . . .

Sen. Blair: I do not understand how you make your distinction between the land itself as property and the superstructure which is upon it, or between the land and the implements that are essential in order to carry on production for the supply of human wants. In other words, I think that in claiming that land should be owned in common you substantially claim that all property which supplies human wants should be held in common.

The Witness: Not at all. As a matter of right, or as a matter of expediency, whichever way you take it, there is a very clear and broad distinction. That distinction is that this property which is the result of labor is properly the reward of labor. You rightfully own your coat; I rightfully own mine, because I have got it from the man who made it and have paid him for it. Nobody can show me a title of that kind to land. So far as the question of expediency goes, to make property which is the result of labor common would be to destroy the incentive to production. If I had to divide whatever I produced with everybody I would have very little or almost no inducement to produce anything. To take from a man that which is the result of his own labor, his own exertion, is to check his desire to labor. But, no matter how much you might make the value of land common, you could not check the production of land; you could not make land any less valuable. It would still have all the properties that it had before. Our present system of taxation, for instance, is a discouragement to the production of wealth. We tax a man according to what he has done, according to what he has added to the wealth of the community. Now, it is really a good thing to add to the wealth of the community. No matter how selfish a man may be he cannot keep it all to himself. The more there is, the more, other things being equal, we can all get; and it ought to be the effort of everybody to stimulate production as far as possible. But instead of that we tax men for producing; we tax a man for getting rich; we tax a man for his economy. What we ought to do is to tax man according to the natural opportunities which they have and do not use. Take that building over there. According to my notion that building is an ornament and a convenience to the city. It does not injure anybody. It is better that there should be a building there than an unsightly vacant lot; therefore I would not tax the man one cent for putting up that building, but I would tax him upon the value of the land upon which the building stands. Under such a system of taxation the man who has that fine building upon his lot would not pay any more taxes than the man who has this vacant lot with the ugly fence around it, and the effect would be to stimulate building, and to induce the holders of the land to take a lower price for it or to let it to somebody who would use it.

Sen. Blair: You would still tax upon the value of the land, you say. Upon its value at what time? Upon the value in a state of nature, or upon the value with all the surrounding improvements?

The Witness: Upon the value at the time the taxation was imposed. For instance, I would tax it in 1883 according to the value of the land in 1883 if the particular buildings upon it were swept away by fire.

Sen. Blair: Then all the land, occupied or unoccupied, would be taxed upon that primary valuation?

The Witness: Certainly. Here you have an enormous population crowded onto one-half of this island. The population is denser in these downtown districts around us here than anywhere else in the world.

Sen. Call: Except in the Eastern countries.

The Witness: They do not build in our way in the Eastern countries. They build low there. Notwithstanding this crowding, if you take a ride up on the Sixth Avenue Railroad you will find any quantity of land in a state of nature; but if you want to build a house upon it you will be met by the owner who will demand $5,000 or $10,000 or $25,000 for a lot. You pay that and put up your house, and then along comes the tax gatherer who taxes you for the house, for the improvement you have made, for the increased accommodation you have furnished for the people of this city as well as for yourself, and in all probability he taxes you more on the value of the house or on the value of the land on which the house stands than he taxes the other land beside it which is lying vacant. I think that is the general rule all over the United States, that the occupied land, especially where it is in the hands of small owners, is taxed, even on its value as land, higher than that which is lying beside it unused. We ought, on the contrary, to discourage this dog-in-the-manger business, these people who are doing nothing themselves to improve the land and are preventing others from doing anything.

Sen. Blair: I was going to ask you whether you would confine taxation of occupied land to the value of the land before it was occupied?

The Witness: Not at all. I would tax it whether it was occupied or not so long as it had a value.

Sen. Blair: Would you tax any other forms of property?

The Witness: I would not. I do not think it would be necessary. I would say to the people, "Produce all you can. The more everybody produces the more there will be to divide, and the more each can get for his share."

Sen. George: In your theory you disconnect the improvements entirely from the land?

The Witness: Certainly.

Sen. Blair: And you would make the land common property?

The Witness: That would be in substance making it common, but I would not in form make it common. I would let the present holders call it their land, just as they do now. . . .

Testimony of R. Heber Newton *

The Witness: To sum up the suggestions which I have to offer:

Labor is at fault, and needs to develop greater ability and interest in its work; more thrift; larger powers of combination and better methods in combination; the substitution of arbitration and cooperation for strikes; the building up in its trades unions of centers of political action.

Capital is at fault, and needs to develop greater personal interest in its employees; to create for them in their surroundings the interest that their work so largely lacks; to bind its men to itself through a system of industrial partnership; to prevent strikes by arbitration; to make out of its brains and means the position of control a real captaincy of industry.

The general world of business is at fault in its anarchic system of industry and trade, alternating between fevers of speculative production and congestive chills, in which labor is left idle in the market; in its vast monopolies of common necessities and common services; in its total disregard of humanitarian considerations in seeking investments.

Philanthropy is at fault in its unwise and obsolete methods.

Society at large is at fault in its thoughtlessness and selfishness, its luxury and extravagance, its manifold wastes.

* See above, page 37.

Municipal governments are at fault in not taking civil administration out of national politics and making it wholly a matter of wise corporate management; in their dishonest and wasteful administration; in the burdens of debt thus imposed on the people; in parting lightly with valuable franchises; in encouraging intemperance, by their multiplication of grog shops; in allowing the poor to be housed as they are.[1]

State governments are at fault in not providing a system of industrial education in connection with the common schools; in legislating freely in the interests of capital while neglecting the needs of labor; in establishing no control of the great corporations they charter and endow with munificent privileges; in allowing the present license of gambling in the necessities of life, and of monopolizing the most important resources of the people; in not establishing labor bureaus.

The national government is at fault in various respects, concerning which I sum my suggestions into propositions, which I should like to see this committee submit to the Senate of the United States:

(1) Tariff reform.

(2) A national bureau of labor.

(3) Legislation concerning the great transcontinental railroads, and the appointment of a national railroad commission.

(4) The establishment of postal savings banks.

(5) The further fostering of industrial education.

(6) A better system of patent privileges.

(7) The limitation of the right of bequest.

(8) The organization of colonization from our crowded centers to our newer regions.

(9) The reclaiming of public lands whose grants have become forfeited, and the return of the old policy of preserving all public lands for actual settlers.

(10) The reservation of future mineral resources as public property.

Back of all which lie the responsibilities of our capitalistic system of industry and of our tenure of land, concerning which the time seems to me unripe for other action than that already suggested.

The propositions concerning the action of the national government are, of course, open to one serious objection — apart from all other criticism that they may deserve. They look to a considerable increase of the functions of the state, already burdened with heavy responsibilities and developing now a dangerous bureaucracy. Our prevailing theories favor the minimizing of state action, and regard any further assumption of offices by government as a reaction, and not a progress; a return to-

[1] The lines of responsibility of civic and state authorities overlap and are not readily separable at times.

wards the obsolete ideal of a paternal government. I recognize the danger in every increase of functions by the state; but I see the danger that lies in the avoidance of such increase of function, an even greater danger, as it seems to me.

Apart from any theorizing, the whole trend of our social life is forcing on our age such increased action by the state, in the very teeth of what is believed to be the gospel of political economy. Doctrinaires prove powerless before facts. England, the home of the noninterference dogma, has been driven on, from one step to another, in the direction of larger state action, out of the felt necessities of the situation.

Thus within a few years we have seen the development of the postal savings bank, the purchase of the telegraph lines, the organization of the parcels post. Within a decade the state has added to its functions the office of banker and telegrapher and expressman, and the country lives and thrives. Wisdom dictates a slow feeling of the way in this direction, which is all that I suggest. The state should avoid assuming any new office until that office is fairly forced upon it, by the demands of the people or the exigencies of society; but, then, it should not hesitate to take up the work thus plainly indicated for it. The work of the Department, in one of whose buildings we are now meeting (the post office) is the best vindication of the possibility of capable and honest administration of a huge business, with which no private company could be trusted.

The introduction of a real civil service reform is the indispensable preparation for such higher functions on the part of government. . . .

Sen. Blair: You think that labor does not get its fair share. I suppose, then, the more wealth there is created the better, because there would be more to divide? — A. Undoubtedly.

Q. Do you believe the proposition somewhat generally received, I suppose, that production ordinarily can be more stimulated under private than under public management? — A. Speaking generally, I do. I believe that has been the function of individualism in the development of civilization. Perhaps another force than individualism is necessary for rightful distribution.

Q. Then, if the proper distribution could be effected, you think it would be better that this combination of the factors of production should remain under private management rather than be consigned to public management? — A. Yes, if that could be secured, except insofar as there are works which from their nature the state is better fitted to do.

Q. In other words, you believe that the individual in society is more capable of successful administration or working of these great factors of production than the mass, the government at large? — A. On the whole, yes.

Q. So it would follow from these premises that if the abuses, whatever they are, that have caused it, now existing in society, could be remedied you would be satisfied with the existing order of things so far as titles and the general administration of social and business life are concerned? — A. Yes, with that very big "If."

Q. Then, all that conceded, I want to ask you to specify such particular direction or particular ways in which there is waste or improper appropriation of the result of production. Certain parties get too much; others do not get enough. Specify a few of the directions in which you think the greatest waste or misappropriation against justice occurs. — A. Capital, as a rule, gets a disproportionate share of production. Figures, I know, are so handled by skillful statisticians as to becloud this fact; but fact I believe it is. The whole mass of labor in a factory, say 500 hands, is balanced against the one capitalist, and then it is said that "labor gets the lion's share." It is enough to look at the wealth so frequently accumulated in manufacturing, and to look then at the general condition of factory labor, to see through all sophisms on this point. Here is a great waste or misappropriation, speaking from the standpoint of society. It would be juster and better to have our capitalists less wealthy, and their laborers more comfortable, better educated, and better housed. Plainly, society's need is of the many getting more and the few less out of production. It is this fact which lends force to the socialist doctrine, that if, say, four hours' work represents the productivity for which a man is paid in the wages he receives, the other six hours represents his labor appropriated to its own benefit by capital.

Then there is misdirection of the results of labor in the huge accumulations of middlemen, traders, merchants, carriers, etc. They serve an equally important function with production proper, but they get a share of reward wholly disproportionate. Thus it is that great fortunes are built up most readily by the men who simply exchange what others have produced. And in securing these great rewards, prices are run up high, so that while the producer gets but a small part of the value of his labor, when he needs to buy back that work, or some other branch of labor's work, he has to pay several times the value it had as a piece of production. Where are the colossal fortunes made? Not in producing, but in exchanging, including in this term, of course, carriage. So in other directions, through which it would take time to track the absorption into others' than labor's hands of the value of labor's own production.

Q. You have mentioned the accumulation of very large fortunes in the hands of individual men. — A. As drawn to do so by direct questioning, otherwise I have not emphasized, I believe, that phase of the subject for more than one reason. These gigantic fortunes arrest attention, and so start questions and rouse antagonism. They serve to objectify a social tendency and to throw it into a strong and bad light. And all this I hold to be well. That tendency is unwholesome, unsound, dangerous, especially in a republic; so we are likely to hear quite enough about "the coming billionaire." But there is fear of overdoing the personal opposition and of concentrating upon a few men, perhaps personally by no means monsters, the indignation which ought to spread itself upon the wrongful social tendency. While the roots are in the ground it is of little use to mow down one crop of weeds.

Q. But generally take the fortunes of $200,000,000 that we read about in particular individuals. Do you think that these fortunes, as a whole, are better administered than they would be if they were vested in the government at large; or, in other words, does it not follow, from the premises we have assumed, that Astor, Gould, Sage, Vanderbilt, Huntington, and others administer their large fortunes better than they would be administered in other hands? — A. Solely as a matter of production, possibly — probably, yes. Most of these men are admitted to have talents of an uncommon order. Commodore Vanderbilt was certainly a rare genius in organization, and Mr. Gould is often called a Napoleon of speculation. Less gifted men could not, perhaps, develop such enterprises as these men have done. But even then there are qualifications to come in. Perhaps no one man could as well manage Commodore Vanderbilt's lines as he did. But a large and well-organized system of officering can possibly do it as well. The Pennsylvania Railroad today is a splendid specimen of corporate capacity, with no one such man at its head. We are increasingly being driven into the peculiar power of administration that lies in well-organized companies. This is the new tendency already making itself felt over the older force of pure individualism.

Then, moreover, it is open to ask how well for *public good* most of these gigantic private fortunes *are* administered? They seek investments solely with reference to dividends, and with an almost sublime indifference to every consideration of what the people most need. A host of urgent improvements may be waiting to be carried out right at their doors; are so waiting, with every promise of fair returns to the capital invested. But huge fortunes rarely care to engage in such enterprises. They are filled with schemes of vast aggrandizement, with dreams of immense combinations, giving unheard-of power. They tend to go out into speculative enterprises; and these stimulate the country unhealthfully and help on the inevitable reaction. They go out "wildcatting" in all countries of the globe and lend kings the power to wage war. English capital has sunk enough, probably, in Egyptian improvements, after Ismail's heart, in floating Turkey and in all sorts of out-of-the-way and generally harmful schemes, to have reconstructed the worst defects of London, while drawing a fair return.

But the question of administration covers that of distribution as well as that of production. And there can be, as it seems to me, but one judgment as to the influence of the sort of expenditure which huge fortunes encourage. It is bad. It gives work, as the same thousands would, however spent; but it gives the work which creates little or nothing, and which enfeebles and degrades the workers. It builds up the classes which minister to luxury, and they are economically unprofitable classes to the community, and socially are undersirable classes.

It is not a question between A's having $2,000,000 and the state's having it. It is a question between A's having it and all the rest of the alphabet having it. If the state ran all Mr. Gould's roads it would be the people who pocketed the dividends in one way or another, if the administration was honest. Men say A. has to put out all his $200,000,000 in investments, except the few thousands he can spend a year. True; but there is a great difference between the way he puts out $200,000,000 and the way 2,000 people would each put out $100,000; as between the way he spends what he can of his vast income and the way they would spend their $6,000 or $5,000 apiece. Here is the root of the matter. Which is the best for the country, the investments and personal expenditure of one man with $200,000,000 or the investments and personal expenditures of 2,000 men each having $100,000, or of 20,000 men each having $10,000? . . .

Sen. Blair: Men popularly known as leaders in the labor movement and organizations have been before the committee, and many of them have given testimony to the effect that evangelical Christianity is very rapidly losing its hold upon the masses of wage-workers in this country. I suppose you have studied that matter from a somewhat different standpoint. I would like to know what your views are as to that, and whether you think that is the fact.

The Witness: I fear that there is too much truth in this view.

Q. How do you explain that fact? — *A.* I explain it to my own mind partly by the intellectual movement of our age and partly by the social movement of our age, from both of which movements the evangelical churches have held back.

There is a general breakup of the old order of thought now going on — a sort of climatic change in the human mind, in which the growth of former periods is disappearing rapidly from the world. The forms of belief of the Middle Ages find the conditions unfavorable for them, and are drying up of themselves; they are becoming unthinkable and unbelievable. About this fact, as a fact, there can be no manner of doubt; it is unquestionably true, and I shall not spend time in proving it.

By this change I do not at all mean a dying out of religion or of Christianity. Religion I hold to be the natural and necessary expression of man's spiritual nature before the mystery of the Power in which we live and move and have our being. . . .

But it may and does need new forms — new growths of thought — higher bodies of belief, in which the old spirit may live on after the death and burial of its wornout "bodies of divinity." And it is the business of the church to see that there is free play given to this natural development. If it does see it, if it changes its thought with the changing knowledge of man, if it grows with his growth, it will never be outgrown.

Now, Christianity is evidently passing through one of these critical stages of death and resurrection. The mass of openminded, intelligent men have already made up their minds about the old theology. They find it simply obsolete. It doesn't translate itself into our speech or represent real thought and true knowledge of our age. If the fact were perceived and owned by the church, and if its doctors busied themselves in thinking the old thoughts over into the new forms made necessary by our age, all would be well. Religion would find forms in which it could live and act, and Christianity would take a new lease of life.

Instead of which the church doctors, for the most part, only repeat the old words more loudly, insist on the old thought more positively, and denounce the new knowledge as hostile to religion. They are simply driving off the intelligence of our age from the evangelical churches. And in this alienation the workingman shares. So much for that half of my explanation.

Now, as to the other half, there is a parallel story of obstructiveness on the part of the church, with similar effect.

Our age is preeminently, perhaps, the age of sociology. Social science — the latest born of the sciences — is felt to come as the natural head of them all. Every other study leads up to the construction of a true social order. And while it is the business of the sciences of political economy, sanitary science, the science of education, etc., to gather the materials of knowledge out of which to build this social structure, and to elaborate the plans by which it is to be reared, it is the business, as I see it, of religion to inspire the spirit which is to energize this herculean task. It is religion's function to waken the enthusiasm of humanity, as the love of God, and to set this omnipotent force at work on the building of the City of God. . . .

The well-to-do classes are not quick to see how completely the Christian church has forgotten its Master's gospel, and become the church of respectability and wealth and "society"; how it has become the upholder of civilization as it is; how it has accepted the anti-Christian dogmas of the older political economists, and in so doing really turned traitor to the ethics of Jesus Christ.

But the workingman sees all this quickly enough, his eyesight, as I said, being sharpened by the sense of wrong. Is it any wonder that he turns away from a church that has no better gospel than *laissez faire*, no better brotherhood than the selfish strife of competition, no kingdom of God for human society here upon the earth, but only one up in the skies; a church which baptizes the kingdom of the devil with fine Christian names and asks the suffering mass of men to accept it as the will of the good Father in heaven? The only wonder is that in such an apostasy from its Lord's life and spirit the church has kept any hold upon the workingman.

But I believe that there is a mighty change going on in the Christian church. One sees the signs of it everywhere. . . . The new movement in religious thought runs into the channel of a new social righteousness.

The Christian Union, which represents this movement in congregationalism, is thoroughly outspoken on questions of monopoly, strikes, etc. Indeed, the new Christianity which is coming on fast is going quite surely to find the old social enthusiasm. It will preach justice and not charity, and will inspire men to seek not so much to save their souls as to save society.

And then I have no fears about the attitude of the workingmen to the church of the Carpenter's Son.

Q. You believe, then, that one of the things essential is for the church to reform herself? — A. I do, most assuredly. . . .

CONCLUSION

Despite the mass of valuable testimony collected by the committee, the investigation produced few immediate results. The four volumes containing the verbatim record of the hearings were published in 1885, but Senator Blair did not even file a report summarizing what had been said or recommending action of any kind.

The most important direct result of the investigation was the passage in 1884 of a bill establishing a federal Bureau of Labor Statistics. A growing number of states had, by that date, created such bureaus. These state organizations gathered and published data on wages, working conditions, and the cost of living, and conducted investigations and made field studies of such problems as unemployment, sweatshops, the employment of convict labor at low wages, and strikes. The valuable work performed by these state bureaus encouraged labor leaders to urge Congress to create a federal bureau. A number of witnesses had pointed out during the 1883 hearings that such an organization was needed to summarize the data collected by the state bureaus, as well as to conduct useful investigations of its own.

Senator Blair therefore introduced a bill creating a federal bureau. Both high- and low-tariff Congressmen spoke in its favor, each group expecting that the statistical studies undertaken would be helpful in convincing workingmen that its position was correct. Since the measure could scarcely do any harm, and since 1884 was an election year, even most conservative Congressmen were willing to go along; when the measure came to a vote it passed both houses by large majorities. The first man appointed Commissioner of Labor Statistics was Carroll D. Wright, who had been chief of the pioneering Massachusetts bureau since 1873. Under Wright's leadership, the new bureau gathered and published much valuable information. At first a number of employers objected to the bureau's "prying" into their affairs, but Wright's thoroughness and fairness soon won him and his organization the confidence of the business community as well as that of labor. The importance of the work of the Bureau of Labor Statistics since its foundation can scarcely be overestimated.

In 1884 Blair also took the lead in the Senate in pushing through an anti-contract-labor bill which had been introduced in the House of Representatives by Martin A. Foran of Ohio. This measure forbade employers to import foreign workers under contract, the theory being that such men were signed up at substandard wages and brought to America to replace higher-paid American labor. Actually, the only persons who were brought in under contract were a relative handful of highly skilled and thus well-paid workers; since the practice was not used by employers of unskilled and semiskilled factory hands, it had little or no effect on the welfare of the mass of industrial workers. Nevertheless, the Foran bill was at least a form of insurance against the possibility that employers would resort to this tactic. It too was enacted into law (1885) over only minimal opposition in Congress.

This was the sum and substance of the response of Congress to the 1883 investigation. When Senator Blair tried to obtain passage of a bill, supported by many labor leaders at the hearings, that would have permitted unions to obtain federal rather than state charters, the effort failed, mainly because many Congressmen thought the proposal unconstitutional. Yet the investigation had established a most important precedent. In later years other studies of the relations of labor and capital were undertaken, and these had far more significant legislative results. And above all, the testimony itself remains, an incomparable record of the problems of industrial workers in the Gilded Age, of the opinions of a small army of persons who had grappled with these problems first hand.